SEX, RELATIONSHIPS, DATING, NUTRITION & GROOMING

WHAT MEN REALLY NEED TO KNOW!

P&J Books

Published by P&J
Peter Goodall, 9-11 London Lane, London, E8 3PR, England
First Published in 2009 as The Numen Programme

P&J Books

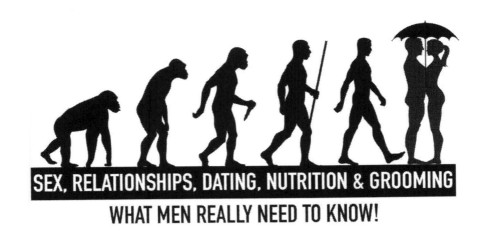

SEX, RELATIONSHIPS, DATING, NUTRITION & GROOMING
WHAT MEN REALLY NEED TO KNOW!

Peter Goodall

P&J

P&J Books

To Dominic
Thank you for believing

I believe in Miracles.
I believe journeys are why we are here.
Did you ever see something and think this is the reason you were put on earth?
Magic is real, it's all around us.
I believe in forgetting about the pain.
I don't believe in fear.
I believe we have a chance to change everything...Take it!
I believe in finding that one thing that sets you free, you just need to believe in yourself or none of this really matters.

Peter Goodall

SUMMARISED CONTENTS

TABLE OF CONTENTS

FODDER FOR THOUGHT

- *Only 30% of women ever achieve an orgasm during sexual intercourse.*
- *The clitoris has 8,000 nerve endings.*
- *The Woman on Top coupled with the right technique can help both of you to reach orgasms at the same time.*
- *If you are concerned about climaxing before your partner does than pull down on your testicles before you cum.*
- *It takes a woman an average of fifteen minutes to become fully aroused and receptive to receiving an orgasm.*
- *The number of erogenous zones that a woman has is actually twelve.*
- *To get into the right rhythm you have to perfect the technique of breaking off contact from her clitoral network.*
- *The neck is one of the best areas to arouse stimulation from your partner.*
- *Having intercourse around three times a week equates to around 7,500 calories a year which is as much as jogging 75 miles over the entire year!*
- *The aim of escalation is to put the clitoris under some more pressure so that your partner can reach the pre-orgasm stage.*
- *Not now darling, I have a Headache! Sexual intercourse releases Oxytocin, which contains endorphins with a sedative property. This is the chemical in the body that relieves us of pain, thus a good session, especially if it includes your partner reaching orgasm, will help to disperse some of the pain.*
- *Avoid the triangle mentality.*
- *The same tissue in the womb is used to create the penis and the vagina.*

- *The vagina is self-cleaning and one of the most pristine and looked after areas on her body. It excretes secretions, which rid the area of bacteria as well as preventing infections.*
- *There are a few techniques you can employ with the tongue, which can help ease a woman into the latter stages of orgasm.*
- *Premature ejaculation affects 30 to 40 percent of men.*
- *The average time a man makes love to a woman (that is to say, where vaginal penetration takes place) is two and a half minutes.*
- *One of the most effective techniques is known as the "Circling Tongue".*
- *There is a movement known as the "cat lick" and it does exactly as the name suggests.*
- *The woman's clitoris is actually made up of 18 parts, some of which you cannot see.*
- *Sometimes the most effective position is for your partner to have her legs in the air.*
- *In general, a woman will experience between five and eight contractions for a "middle-of-the-road" experience.*
- *Some women's capacity to reach orgasm is heightened when she is menstruating.*
- *This position still allows you to use your tongue for the strokes needed for that all important rhythm whilst adding some much needed pressure to the commissure!*
- *Normally, the fluids can taste somewhat bitter but as a woman's body prepares for orgasm, they become a little bit sweeter. There may also be an increase in the warmth of the fluids.*
- *In order to give her the optimum orgasm, you will need to change your position in order to bring her legs closer together.*
- *Her breathing will increase and she will take short, shallow breaths on the immediate cusp of the first wave of pleasure.*
- *The back of the knee is a particularly sensitive and erotic area for women.*

- *The CAT technique.*
- *Kegal exercises strengthen the muscles that are used during intercourse.*
- *Scientists in the 18th century did believe that the female orgasm was a fundamental part of the act of reproducing*
- *75% of women have faked an orgasm at some point in their lives.*
- *Understanding that women have different physical and emotional expectations will allow you to start making some important changes.*
- *The key is to identify your agendas and to treat the whole process of outercourse as its own entity.*
- *Coreplay is the practice of focusing and giving attention to your partners' genital area and can be broken down into six stages.*
- *There are certain positions and techniques that you can adopt to make sure that you are aroused but also focused solely on her pleasure.*
- *Pre-orgasm and orgasm encourage you to maintain the rhythm, tension and balance in order to bring your partner to orgasm. By keeping the pressure and rhythm heightened, you will allow her to achieve climax!*
- *Moreplay describes further activities resulting in your partner climaxing after intercourse has transpired.*
- *Once you have established your rhythm and the right amount of tension using the skills above, you can now step it up a gear!*
- *The aim of escalation is to put the clitoris under some more pressure so that your partner can reach the pre-orgasm stage.*
- *I want to talk to you a little bit about the infamous "G-spot".*
- *One method is to replicate the method used by a frog when it sticks out its long tongue to catch prey.*
- *There is a technique known as the "Jackson Pollock", named after the famous artist.*

- *The Coital Alignment Technique and the woman on top technique are two of the best ways to achieve simultaneous orgasms.*
- *A great lover's hands are never motionless. Whether it is a light touch on the shoulder, a sensual massage or manual stimulation of the clitoris, women like to be touched. It gives them a sense of connection with their partner and makes the entire experience more pleasurable.*
- *The Orgasmic Fingerprint!*

- *As men, we are often inclined to repress emotional awkwardness as a result of infantile social stereotypes.*
- *No one is ever right or wrong: they are just unheard.*
- *The heightening of some deeper issues aligned within your subconscious, moulded through decades and decades of reinforcement with the consequences being the development of discernible self-esteem and an avoidance of trust.*
- *Interdependence becomes essential which maintains secular lifestyles whilst still remaining in a partnership.*
- *You cannot find fulfillment if you are beset with hidden agendas and are unable to vocally commit to them.*
- *Women utter on average about 30 000 words per day in comparison with a man's' meagre 10 000.*
- *The mindsets of inferiority complexes result in continual antagonism with the intent of making the other person feel ill equipped.*
- *Successful long-term relationships cannot succeed unless both parties are willing to adapt to certain changes.*
- *If you are dependent on alcohol or drugs, your relationship exists with the dependency and not with your partner.*
- *The belief that emotional exploration should be a feminine characteristic is incongruent with a happy relationship.*
- *Your discoveries are communal and there is nothing unique about the negative traits you will find.*
- *The difference in development comes down to the meaning attached to events and not the events themselves.*
- *Individuals with low self-esteem sabotage their relationships in order to justify their own diminished personal opinion of themselves.*

- *Your past does not define who you are.*
- *Assertive behaviour embodies respect and a willingness to avoid control.*
- *There is no point in agreeing to something your partner has requested, with the intent of harbouring resentment and fulfilling your obligation with animosity.*
- *It is not about a winning or losing outcome but rather the meeting of two minds with the single intent of benefiting both parties.*
- *Negative opinions that you have allowed to define you are nothing more than expressions of others dealing with identical diminished levels of self-esteem.*
- *Everybody is worthy of loving and being loved.*
- *Women are looking for a partner who views them as an equal.*
- *Where men embattle to find a solution to every obstacle, women are more aligned to share the experience rather than pursue its clarification.*
- *Trying to embody the characteristics of someone who you think your partner will find attractive is short term and leads to inconsistency.*
- *We are affected by our understanding of love, which was formulated in our youth.*
- *Many men struggle to deal with the emotional aspect of pain as a result of the social expectations of remaining strong and in control.*
- *When the conversation seems meaningless in terms of providing resolution to a particular obstacle, remember that this is how men are geared in terms of problem solving, and not women.*
- *It is important to understand that sometimes love is not enough for a relationship to survive.*
- *Men can be more indifferent than women in terms of their emotional sincerity and what often develops is an unhealthy and unloving relationship.*

- *After approximately 18 months, the in-love symptoms fade and the relationship either ends or develops into a more meaningful state.*

- *The concept of the Alpha Male – the leading stock – was to be aspired towards, exuding control with the incapacity to exude emotional discomfort.*

- *Love as opposed to lust, is a choice rather than an infliction.*

- *It is a human preoccupation to imagine other realities as healthier, happier, more meaningful and consumed with the 'in love' phase.*

- *Can you learn to love someone who you are not attracted to?*

- *Numerous partnerships break down, not because of diminished love, but because one party feels he or she is not being heard.*

- *Many couples talk over each other, often agreeing on similar principles, yet unable to hear the meaning behind the others expression.*

- *Breakdowns result, not from dramatic acts of indifference, but rather small seemingly inconsequential build ups that can be best defined as 'the straw that broke the camel's back'.*

- *Communication is about reinforcing the security blanket surrounding your relationship.*

- *Minor victories will often result in major catastrophes. It can be more rewarding to remain selfless and concede, than to remain perched on a pedestal.*

- *You will find that most of the irrational fears causing you to become heated will dissipate with time and thought. Welcome to thinking time and the concept of taking a 'Time Out'.*

- *Your subconscious steers you towards or away from people as a result of formative reinforcement.*

- *Successful relationships are based on choice and not need.*

- *Negative thoughts result in negative actions. They feed off each other and stimulate irrational set type behaviours resulting in dysfunctional mindsets and animations.*

- *Right or wrong is a perception and not a reality. It does not exist outside of opinion.*
- *Relationships require work and a serious level of commitment. The 'happily ever after' mindset is an illusion that will constantly keep you disappointed if it is an expectation.*
- *It is human nature to look into the windows of other lives and imagine a more fulfilling existence. Why? Because we are introduced to fragments of their existence, which are actively designed to express all the highs and none of the lows.*
- *Along with dismissive splendour of water out of a tap, heat or light at the switch of a button and shelter at the end of each day; so do we escape the wonders and joys of having a unique and committed individual in our lives beset on loving us along with all our inadequacies.*
- *By learning to embody successful communication skills you will develop a resource for overcoming conflicts and creating more positive outcomes.*
- *We are social beings with a predisposition for being adorned, cared for, thought of, depended upon and provided for. It is a symbiotic relationship, which leads to open and meaningful revelations, as we grow older.*
- *You should realise that relationships require attentive work and that the natural progression for the spark to fade is as normal as biting into an apple.*
- *The reality exists that we can retrain our brains and the associated meanings attached.*
- *Our particular type of behaviour incorporates the thoughts, actions and methods we adopt in approaching situations and can be directly proportional to how well you fair in a relationship.*
- *You should be looking to embody is a sincere level of assertiveness in your personal mainframe where equality and empathy are the benchmark. Your understanding of control is that it rarely exists and even when it does, it is not a prerequisite for happiness.*

- *Being angry whist remaining assertive, embodying respect and equality, is an essential method of communicating disapproval of certain behaviours. But always remember to indulge in its deliverance as you would expect to receive it.*

- *Successful relationships have cycles and just because you and you partner decided to go your separate ways, does not mean the partnership itself was not successful. The most important conclusion to reach is not one of failure, but rather of intrepid experience with the result being insight and wisdom to engage in future relationships.*

- *Incorporate respect, empathy and understanding into conversations and give up the need to be right or look good.*

- *There are particular reasons why someone has chosen to love you, have faith in her decision and embrace the idea that you are worthy of being loved.*

- *Old-fashioned beliefs do not work in the current game. Nice guys, who hesitate, do not succeed with women.*
- *You do have control over the direction you're heading, and that is your responsibility. When you embrace this, you will know what you're about and in turn, you will know what you can offer someone else.*
- *Self-acceptance plays the leading role in creating your self-image, which is a pre-requisite for genuine unaffected confidence.*
- *The fact that most people have an aspect of 'self depreciation' is not going to win any awareness awards. The great thing about attraction is it does not matter at all.*
- *Attraction is about confidence and inner comfort, and when you exude that, there is nothing that can undermine you.*
- *Self-Esteem can be built through constant exposure to new experiences and people.*
- *Men with a healthy self-esteem never concern themselves with the notion of being right. It is about the interaction and sharing of opinions and this kind of self-acceptance is infectious and humbling. Get this right – and you will attract.*
- *Commit to taking the action, regardless of irrational fear.*
- *There is no guy in the planet that approaches a girl he likes, absolute of fear. It's in all of us. If we like something, we want it and there is an innate reaction, which links us to loss or rejection. There is one simple solution to it all. Do it anyway.*
- *Worrying is a habit. And habits are as easy to break as they are to create. They exist because of the unknown.*
- *That's an interesting term there… "Self fulfilling prophecy of Failure"*

- *Winning is not a conclusion, it comes before that. You've heard the saying, "Seeing is believing". Well I'm here to tell you it's not true. "Believing is seeing".*
- *The women you really do want, the ones that are not superficial, are attracted to the guy with the positive attitude who embodies the "potential" for success.*
- *It is likely and reasonable to place yourself in a position where future ambition and not past reality become your shaping mechanism.*
- *The key to making a lasting impression on someone is being in complete control of what you reveal.*
- *As human beings we are attracted to confidence and assertiveness; it's about control and the ability to protect.*
- *Fear of judgement remains constant until those first words come out of your mouth and the irrational fears that were manifested through the imagination become fictional.*
- *In the game, as in with life, you are judged not on your thoughts, but by your actions.*
- *Get these principles under your belt and you will exude a greater confidence when approaching a woman you are attracted to.*
- *The first rule when talking to the opposite sex: do not fake expertise.*
- *Self depreciation is always well received, but be sure to make it funny and not sad.*
- *Being aggressive is also a sign that you lack communication confidence.*
- *Actors and singers learn this trick to optimise their voice and get rid of stage fright instantly.*
- *As long as your posture is fine, your feelings of self-assurance will supply the rest of the body language signals you need to exude.*
- *The ideal voice is slow, calm and assured. Surveys suggest the sexiest voice on our planet belongs to an old Bond actor, Sean Connery.*

- *Shyness is not the same as having low self-esteem.*
- *Introverts tend to be the most creative people out there, so the assumption that dating is an activity for extroverts alone is a fallacy.*
- *In the dating world an attractive woman is inundated with pseudo alpha extroverts, so the unique opportunity to offer her something which is real and unobtrusive can be refreshing. You are "peacocking", standing out from the crowd, whether intentional or not. This is an attractive quality.*
- *"Fake it till you make it" - You can feign self-confidence to increase your confidence without anyone noticing it's a put on. Actors live and breathe this principle when delving into character portrayals.*
- *The quickest way to project self-assurance is to alter your body language.*
- *We elevate the action of approaching an attractive woman to a pedestal it does not deserve.*
- *If you deal with approach anxiety, you can increase your social value and interact with pretty much anyone out there.*
- *Socialising opens your mind as you pick up on habits, interests and thoughts of people with different beliefs and unique idiosyncrasies.*
- *You will learn more about yourself by being in the company of others.*
- *Emotional stability is an important aspect of personal excellence and attraction. Understanding that the goal is in the interaction itself and not the result creates a disregard for being right or wrong, which enables two people to make a connection.*
- *Women are attracted to the potential of men, and not their current status.*
- *What is essential is that you attempt to do something you have never done before.*

- *You do this again and again, until your brain begins to identify that this entire experience is safer than you initially imagined. What ensues is a more rational physiological experience through the power of habit.*

- *Mates, wingmen, advisors…whatever you want to call them, can be more debilitating in terms of getting you your date.*

- *The outcome has nothing to do with the success or failure of the objective.*

- *There are dating development programmes out there that will give you sixty guaranteed one-liners to get her into the sack. It's garbage! A girl who seems sullen or bored might not react well to a cheesy joke, but she might respond positively to a smiling "hello" and a sincere "how are you feeling".*

- *Free your mind from the worry brought about by the "what if" scenario and give yourself the chance to find out whether or not you can develop some attraction with her.*

- *Her interest is aligned completely with where you are going, what your ambitions are and the potential you possess.*

- *The simple fact remains that being open to new experiences and straying from your comfort zone will improve your social life drastically, and this is the first step you need to take if you want to get rid of Approach Anxiety….*

- *In the modern multi-channel world we live in, technology has actually made us more insular and less social. Think about it like this. In terms of communication, seven percent is conveyed through words, thirty eight percent through vocal elements like tonality and fifty five percent through non verbal elements like facial expressions, gestures or posture. Yet we have defined communication in the modern era as an email, a status update or a text message. We have become less social and rely on technology as an alternative which flatters to deceive.*

- *Do not rehearse negatives scenarios in your head.*

- *In order to genuinely alter your state; you will need to realign your thought patterns.*
- *Anything and everything is possible, dependant on the thought you choose to associate with it.*
- *This is the start of the rapport process. In order to be successful, you will need to align your thought pattern with a positive outcome.*
- *You know those people that walk into a room and create a buzz, a rapport with anyone and everyone around them. This is the mantra they use to create attraction and interest.*
- *The most important qualities to portray under these circumstances are calm, cool and collected.*
- *People use stereotypes for comfort and the act itself is driven purely out of fear.*
- *It is critical to understand that you are judging yourself far more cruelly than anyone else would.*
- *The outcome is not what is going to make you grow; it's the action you take in trying to achieve the outcome.*
- *There is a big difference between initial attraction and long-term attraction.*
- *Women have a different agenda to men.*
- *The number you are looking for should be one, and not one hundred, as the latter is not going to lead you anywhere fulfilling.*
- *You highlight the traits that women associate with the things they want from a man who they would consider to be a long-term prospect.*
- *Latent attraction is the kind of gravitational energy that is present in any interaction between men and women.*
- *There are certain things that have to be in place before it can be released from its dormant state.*
- *If attraction isn't present you can generate curiosity, which in turn will lead to interaction which can then lead to attraction.*

- *Whereas we are stimulated by their physical prowess, they are on the lookout for men who have visible traits of a potential partner which has nothing at all to do with looks.*
- *Men who get noticed as soon as they enter the room or a woman's line of sight look comfortable, confident and charismatic. The three C's embody the characteristics of an Alpha Male.*
- *Research has shown that women are aroused by broad chins, high cheekbones and large eyes and recognise a good body as indicative of discipline and control.*
- *The more relaxed you are, the more attention you attract.*
- *In terms of eye movement, you are going to need to keep a neutral gaze. Do not react to the environment.*
- *Women are attracted to men who are passionate about their purpose in life, and men who seem to control their own destiny.*
- *This attitude appeals to women because of what it represents… freedom from judgment.*
- *Women are acutely aware of the pressure to conform.*
- *To start a conversation with a stranger, you must develop your approach confidence and your rapport skills.*
- *Apart from your body language, this is one of the initial impressions that will make or break your approach.*
- *Thinking of the end result will only create internal pressure.*
- *Your success is about making an approach and not the outcome.*
- *It creates a unique bond between the two of you by exploiting commonality.*
- *The guy who buys all the drinks, tries the hardest and seems the sweetest, has the lowest value.*
- *"You"-centred stories are your best dating props.*
- *Never be negative or bitter when you're describing something that happened in your past.*
- *Arrogant men turn women off. But cocky and mischievous men are attractive.*

- *You will start emotionally connecting with a woman if you relate to her in terms of commonality as well as showing character traits that she values.*
- *People gravitate toward familiarity because it makes us feel safe.*
- *Use Scarcity as a tool.*
- *I want to dispel the myth that approaching women is an exclusive exercise for extrovert personalities.*

- *Thoughts, motivations and desired energy levels are directly proportional to what you eat.*
- *A nutritional guide that is known to offer you a far better lifestyle and greater chances of increasing your life expectancy.*
- *My aim was to conceive a diet, which would provide confidence, weight loss and longevity in terms of life expectancy.*
- *Certain types of foods can have a significant impact on your energy levels and general state of mind.*
- *All three of the macronutrients are vitally important to your diet, and you will be able to identify the very best sources to obtain optimum nourishment.*
- *Dairy products are known to be associated with severe medical problems.*
- *If you are looking to lose weight, pay particular attention here, as it is a sure fire way to get you dropping those unwanted pounds.*
- *If you become accustomed to eating all the wrong types of foods, your body gets used to this and will essentially crave more of the bad stuff, which results in exhaustion and fluctuating blood sugar levels.*
- *Protein forms an essential part of our diet and you are likely to be surprised at the number of ingredients that contain sufficiently high levels of this macronutrient, as an alternative to meat derived products.*
- *It has been scientifically proven that these food types contribute towards stress, anxiety and depression.*
- *Whole grains are one of the best sources for the full spectrum of the key vitamins for energy generation, especially the B-vitamins.*
- *If you are not getting enough Omega 3 & 6 (walnuts and flaxseed), vitamins B1 and B3 (Brown rice), vitamins B6 (Whole Grain*

Oats), Vitamin C and Folic Acid (Cabbage) and selenium (Molasses and Nuts), you are asking for a whole heap of depression.

- If you want to reduce the risk of heart disease you will need to balance your diet with less saturated fat from red meats, more fresh fruits and vegetables, less sugar and more fibre.
- Foods that are high in fat and sugar work on our brains like opiates – painkillers – and the more we eat, the more we want. This consequence is also increased by the "empty calorie" effect of junk food. It fills us up for a short period of time, but then, like any addict, we begin to feel tired, depressed, and hungry all over again, and we keep coming back for more of the same.
- A healthy mind is proportional to what you decide to put in your body.
- Farming animals for food causes forty percent more green house gas emissions than cars.
- Ninety percent of dieters regain the weight they lose in less than a year.
- This is an optimal diet that is proven to provide you with far more energy, positivity and a healthier lifestyle.
- Eating a low carb diet only helps with temporary weight loss and can lead to some serious health problems.
- Carbohydrates provide energy to the muscles, nervous system and specifically the brain, which relies completely on carbohydrates to pump in the glucose, which is essential for its functioning.
- Simple carbohydrates are not the best types of carbs to include in your diet because they can cause an increase in your glucose and insulin levels. These then trigger off hunger pangs leading to overeating, resulting in fat accumulation.
- Although fibre does not play any role in the production of energy, it helps in digestion, bowel movement, reduces heart problems, maintains sugar levels and is equally essential for you.

- *If the body lacks carbohydrates it makes it difficult for fats to burn normally.*
- *A high protein diet, especially one that you get through meat, can lead to heart problems and a lack of calcium causing osteoporosis.*
- *55 to 60 percent of the calories should come from carbohydrates alone.*
- *Complex carbohydrates are considered far better, as they digest slowly and provide energy for a longer period of time.*
- *When you fail to take carbohydrates, your brain ceases to organise the production of serotonin, a substance produced in the brain that stimulates the mood and reduces hunger pangs.*
- *Your diet must contain more complex carbohydrates and fibre and a small amount of simple carbohydrates.*
- *Use the diet diary to honestly acknowledge the way in which you're affected by the foods you eat.*
- *Whilst the human body can store fats and excess carbohydrates, it is unable to store excess protein. So aim to get your balance just right.*
- *There are more efficient protein-rich sources of foods, which do not require you to eat copious amounts of saturated fats at the same time.*
- *Saturated fat is found to increase cholesterol production by the body. It also decreases insulin sensitivity, which causes the body to store food more often as fat.*
- *Coronary heart disease is the most common cause of death in the UK and it is suspected that large amounts of meats, prevalent in our diet, are to blame.*
- *Protein can be just as prevalent in plant-derived foods as their animal counterparts.*
- *Look at low fat Soya flour as an example; where nearly half of its overall mass is devoted to protein. No animal-derived food source gets close to this.*

- *In the UK we spend around £1.2 billion on pre-sliced, pre-packaged bread each year and if bread protein is combined with certain other plant foods, it will produce a complete protein source that your body requires.*
- *There are literally thousands of uses for protein with cell renewal being the most important.*
- *Look at the amount of saturated fat you find with products that are high in protein (animal-derived). Then compare these with plant-derived high protein foods.*
- *It is vital for men to consume a certain amount of fat each day.*
- *Fat is the one type of macronutrient that the body is able to store which translates into excess weight.*
- *The creation of trans fat occurs when liquid oils solidify by partial hydrogenation, a process that stretches food shelf life and changes "safe" unsaturated fat into dangerous fat.*
- *Heart disease, clogged arteries, and high cholesterol are the main health risks, but some studies indicate trans fats as triggers for diabetes and various forms of cancer as well.*
- *Monounsaturated and polyunsaturated fats actually help lower your cholesterol and in turn put you at a lower risk for heart disease.*
- *Butter could not be any worse for your health as it contains numerous different types of saturated fats.*
- *As a general rule of thumb, the harder and more solid the type of fat, the worse it is for you.*
- *Olive oil and sunflower oil are an excellent substitute for animal and vegetable oils as they are high in essential monounsaturated fats and other antioxidative substances.*
- *You can create healthy habits, which will bring as much pleasure to your palette as the negative alternatives.*
- *People are more likely to neglect the intake of adequate amounts of micronutrients, than they would with the macronutrients. Their*

education of protein, fats and carbohydrates tends to extend a little further than vitamins and minerals. But it is important to understand that our bodies need them in small amounts, to support the chemical reactions our cells need to survive. They affect digestion, the nervous system, thinking and various other body processes.

- *Your body is not able to store water soluble vitamins and thus you need to ensure that you consume regular and sufficient supplies.*
- *Vitamin H (Biotin) is essential if you are looking to prevent baldness.*
- *Let's take a look at the types of minerals that are imperative for our health.*
- *It is a myth to think that calcium can only be obtained from dairy products.*
- *These plant-based sources are thought by many to be superior to dairy, because they are also excellent sources of antioxidants, fibre, folic acid, complex carbohydrates, iron and other important vitamins and minerals which you won't find in milk products.*
- *Approximately 85% of the body's phosphorus is found in bone and it is essential for the creation of DNA in our bodies.*
- *This micronutrient is essential for the conduction of nerve impulses.*
- Females require a higher amount of iron than men because they use up reserves of iron in their menstrual cycles and it is much more common for women to suffer from anemia (lack of iron), than men.
- Zinc used in combating problems on the skin, like boils or acne, as well as aiding muscle growth.
- *With genetic manipulation and intensive production technologies, it is common for modern dairy cows to produce 100 pounds of milk a day, 10 times more than they would produce in nature. Growth hormones and unnatural milking schedules cause dairy*

cows' udders to become painful and so heavy that they sometimes drag on the ground, resulting in frequent infections and overuse of antibiotics.

- *They are also likely to be contaminated with antibiotics, hormones and other chemicals such as dioxin, one of the most toxic substances in the world.*

- *Soya milk is an ideal alternative to cow's milk. It contains vegetable proteins, which results in less calcium loss through the kidneys.*

- *70% of the world's population is lactose intolerant.*

- *We have always blamed carbohydrates for causing obesity. It is in fact high protein diets and fats that are responsible, with excessive meat in our diet topping the list.*

- *Red meats are accepted as being a contributory factor towards a lower life expectancy.*

- *An area of rain forest the size of seven football fields is destroyed every minute to make room for grazing cattle.*

- *About 20 percent of the world's population could be fed with the grain and soybeans fed to U.S. cattle alone.*

- *Since the digestive process of meat is slow, heavy oxidation takes place and can result in a large accrual of free radicals.*

- *It is estimated that nearly eighty per cent of land is used for cattle rearing food consumption.*

- *Livestock accounts for more than 18 per cent of all greenhouse gases.*

- *The average person can be responsible for consuming more than 2,000 livestock in a lifetime.*

- *Studies have actually revealed that people who live on meat-free diets have a longer lifespan than meat eaters.*

- *Excess sugar is converted into fat, returned to the bloodstream and then stored as fat in the stomach, butt and chest.*

- *The raised insulin levels, caused by sugar, depress the immune system, which results in an inability to fight diseases. On top of this, as refined sugar contains no vitamins and minerals the body ends up drawing on its reserves.*

- *Sugar speeds up the ageing process.*

- *Soda has high levels of phosphorous, which increase calcium loss in the body.*

- *Research has shown that the combination of this substance with carbohydrates leads to decreased serotonin production. Bottom line – you will drink yourself into a depression.*

- *We have become far too dependent on fast food and products containing synthetic additives and sugar. There is little or no nutritional value in these kinds of meals. Our bodies are in truth being starved and a large part of the problem is being ill informed.*

- *The single biggest killer of men in the UK is the heart attack. By eating foods that are lower in cholesterol such as oatmeal, walnuts and plant derived foods with omega 3, you can keep this at an appropriate level.*

- *The tomato, which contains a phyto-nutrient called lycopene, has been hailed as one of the best weapons against prostate cancer.*

- *For heart disease and cancer alone, eliminating the meat and dairy elements of your diet can reduce the risk of developing them by as much as 57%.*

- *Eliminating all of the trans-fatty acids and saturated fats that cause you body to deteriorate will shed those unwanted pounds at an incredible rate.*

- *Red meat is full of fat, which turns testosterone into a powerful hormone known as DHT. This hormone attacks the hair follicles and basically kills them off. If you were to cut out the meat from your diet, hair loss and baldness could be slowed down to a natural pace.*

- *It is a common case that as many as three out of four men, by the age of 23, already have blocked arteries.*

- *Men are 16% more likely to develop cancer than women. And to scare you even further, 40% more men die from cancer than women.*
- *The lowest cancer rates occur in Third World Countries, where plant based foods are predominantly consumed.*

- *Positive or negative actions became reinforced leading to continual habits being formed, resulting in your personal definition.*
- *The formation of good habits become your most potent tool in terms of developing self-esteem and positive perceptions of the self.*
- *Identify some of the more harmful substances that can result in premature ageing.*
- *First impressions are formed within 30 seconds.*
- *By doing this daily, you are blotting away the excess oil that makes the skin look shiny and unhealthy.*
- *Make sure your moisturiser is oil free as this means it will not clog your pores.*
- *To maintain firmness and elasticity, you should also use toners.*
- *This helps to reduce the puffiness or bags under your eyes.*
- *Face scrubs with fine granules are a lot better for your skin because they clean your skin more effectively, particularly in problem areas (between your nose and your cheek). A good scrub will remove dead skin cells too.*
- *Make sure the brands you choose for general skin cleansing are free of chemicals and preservatives.*
- *Toners with alphahydroxy and glycolic reduce pore size. Always look for skin friendly toners that contain substances like aloe and omegas.*
- *Research has shown that many skin care products that make products just for men, have the same ingredients as women's products.*
- *You shouldn't use deodorant soap on your face, as they have harsh ingredients.*

- *A crucial step to caring for your facial skin is getting to know your skin type.*
- *Your pores NEED to be cleaned or else your skin will become irritated and dehydrated, which can cause pimples, blemishes and blackheads.*
- *Men's facial skin generally has larger pores compared to women's, which results in the accumulation of more dirt and the production of more oil in the pores.*
- *Testosterone is the chemical in men's skin that makes it thicker.*
- *Age spots appear due to the sugar in the system binding with collagen and causing a chemical reaction called glycosylation.*
- *Free radicals are unpaired electrons that attack healthy cells in our body.*
- *Damage to healthy cells is through a reaction called oxidation and thus leads to skin damage as well as premature ageing.*
- *Since these free radicals are oxidants in cells, the best way to control them is by drinking supplements and foodstuff rich in antioxidants. Some examples of these include fruits (particularly berries), ascorbic acid tablets and vegetables.*
- *The blood absorbs carbon monoxide 200 times faster than oxygen, which results in a lot of oxygen being displaced.*
- *Your skin consists of 90% water.*
- *Warm water can get rid of black heads and makes large skin pores smaller.*
- *Excessive drinking of alcohol will lead to the development of telangiectasias or chronic dilation of the capillaries and a permanent flush on the face will appear.*
- *Alcohol depletes the body of vitamin A, which is an important anti-oxidant.*
- *For combination and oily skins, clay works a treat by absorbing the toxins and balancing the oil.*

- *The average person smiles up to 50 times a day.*
- *The best whitening toothpaste brands according to the British Dental Journal are Macleans Whitening, Aquafresh, Rapid White and Super White.*
- *Regular consistent flossing is your best weapon against plaque – maybe even more important than your toothbrush.*
- *Certain foods tend to produce volatile sulphur compounds, which are the culprits behind bad breath.*
- *The general rule is that the oval face shape is the most appealing to women, so tell your hairstylist to create a style that will make your face more oval in shape. If your face is long, you need to create the illusion of shortening, while wide faces need to create the illusion of lengthening.*
- *Short hair works for most faces barring the square shaped face.*
- *If you have an oblong face, medium length hairstyles are probably the most suitable.*
- *If you have a big nose a fuller style helps draw attention away from it. Make sure the cut is more voluminous in the front than the back. Also, stay away from a centre parting as it draws attention to the centre of your face.*
- *If you are new to hair colouring it is advisable to take a cautious approach. Consult experts if you are looking for a procedure that requires double process techniques (bleaching and toning).*
- *Temporary colours work best on blonde or light-coloured hair.*
- *Although permanent hair colours will give you the look that you want without it washing out, it can cause unwanted damage to the hair.*
- *A dirty scalp will be a conducive place for a micro-organism called pityrosporum-ovle to breed.*
- *Numerous surveys state women find too much body hair unattractive. Not a revelation, is it? They much prefer the smooth and sexy image of a sleek look.*

- *Always shave in the shower or after you have had a bath so your skin is clean and smooth when you shave. The steam from the shower also prevents skin irritation and softens the hair on your face*
- *In a survey by aftershave manufacturer Lynx, the following information was revealed: beards, moustaches and goatees are a huge turn-off for women, particularly when left unkempt and dirty. Here are some statistics.*
- *Avoid putting on cologne that contains alcohol after you shave, as this will dry the skin out.*
- *If you suffer from itching it can be a good idea to rub some organic olive oil into the skin and beard. Be careful not to use too much.*
- *Make sure the style is symmetrical.*
- *In this day and age it is advisable to ignore the moustache and the goatee.*
- *Hair growth is longer, faster and thicker on the back and chest.*
- *If you don't want redness, swelling and scarring because of a trapped follicle (Ingrown Hair), you can use skin care products that contain salicylic acid. It is basically a dermatological-grade ingredient that helps in exfoliation*
- *Adult nasal hair grows at a rate of approximately 0.35mm per day, approximately 1 cm per month.*
- *Big bushy pubic hair is very unattractive.*
- *Eyebrows need to be trimmed regularly to "open up" your eyes.*
- *Bath salts are also excellent for a tired and sore body.*
- *Body products made from plant ingredients are most effective for dry and tired skin.*
- *A number of lifestyle magazines highlight the fact that hands are something women notice most often when they are on a date.*
- *You need to clean your feet at least once a day in order to prevent bacterial build up, which can result in bad odours.*

- *Make sure you buy one that encourages the pigmentation process and not one that just dyes it.*
- *Make sure there is no alcohol in your deodorant as this can often cause rashes and swelling of the skin.*
- *You can also use talc body powder on areas where you sweat profusely. This will help absorb any excess moisture and control odours.*
- *You will need to replenish the moisture your skin has lost by applying a light aloe Vera, eucalyptus or mint containing lotion.*

INTRODUCTION TO "SEX, RELATIONSHIPS, DATING, NUTRITION & GROOMING" WHAT MEN REALLY NEED TO KNOW!

INTRODUCTION

"Sex, Relationships, Dating, Nutrition & Grooming" What Men Really Need to Know! was born out of opportunity and a desire to understand my own mistakes on that journey personifying personal freedom. Fortune created time for me to research five essential areas that if understood and acted upon, would transform a man in terms of being a great lover, fix his broken relationship or avoiding getting his relationship to that stage, create genuine confidence in the dating game, lose weight, live longer by being healthier and look great in a way he could never imagine. These five areas were chosen as a result of an abundance of research, identified out of necessity, as this is where men fail and fail again and will continue to do so unless acted upon. The bottom line is women play such a large part in our lives, yet there seems to be a common thread of miscommunication and misunderstanding which inevitably leads to bad sex, bad relationships, bad habits and men with severe levels of low self esteem getting fat, lethargic, hopeless and wondering what might have been.

Men are never taught the rules of engagement when it comes to dating, sex or relationships and the results are often farcical and congruent with complete and utter disappointment. You're rubbish in bed, she's probably faking an orgasm and you're sabotaging your relationship whether it is conscious or not. You're also eating junk which makes you fat and unhealthy which in turn is killing any little bit of self esteem you have, if you're single you're petrified of walking up to a woman and saying hi and lastly...you do not know how to look attractive. Notwithstanding these truths or untruths, however you wish to perceive your life, there remains a desire from me to provide you with the best possible opportunity to find the truest version of yourself. Why? Simply put, so she can climax every time you have sex, so you can fix your broken relationship or better yet, not get to that point, so you can drop two stone by eating a healthy well balanced diet and live longer, and do so in less than four weeks, so you can see a girl you are attracted to and be fearless in approaching her and so you can know what works and does not work in terms of looking attractive. The bottom line is this! You will elevate your self esteem and stop destroying that excellent version of yourself that exists somewhere inside of you.

Bear this in mind; I am not the expert, but rather the student who needed to learn as a result of his own personal shortcomings and a desire to overcome them. This book was first published in 2009 and re-published in 2014 with thousands of articles investigated, hundreds of books read, specialists consulted and it remains the common thread that each and every one of those resources provided. There is so much bogus information out there on the internet, but if one of the leading psychologists in the UK said **"Every single man should have this book by his bedside table reading it night after night"**....well...it's the real deal. Read the book and follow the principles that apply to you and I can promise you one thing, you will reach heights you only ever dreamt of.

The intent of this book is simple. Not for you to follow every single piece of advice contained within, because that would be setting yourself up for failure. But to try to follow the principles that apply to you and apply them so they become habits which change your life. What's the end result? You'll feel like a man in bed because your partner will have an orgasm every time you have sex, you'll understand the solution to your relationship problems and re-ignite the love that is still there, just hidden. If you see an attractive woman in a coffee shop, grocery store or on the street...you will have the balls to go say hi and ask her for her number. If you are obese, fat, slightly overweight and want to get lean and stay that way, you'll do it in four weeks and finally, you'll shave that tash and groom yourself so women actually notice you through unique separation from the rest of the ungroomed herd. So, if you want to look younger, healthier, attractive, assertive, and confident, be excellent in bed and developed in terms of not demolishing your relationship...read on. These five sections on sex, relationships, dating, nutrition, and grooming are here to change your sex life, love life, loveless life, fat body, health, fear of the opposite sex and the way you look and feel.

By addressing these five sections, and the elements that apply to you, I can promise you five things.

- You will bring whoever you are having sex with to an orgasm!
- You will fix your broken relationship or better yet, avoid getting to that place!
- You will be able to attract any woman you want!
- You will drop two stones in four weeks if you follow some of my advice!
- You will live longer by eating healthier!
- You will look more attractive than ever before!

This book is about displacing negative self-beliefs and attaining genuine levels of self-esteem through actions, not words. I reference self-esteem on a number of occasions in this book because quite simply, when you are a great lover, a great partner, fearless and attractive, the end results speak for themselves. The development of this self-esteem and fulfilment however goes beyond your individual boundaries.

The section on SEX is about being able to pleasure your partner and make her have orgasms! This has to be one of the most gratifying personal feelings a man can have. Again, this is an area which is least understood by men. You've watched the porn, you think she's enjoying it and I can assure of one thing...its garbage and she's not. This is not a simple biology lesson on female anatomy. It is a detailed understanding through exploration and volumes of research, providing you with the essential tools to being an excellent lover. It provides you with techniques that will elicit genuine orgasms from her. I also cut the crap on all the myths regarding intercourse. In a nutshell, this is going to be your blueprint for understanding the female body and all of her wonderful erogenous zones. At the end of this section you are going to be able to send her to cataclysmic orgasmic heights.

The section on RELATIONSHIPS teaches you how to stop fucking up your relationship by avoiding conscious or subconscious sabotage. It provides you with the tools to make your relationship work or fix your broken relationship. If you have any doubts about this, think about what that senior psychologist said. **"Every single man should have this book by his bedside table reading it night after night!"** You will understand what a healthy and loving relationship is and what you need to do to get one.

The section on DATING is to simply action a famous quote: "Everything you want is on the other side of fear". There are masses of literature in terms of dating, which embody manufacturing fictitious versions of yourself to get women interested in you. They also revere multiple conquests as the definition of success. It's bullshit, and I am yet to find a single guy who sleeps with over a hundred women a year...happy. If you want to use this section for that, go wild, but let me know how complete it makes you feel afterwards. This section is about being your true fearless self and getting the girl you want. It's not about bedding hundreds of women a week. It is about being able to get the **one** woman you truly want. How? By using attraction as a verb, a doing word, a choice and deleting 'approach anxiety' from the memory bank so you can get any woman you are attracted to. Through this, you will develop rapport and elicit a genuine emotional connection with her.

The section on NUTRITION focuses on you losing weight by cutting the crap out of your diet. You do this by following what you can in the Optimum Male Diet. We examine all the essential macro and micronutrients that are essential for your health and wellbeing and eradicate all the myths about carbohydrates, proteins, fats, dairy and meat. The aim of this section is for you to get lean and trim, stay that way and embark on a nutritional lifestyle that is healthy. The result is simply looking and feeling better than ever before and living longer.

The section on GROOMING, gives you the best advice on looking after your skin and body and what women genuinely find appealing. It highlights the essential elements in accentuating the more attractive physical qualities you have, an example being the type of cuts to suit the shape of your face. We also look at a number of factors that can help you maintain a youthful appearance.

I wish you much success on your journey. Apply what you read into actions, and you will make whoever you are having sex with cum, fix your broken relationship and reignite the love that once was there or better yet, avoid getting to that place, attract any woman you want, drop two stones in four weeks and become most attractive version of yourself you possibly can.

Good Luck!

SEX

Sex

Being in a relationship with a woman can be incredibly fulfilling for both parties and even more so when you are able to satisfy each other. As well as the commonalities of respect, kindness, understanding, equality and supportiveness, it is important to recognise equality in terms of sexual response. Many of us think that we are doing quite well in the bedroom department, but you may be surprised that there is a lot yet to learn. And taking the time to boost your knowledge of how your partner works will make you a far better lover!

The Aim of this Section: Sex

The female body is something that is thrown at us almost every day, whether it is on television, films, newspapers, magazines or a quiet glance on the tube. Although we can admire the female body, let's be honest, we don't really have that much of a clue as to how it really works or what makes her tick! Women are incredibly complex creatures and it can be a daunting task to fathom the intricacies of her pleasures and potential pitfalls. The extent of our knowledge lies in their capacity to give life and a few minor biology lessons at school regarding the vagina, clitoris and the capacity to breast-feed.

The aim of this section is to give you all the information you need to understand the woman in your life in terms of her sexual needs, wants and desires. We are going to focus on giving you the tools to deliver the utmost pleasure to your partner – which is something that she thoroughly deserves! I promise you that by reading this section and putting all of the information to good use, you will escalate your relationship with your partner in the bedroom department to new heights.

In Sex, Chapter 1, we are going to discuss why it is so important to pleasure your partner and identify if you are really pleasing her.

In Sex, Chapter 2, we are going to look at the differences between outercourse and intercourse as well as listing all their benefits and potential pitfalls.

In Sex, Chapter 3, we are going to discuss foreplay, coreplay and moreplay. We will also delve into some of the aspects of cunnilingus.

In Sex, Chapter 4, you are going to find out all about rhythm, tension and escalation.

In Sex, Chapter 5, we will spend some time discussing the pre-orgasm and orgasm stages of sexual response as well as identifying her signs of readiness.

In Sex, Chapter 6, you will develop some insight into the concept of simultaneity. You will also learn about the most favourable positions in reaching this state.

In Sex, Chapter 7, we are going to identify all those essential erogenous zones.

In Sex, Chapter 8, we'll get you started on some exercises to get you primed for her pleasure.

In Sex, Chapter 9, you are almost on your way to becoming the perfect lover.

THE HISTORY OF SEX

Many of us who were born into the current generation recognise to a certain extent, that women deserve equality in and out of the bedroom. This has not always been the case though. Through the ages women have been treated as sex objects and nothing more. We have also had media pressing for women to look and act in a certain way, more often than not, incongruent with the reality of happiness.

It may interest you to know that in the earlier days of man, women were revered for the sexual beings that they are. There were many goddesses that were worshipped for their immense sexuality; their power to bring life onto this earth. There were even celebrations which involved costumes, music, feasts and sexual rituals! One of the Empresses of China, during the Dynastic years, used to order visiting politicians and dignitaries to perform sexual acts on her – and most of them willingly obliged. This was a significant show of how much power she had and reinforces the link between power and sex, which is still current today.

We lost the importance of a woman's sexuality somewhere along the way, until the early 17th century. Those days when Greek warriors could claim the wife and children of their dead opponent as their own? Or when landowners could claim "Prima Nocte" – the first night with a bride after she had been wed, particularly if the girl was a peasant or surf?

We found ourselves conducting sexual activity purely for reproduction up until the Industrial Revolution. This is partly due to the fact that religion played a much stronger part in dictating our decisions. The Victorian period was attributed with being the "watershed" era, which found cultures mixing, due to the Industrial Revolution, and attitudes of sexual enjoyment came to the fore.

We delved into the beauty and sexuality of women during the sexual revolution of the 1950's, 1960's and 1970's. The 1960's empowered women with the creation of the contraceptive pill. There was no longer the worry of falling pregnant out of wedlock and women were free to indulge in the sheer pleasure of sex in the same way as men did. This ultimately led to equality of sexual response that we are experiencing today.

IS THERE EQUALITY IN YOUR BEDROOM?

You may have read this chapter so far and think that you are a very loving and giving sexual partner. I aim to show you that although you may think you are pleasuring that special woman in your life, you actually aren't! There is good news though. You are en route with the aid of knowledge, dedication, patience and of course, lots of practice to making her orgasm more than she could ever have imagined.

Firstly, ask yourself this question; "Do I always make sure that my partner is fully satisfied before I turn my attention to myself?" I am guessing that having thought hard about this question, the conclusion that you have reached is NO! It is usually the case that men assume women are happy with some groping and a lot of vaginal penetration until he reaches orgasm. Thus, the male orgasm is the ultimate highlight of the encounter.

We see vaginal penetration as the be all and end all; we thrust like we have never thrusted before...with the end result being more of the same. But have you ever considered that this may not be the best experience for your partner? Later on in this section we will examine why vaginal penetration is not the best way to make your partner orgasm; nor is it the most exciting part of the sexual experience for a woman. Yes, I am stating that the things that are important during the sexual process for men and women are different. For the moment, leave your mind open and take a step back from the idea that vaginal penetration is the best thing since sliced bread for the woman in your life.

INTERESTING FACTS THAT WILL BLOW YOUR MIND

As I have said, a woman's body is a complex and amazing thing. We have also acknowledged that we know pretty much nil about it. How many erogenous zones can you name for example? Do you know how to spot a fake orgasm? Did you know that the clitoris has 8,000 nerve endings? This last fact, I'm quite sure, has left you with your jaw agape. How can something that small have so much sensitivity? Let's take a closer look.

The woman's clitoris is actually made up of 18 parts, some of which you cannot see. Many people, including women, think that the clitoris is the small nub or head situated above the vaginal opening. This is actually the powerhouse of the whole clitoral network, but it takes many hotspots throughout the different internal and external parts of the network to create an orgasm. Each part has a different role to play in a woman's sexual response and many of these are seriously overlooked.

Now, as I also said, a woman's clitoris has 8,000 nerve endings. This is actually double the number that is found on a man's penis. So, when we are feeling that sexual tension and intensity just imagine what it must be like for her!

Scientists have also confirmed that the same tissue in the womb is used to create the penis and the vagina, within the first three months of development. So essentially, you could state that the clitoris is the female version of the penis. This is not altogether true though, as the clitoris has no other function except pleasure. It plays no part in the reproduction process and is in fact, situated too high up on the outside of a woman's body to be of any other use. Interestingly, doctors and scientists in the 18th century did believe that the female orgasm was a fundamental part of the act of reproducing but science has come a long way since then. We now know that the clitoris is purely an area that is designed to match the intensity and sexual release that us men feel every time we ejaculate.

For those of you who are a whiz at mathematics, this next point will be easy to calculate. The average time a man makes love to a woman (that is to say, where vaginal penetration takes place) is two and a half minutes. Now take the fact that it takes a woman an average of fifteen minutes to become fully aroused and receptive to receiving a phenomenal orgasm. Herein lays a slight problem in the equality of sexual response, certainly in terms of the way most couple's routines do not allow for fifteen minutes of foreplay, never mind any outercourse, coreplay or pre-orgasm stages (don't worry too much about these terms at the moment; they are important but you will find out all you need to know about them in the coming chapters!).

STRIPPING AWAY THE MYTHS

There are many myths and stereotypes that befall a woman when it comes to pleasure and sex. We have to remember that all women are different and what one may find enjoyable, another will find a complete turn off. The best way to find out what turns your partner on is to take the time to actually ask her. Sex can still be a fairly taboo subject, even between men and women in serious relationships. Unfortunately this means that we tend to listen to all of the female sexual myths to identify what works and what doesn't.

We wouldn't be men if we did not look at pornographic materials – no need to hide it under the mattress here. We are visual creatures and this is one of the best ways for us to get turned on. Secondly, it can be educational when we are looking for new things to try with our partners.

Basically, whatever you are looking for, you will find a magazine or DVD that has it and some more.

As enjoyable as a dirty film is for us, there is an important simple realisation to make. Almost everything that you see or read is exaggerated for the purpose of sales. If you watch a film where a woman is screaming her way to orgasm in the lotus position, it is 99.9% certain that she is performing for the camera. The same can be said of a woman in a porn flick having multiple orgasms at the drop of a hat. In other words, how you see a woman reacting in a pornographic movie is not a true reflection of what women enjoy in their sexual encounters.

Most films show off couples climaxing together through intercourse and women shuddering with multiple orgasms. The truth, only 30% of women achieve an orgasm by way of vaginal penetration; the rest rely on stimulation of the clitoris by hand or tongue. Some more food for thought; whilst it is scientifically achievable for all women to have more than one orgasm during a sexual encounter, the majority are satisfied with one. Although she can recover reasonably quickly after having the orgasm, the clitoris is still a very sensitive area and requires some respite. It is exactly the same for us mere men – we need time to recover before we can get our penis ready for action again.

ACTIONS

Keep a Note of Activities

In order to identify the key areas for improvement, I want you to keep a note of your routine in the bedroom department for the next two weeks. Write down some thoughts on the entire sexual experience. Did she climax? Did you try something new? Was there foreplay? I also want you to pay attention to the times you go down on her, that is performing oral sex.

Take the Bull By the Horns

The next step is to grab the bull by the horns and ask your partner if she is satisfied in the bedroom department. It is likely that you will get a "fine, it's wonderful" reply with a beaming smile. Do not accept this as gospel. We all know that sex can be a difficult subject to discuss, even with long-term partners and it is unlikely that she wants to rock the boat. Make sure that you encourage her to give you an honest answer; show her that you are interested in hearing her thoughts and opinions about your sex sessions together. It is also important that you ensure your partner that you will not be offended by anything critical that she has to say. It may be a bitter and hard pill to take if she does have some negative comments. Just remember that you are now open to learning how to put this right and once you have mastered the process of really pleasuring her, you will be taking your relationship to another level.

Do A Bit of Research

Without freaking your partner out too much, try and take a closer look at her clitoral network. I am sure after explaining the reasons behind your interest; she will be more than receptive. Maybe stun her with a few facts that you have learnt about the female body. Alternatively, any good biology or human anatomy book will give you wonderfully in-depth diagrams.

The Glans – This is the part that is known as the head or the clit. You may also call it the nub, love button, the love bud or the jewel in the crown! This is the visible part that has most of the nerve endings and is ultra sensitive. There is a hood that surrounds this delicate area, which protects the glans during stimulation.

Labia Minora – This is the part that is commonly referred to as the "little" or "inner" lips of the vaginal area. Their job is to protect the vaginal entrance, the glans and the urethra. They contain layer upon layer of oil glands and have many nerve endings. They play a crucial role in the arousal process.

Labia Majora – These are what are deemed to be the "outer" or "bigger" lips of the vaginal area. They have pubic hair on the outside and sweat and oil glands on the inside. This area is not as sensitive as others in the clitoral network but respond during the sexual process by filling out with blood when a woman is aroused.

Mons Pubis – This is the "fluffy" area often referred to as the "love mound". It has layers of fatty tissue, which lie above the gland and is covered in pubic hair.

Perineum – This is the small area of skin that lies just below the entrance to the vagina and above the anus. It is a very sensitive area that can be a great source of arousal when used in foreplay and coreplay techniques.

SEX, CHAPTER 1: WHY IT IS IMPORTANT TO PLEASURE YOUR PARTNER?

Summary: This may seem like an obvious point – of course you want to make sure that your partner enjoys sexual experiences as much as you do. But women view their sex life and the fulfilment of it in a completely different manner to men. This chapter will show you how you can ensure that you are giving her the best pleasure possible and ultimately, what this means for you.

IS SHE TRULY ENJOYING THE EXPERIENCE?

I'm sure most of you have had sexual experiences where you felt a bit deflated afterwards. Maybe you came too quickly or she was unresponsive and looked bored. Remember how that made you feel? Guilty and certainly not feeling like an Alpha Male!

The point I am trying to make is that the success of the encounter is largely down to whether your partner is able to orgasm or not. This is the precedent for its success or failure. If she enjoyed herself, you will no doubt too. But the primary focus must be on pleasuring her...and not yourself.

THE BENEFITS FOR YOU

It is disparaging to say the least, when you feel as if you are not fulfilling your wife or girlfriend. It leads to thoughts of inadequacy and ultimately it is a broken spoke in the wheel. The opposite can be said when your partner is enjoying the experience and on the receiving end of numerous orgasms. You feel like a provider and resolute in terms of your relationship.

The bottom line is that you want to feel like you are a great lover and the only way to ensure this is by putting her needs before yours. Whilst it is important that there is equality in these stakes, the satisfaction should be such that she is truly sated before the end of each sex session. The thing about women is that they are not very vocal with regards to the extent of their enjoyment when it comes to sex. As women are more emotionally wired, they prefer to sit on the fence and claim that the earth moved for them, even when it clearly didn't. This ultimately leads us to thinking that there is no need for improvement.

This is a cycle you need to break if you are genuinely interested in her being sexually fulfilled. The benefits of embarking on this selfless approach are numerous. Firstly, our egos are done no damage by being classed as an amazing lover. Secondly, the process will become reciprocal. She will want to understand your desires and push the very buttons that make you tick. Thirdly, it goes without saying that a healthy sexual relationship is the cornerstone of a fulfilling relationship.

THE PHYSICAL IMPORTANCE

As discussed earlier, it takes 15 minutes for a woman to become fully aroused. What this means for you is simple. Foreplay needs to incorporate a lot more than a 5 minute fondle followed by penetration. If you ignore this, her sense of stimulation is thwarted which results in no lubrication and ultimately a very uncomfortable experience for her. Her response to touch and the intercourse itself may be painful resulting in her feeling reluctant for future sexual endeavours.

It is paramount to understand that in order for a woman to truly enjoy sex, she needs to be psychologically and physically ready. This is achieved through taking time in the build up to make sure she has acquired the same level of arousal as you have. As visual beings, we do not require as much as she does to bring us to this state of intoxication. Being aware that she does, and making inroads into her achieving these states of arousal will generate a sexually fulfilled partner.

THE PSYCHOLOGICAL IMPORTANCE

Although it is naïve to maintain men do not go through a range of emotions when it comes to sex, it is fair to say that women experience them in a more complex manner. She has more to lose at the end of the day; being labelled a slut whereas you will be elevated to a studly status or even her biological concerns of falling pregnant. This adds another dimension to the success of the encounter and results in it being imperative that she feels safe, secure, wanted, loved and truly bonded with the man she is about to indulge.

Of course I am well aware of one night stands, but I am more interested in the genuine interest of pleasing someone you care about. When a woman has made that decision to settle down with someone, she develops a bond and her emotional intensity is heightened in the bedroom department. She will want to feel that you are interested in pleasuring her for your own reasons and that you generate a lot of pleasure out of the act.

When it comes to activities such as oral sex, many women feel that their partner is doing it just to please them and not because they want to. This can lead to a big psychological issue and an ultimate barrier to women; this is something that we will explore in much more detail in the next chapter.

Self-image and self-belief are two major factors that affect a woman's sex drive and the resulting pleasure from each sexual experience. If a woman feels unattractive or inadequate in the bedroom department, then it is very difficult for them to fully indulge themselves. It becomes a routine or a chore that needs to be done. This in turn can result in the male feeling inadequate. The point is that you need to indulge the psychological aspect of making her comfortable. Being positive and elevating her self-esteem will create comfort and security, which is paramount in terms of heightening the sexual encounter itself.

Increasing her confidence with genuine intent, will allow her to concentrate on her own personal gratification, which will result in a less inhibited sexual experience. For example, assurance is needed when you are about to go down on her that this is something that you derive sincere pleasure from. And I can't see why you wouldn't. Heightening the state of your partner should be a highly exhilarating experience. The downside of not being able to provide this psychological comfort is a withdrawn, self-conscious and cynical woman in the same bed as you.

COMMUNICATION

There is no such thing as a successful relationship without communication. This is no different when it comes to sexually fulfilling your partner. The key element to remember here is that sensitive and assertive conversation will unlock a number of unnecessary inhibitions.

It may shock you to know that 75% of women have faked an orgasm at some point in their lives. The inability to approach the topic of likes and dislikes results in the manufacturing of an experience. It is essential to open communication to a level of sincerity and honesty, which will result in both of you expressing your true desires. With only 30% of women achieving orgasm through vaginal penetration it is important to explore other alternatives available, no matter how incongruent they may seem with comfortable conversation.

How Do I Know If I Am Pleasing Her?

For many men this can be a difficult question to answer. With so many faked orgasms being blasted through the rooftops every night, how is it possible to identify whether she is being satisfied or not?

The first sure-fire way to know that she has had an orgasm is by way of vaginal contractions. You will be able to feel these pulses, of which there are generally six to eight after she has climaxed, if you are inside her. There is usually some ejaculation fluid or just secretions from the vagina. If you can feel the pulsing and her vaginal walls tighten around your penis, you can pat yourself on the back because she has had an orgasm.

Other visible signs of a woman having an orgasm include breathlessness, the abdomen and thighs tightening and her skin flushing. She may tilt her pelvis against you to increase the pressure on her clitoris so that the orgasm becomes more intense.

If you are a fan of making your partner orgasm through the process of cunnilingus, by far the greatest method at our disposal, then there is also another noticeable sign that she has truly come. The clitoris will retract back under the clitoral hood when she is very close to orgasm. If you have also inserted your fingers into her vagina, you will be able to feel the pulsing that has been mentioned above.

It can take a woman several moments to come down from experiencing an orgasm and regain her composure. If she recovers very quickly, then there is the possibility that she faked it! As the clitoris is also very sensitive, she will be incredibly sensitive after having a real orgasm. Even a woman who likes multiple orgasms will require that bit of downtime before she is able to handle her second or third offering.

REDUCE THE POSSIBILITY OF STALENESS AND BOREDOM

Sexual exploration is paramount in terms of satisfaction. Common sexual routines can often become comfortable and safe for us, resulting in a severe lack of exploration. We continue with the same techniques and routines that have more often than not, provided very little pleasure.

Another key element to becoming a great lover is abandoning the monotony of the past and exploring new preferences and pleasures. There are an abundance of different positions, toys and games that can heighten the experience for both of you.

Engaging in role-play or purchasing some sexy lingerie for her will raise her libido immensely. Being an excellent lover is about heightening and drawing out the entire experience to include all of the little innuendos, flirtations as well as the final act of intercourse itself. Creating a new enthusiastic environment where both of you are able to explore each other more freely will result in a heightened experience.

It basically comes down to drawing the level of stimulation out for as long as possible. Let's say she brought home some sexy lingerie…your initial impulse would be to rip this off as quickly as possible and get stuck into the intercourse. But think about a couple of things here. Firstly, she has spent all day choosing the right lingerie in anticipation of an erotic sexual experience with you. She will have agonized over what makes her look and feel good, and what you will think about it. She wants to be able to show it off and enjoy the reaction it has on you.

By going in for the kill you will only make her feel self-conscious and inevitably this will result in a serious downpour on her self esteem. As discussed earlier, her self-esteem is essential to the success of your sexual exploit. The moment should instead be seen as one to savour for as long as possible, exploiting your appreciation for her endeavour. This will result in an inner comfort that is conducive to a memorable orgasm.

KEEP THE PLEASURE HEIGHTENED

If you have realised that penetration is not the ultimate tool in arousing your partner to a point of climax, then you are a step ahead of the game. Understanding that women have different physical and emotional expectations will allow you to start making some important changes. The key is to keep the pleasure heightened for as long as possible and to draw out the entire experience. Not that it becomes monotonous, but rather that it entails discovery and a loss of inhibitions.

But bear in mind, the essential elements required for this are intimacy, trust, sensitivity and attention. For the entire experience to be truly gratifying, you are going to have to support the psychological element of sex. It is perhaps one of the most essential areas in a relationship, yet it is also the one least talked about. So your endeavour should be to communicate openly about ways in which she can be fulfilled.

ACTIONS

Identifying Pleasure Gaps

Take a detailed look at all the sexual encounters you have had over the last few weeks that you have been making notes on. Carefully read through all of the activities that took place during each of the sessions and highlight the ones that were purely for your partners' pleasure, for example cunnilingus. Now go through the list again and think about the activities that could be identified as solely being pleasurable for you, again as an example, fellatio. Take a final look through the list and determine which activities were pleasurable for both of you simultaneously.

Once you have done all of this, begin communicating your findings with your wife or girlfriend. Talk as intimately as possible to establish where the pleasure gaps lie. There may have been an activity that you considered ecstatic that was in fact not. Through this action you will begin to highlight the areas that both of you find most fulfilling.

Check Out the Pulses!

As you are now armed with the knowledge of determining a real orgasm, take time out to test it. You can do this very discreetly and your partner does not need to know that you are checking!

The number of "contractions" you will feel will differ from each experience to the next. The quantity will vary dependant on the intensity of the orgasm she has experienced. A woman cannot fake these pulses, so if you can determine which activities helped her to climax, you will be able to build on this newly acquired knowledge.

It may also be a good idea to ask your partner if she has ever faked an orgasm with you. If she has, take it with a pinch of salt and regard it as valuable feedback. Remember, she did this to try and please you so don't go off in a huff. It is part and parcel of open communication, which will inevitably result in your sex life being improved dramatically.

Experiment with Lingerie

Change your approach when she is dressed in some sexy underwear or lingerie. Resist the temptation to rip it off and appreciate the effort she has made in looking appealing. Remember, time is not an issue here and you will be able to explore, touch, kiss and penetrate later on.

Sex, Chapter 2:
Outercourse and Intercourse –
The Difference

Gone are the days where sex is a one-dimensional procedure for the purposes of reproduction. There are a myriad of categories to describe different sexual activities and acts that we can all indulge in. And the great news is that outercourse can be just as much fun for both of you. It essentially heightens the final act of intercourse and results in a sexual experience of extreme pleasure.

Sex is not as it used to be – oh no! Unlike our parent's younger days, it is no longer just about a bit of foreplay, sexual intercourse and the post-coital cigarette. In this day and age the terms and jargon associated with sex can be confusing and in the next few chapters I am going to unravel some of their mysteries. By the end, you will know your outercourse from your intercourse and realise why they are both so essential to your success in the bedroom

So what is Outercourse?

There are times when neither of you feel like having intercourse, but still want to pleasure each other. One of the ways to achieve this is to indulge in outercourse. This is now a scientific term that is used for sexual acts and activities that do not involve vaginal or anal penetration. Outercourse is similar to foreplay except that the activities are not designed to lead to either vaginal or anal penetration in the way that foreplay does.

Many couples indulge in outercourse to strengthen their relationship. Emotionally, it can bring the two of you closer together and create freedom to explore each other without the intensity of intercourse. It can also benefit new couples as they can begin to build a connection and trust without committing to the act of sex.

WHAT ACTIVITIES ARE CLASSED AS OUTERCOURSE?

Okay, so you are now asking yourself, what constitutes outercourse? Well, holding hands kissing or cuddling are all the simplest forms of outercourse. Other "heavier" forms include masturbation, erotic massages, oral sex, talking "dirty" to each other, using sex toys for masturbation and body rubbing. You may even include erotic role playing in the genre of outercourse!

STAYING CLOSE BUT NOT THAT CLOSE!!

There is obviously an element of willpower required when performing outercourse. Although the focus should be on getting to know your partner's body, her likes, dislikes and forming an emotional and lasting bond, it can be tempting to go further. The key is to identify your agendas and to treat the whole process of outercourse, as its own entity. In relation to pleasure, it is an essential part of any healthy sexual relationship.

Outercourse is hugely beneficial in an exploratory way. It is the process of learning about your partners' body in a completely comfortable and non threatening undercurrent. You are able to explore techniques, erogenous zones and anything else that relates to her heightened sexual satisfaction. It is an essential starting point in creating the perfect dynamic between the two of you. In essence, it is the ultimate form of connection and will allow you both to sexually develop together.

WHY YOU SHOULD CHOOSE OUTERCOURSE

The ultimate gratification she will achieve is obviously 'the orgasm'. As discussed, this is rarely achieved through penetration due to the positioning of the clitoris. In fact, no female orgasm can be reached without the clitoris and clitoral network being stimulated. Thus, it is the key to her ultimate arousal and some of the best methods for her to reach this pinnacle are finger stimulation, sex toy stimulation or cunnilingus (oral sex performed on a woman). By utilizing these outercourse techniques, you will help her to climax every time you are involved in sexual activity.

It also goes without saying that the process of outercourse aids in developing trust and ultimately heightens the bond between the two of you. Women often feel emotionally detached during intercourse because there is no meaningful affection beforehand. Outercourse eradicates this and provides the necessary support in heightening the experience. By focusing purely on each other's pleasure, a selfless environment is created which imbues the breakdown of inhibition.

OF COURSE THERE IS INTERCOURSE!

Intercourse may be something that you think requires little explanation. But it is not that cut and dried. There are a myriad of positions and it is the ultimate method for the men achieving an orgasm, other than masturbation. Of course, the fundamental reason for intercourse is reproduction, but more often than not it is a basic recreational activity, designed to give us sheer pleasure and excitement.

THE RISKS OF INTERCOURSE

I think we only need to cover this briefly as we are a lot more informed nowadays. We all know that we are at risk of Sexually Transmitted

Diseases or Infections if we do not practice safe sex, particularly with a new partner. There is a rise in recent years of asymptomatic infections and diseases such as Chlamydia, HIV and Gonorrhoea. It is also important to note that women can suffer more from these infections as the bacterium has a moist internal environment in which to breed. A man's penis is exposed to the air and is able to dispel moisture, which can kill off bacteria.

It is also vital that you keep your eye on any mixture of vaginal and anal penetration during intercourse. Tiny particles of faecal matter from the anus can be transmitted into the vagina. This can lead to some seriously nasty infections and diseases; if you are trying these activities out make sure that you wear a condom and change it before swapping orifices. The anus will also require condom-friendly lubricant, as the anus is not able to lubricate itself. Water based lubricants work best with condoms; oil based lubricants are to be avoided as they can cause the condom to deteriorate.

THE BENEFITS OF INTERCOURSE

Obviously it goes without saying that intercourse is a critical and essential part of every successful sexual relationship. The purpose of this section is not to dethrone it, but to elevate its context by understanding the other activities that are more pleasurable to your partner. There are a number of benefits to the age-old method of inning and outing.

Whereas outercourse focuses on intense stimulation and emotional bonding, actual intercourse has been found to be very good for our health. A frenetic session of intercourse can burn anywhere between 50 to a hundred calories. I can just see all of you now jumping onto the scale after each session. This equates to around 7,500 calories a year if you have intercourse around three times a week. That is as much as jogging 75 miles over the entire year! Other health benefits include lowering cholesterol, lowering blood pressure, cutting the risk of strokes and increasing oestrogen. Oestrogen levels that are high in women can help to lower their cholesterol, prevent brittle bones while keeping their skin supple.

Intercourse has also been scientifically proven to boost our mood. We release endorphins, a feel good hormone which is also released when we do vigorous exercise. This is why we can feel happy and in an exulted state for hours after a good intercourse session. Some recent scientific studies are also exploring the possibility that semen acts as an antidepressant and can help people who are feeling depressed.

You can also catch your partner out next time that she tells you that she has a headache! Sexual intercourse releases Oxytocin, which contains endorphins with a sedative property. This is the chemical in the body that relieves us of pain, thus a good session, especially if it includes your partner reaching orgasm, will help to disperse some of the pain.

INTERCOURSE IS NOT ALWAYS THE BEES KNEES

Vaginal and particularly Anal presentation are definitely overestimated in terms of pleasuring a woman and the hard cold truth is that she is inclined to come more effectively and regularly through other techniques. It is fair to say that us men have a preference for it, as it's the easiest way for us to climax. In fact, clitoral stimulation and the subsequent orgasm are rarely achieved through penetration.

The process of intercourse is aligned with a number of its own pressures. You are trying not to climax too soon as well as endeavouring to lead your fair lady into a multitude of orgasms. This is how it has been portrayed in pretty much every successful love scene on television, so how come it doesn't fit the bill with you? The expectation is a false one.

If the countless directors had been true to life, they would have included a 15-minute session of outercourse. But the ultimate outcome of intercourse remains the same. You come, she is left wanting more and the lights get turned off.

So we need to distance ourselves from the social stereotypes that surround sexual intercourse and make sure that even though it is a significant part of the sexual experience, it is not the only one. Regard it as the finale of the entire show. Delaying your gratification is obviously selfless and she will reward you with a more intense experience when it is your turn to climax.

OUTERCOURSE VS. INTERCOURSE

When it comes to pleasuring your partner and enhancing her own gratification, outercourse is by far the preferred method. You are connecting on an emotional and selfless level, which is an incredibly erotic experience for women. Outercourse is recognised as a fundamental part of ensuring women achieve equality in sexual pleasure. But there is a massive upside to the endeavour itself. We no longer have to feel the pressure of attempting to bring our partner to climax during intercourse, which by now you know is not an easy feat. Once she has climaxed through outercourse, we are able to relax and enjoy the penetration for ourselves. She at this point will be sexually heightened and receptive to every thrust you make.

Vaginal penetration will always have its place in the grand sexual walls of fulfilment. The important element is to remember that it is part of the entire process and not the process itself. Women love it and it is our most effective method of reaching orgasm. It has its own unique savour in terms of connecting with the person you are with and should never be ignored. It is in essence about balance. Finding the right techniques that work for both of you through open and honest communication and loads of practice.

In terms of foreplay, coreplay and moreplay, we will be discussing these activities in more detail in the next chapter. You are now several steps closer to being a better and more thoughtful lover.

ACTIONS

Research Some Other Outercourse Activities

Although there is a fair selection mentioned above, there are several more outercourse activities that can be used during sex. Take some time out to research the different options available to you both on the Internet. Make a note of all the advantages and disadvantages they bring and whom they are most beneficial to. Remember, outercourse activities are something that will truly stimulate your partner in ways you never thought possible.

Try It For Yourself!

It goes without saying that this is a practical book. So try it out. Take an evening out of the week where you can both dedicate some time out for sexual exploration. Make a decision beforehand to ignore intercourse for the night and embark on making each other climax through some of the activities you researched. This will allow you both to understand and discover more about each other's bodies as well as all of the intimate regions or hotspots. Talking through the entire process is also encouraged. Think of it as a tutorial in pleasing your partner where feedback is welcomed.

I suggest trying this activity first. Ask your partner to masturbate in front of you. As she is aware of her body, she will provide invaluable visual feedback as to what genuinely turns her on. It is an incredibly erotic experience for both of you and one that will harness the trust aspect.

Jazz Up the Intercourse

Intercourse can become very methodical and routine like if you are not careful. There are normally two or three positions we find favour with which result in common practice. Try out some different more sensual positions, ones that will generate more pleasure for your partner. This is easy to research on the Internet.

SEX, CHAPTER 3:
FOREPLAY, COREPLAY AND MOREPLAY?

The world of sex is full of different terms nowadays and it can be confusing. Many of us are already familiar with the term foreplay, but what about coreplay and moreplay? In this chapter we will look at each of these in turn and you will then be able to distinguish which sexual activities fall into which category.

Gone are the days of simple foreplay followed by a little intercourse. Sexual therapists have broken the entire encounter into intercourse, outercourse, foreplay, coreplay and moreplay. Let's take some time out to understand the benefits and the latter four.

FOREPLAY

When you think about foreplay, you mind probably wonders to a little breast fondle and some neck play. It is in fact a lot more intricate than this. Any sexual activity that comes before actual penetration is deemed to be foreplay. So what is the key element to remember here? Make the entire process as drawn out and heightened as possible. Embark on giving her a tongue bath and keep this practice going for as long as erotically possible. Remember, it takes her at least 15 minutes to reach sufficient arousal before you can consider taking it to the next level.

SO WHAT CONSTITUTES FOREPLAY?

Kissing, cuddling, massages, dressing up, phone sex, light bondage and even talking dirty can all be classified as foreplay. The list is effectively endless as it incorporates anything and everything that precedes intercourse. Some people also regard oral sex as a form of foreplay, but I am going to talk more about this later on.

WHY FOREPLAY IS OF PARAMOUNT IMPORTANCE

Well it goes without saying that it essential in getting your partner into the right state of mind before actual intercourse. On a physical level this involves her being turned on enough to be lubricated. It is also an additional mechanism in developing the bond and trust between the two of you. It highlights your attraction to her in terms of not wanting to purely satisfy yourself. The most common problem with foreplay is that not enough time is spent on it.

COREPLAY

Coreplay is the practice of focusing and giving attention to your partners' genital area. It involves a lot of work in stimulating the clitoris and helping her to achieve an orgasm. The main activity that is linked to coreplay is cunnilingus (the scientific term for oral sex on a woman). You may already involve cunnilingus in your sexual activities, but there are certain techniques that can help to make the activity more stimulating and enjoyable for the woman.

Most female complaints with regard to cunnilingus are that men are too rough, sloppy or in a rush. It is regarded as the appetizer rather than the main course. The concept of coreplay makes the connection; that cunnilingus should be seen as a whole process of bringing a woman to orgasm. Cunnilingus is one of the few ways in which you can start it as a foreplay activity, take it all the way to that first orgasm and then right through to the multiple orgasms of moreplay. Instead of viewing it as just a quick "dip" to get your partner ready for intercourse, coreplay should be seen as a whole sexual experience in itself.

THE DOUBTS ABOUT CUNNILINGUS

When it comes to cunnilingus and coreplay, there are doubts and barriers that prevent many men and women from treating it as a long and savoured activity. Women are insecure about the way that they smell, taste and the thought that their partner is simply not enjoying giving them cunnilingus. This is why many women learn not to expect to receive oral sex and prefer to focus on performing fellatio on their partner instead. The media consume women with the idea that they can perfect their technique and please their partners no end by giving good head. There is, however, very little encouragement in the same quarters in terms of expecting good oral sex from the man in their life.

Men on the other hand have their own inhibitions. They are concerned about the taste and smell, feeling incompetent in terms of their technique and downplay the importance in terms of the satisfaction it garners. The truth is women love cunnilingus; it's just the psychology of communicating their preferences that elude us men. This in turn results in our preference for intercourse, which as I have previously stated, is not the most effective method in making her orgasm. By taking time out to learn the fundamentals and practicality of pleasurable oral sex, you will not only enhance your sexual repertoire but also guarantee her one hell of an orgasm.

POINTS TO REMEMBER REGARDING CUNNILINGUS

One of the biggest hang-ups for both men and women, when it comes to oral sex, is hygiene. Some women abstain from allowing men to go down on them because of their fear of emanating ghastly smells. So let me clear this up. The vagina is self-cleaning and one of the most pristine and looked after areas on her body. It excretes secretions, which rid the area of bacteria as well as preventing infections.

85

Most men love the taste of their partner. It can be extremely erotic to be allowed to delve into this sensitive area. The essential point I am trying to make is the importance of reassuring her that this is something you enjoy and want to experience. It is necessary to convey that it is not pressure related and an act that you are looking forward to partaking in.

If there are genuine concerns regarding cleanliness or taste, then integrate this into the foreplay. Have an erotic bath together while gently washing her from head to toe. If there is a more stagnant odour then she could be suffering from thrush or bacterial vaginosis. Get some medical attention and as soon as the infection has cleared up, you can get back to pleasuring her again.

ADVANTAGES OF COREPLAY FOR MEN

Coreplay allows you to identify exactly what turns her on as well as ensuring she reaches an orgasm. If you suffer from premature ejaculation, like approximately 30 to 40 percent of men, coreplay and in particular cunnilingus are your number one remedies in ensuring her satisfaction. There are also certain positions and techniques that you can adopt to make sure that you are aroused but also focused solely on her pleasure. These methods help you to control your ejaculation and prevent the physical contact that usually contributes to you coming too soon.

Cunnilingus is an intense and very intimate process, which can ensure that you pleasure her first. As well as this it will boost your confidence and eradicate any unnecessary pressures associated with coming too quickly. Understanding that she is completely fulfilled on an emotional, psychological and physical aspect will create a dynamic atmosphere concentrating solely on the pleasure aspect of sex.

Let's face it; performance is one of the biggest concerns that us men have when it comes to sex. Coreplay is a way of employing patience, concentration and focus which all helps to improve your longevity and sense of sexual purpose.

THE SIX STAGES OF COREPLAY

As I mentioned above, the coreplay process has been identified as having six definite stages. Learning about the whole process will help you understand how to make sure both you and your partner get the best out of the experience. You can start with foreplay, move onto coreplay and finish with moreplay activities.

The first step of coreplay is moving from foreplay to the first clitoral kiss. This event signifies the end of foreplay and the start of the intimate and pleasurable process of cunnilingus. After the first kiss, you can move onto using your tongue strokes to get her clitoris further aroused. Establishing a rhythm is part of the second stage.

The third stage focuses on building the tension needed in order for your partner to follow through to reaching orgasm. You need to employ manual stimulation techniques and turn more attention to the glans (clitoris). At the same time you will need to focus on stimulating the hidden parts of her clitoral network by using fingers, thumbs or sex toys in the vagina. Remember – do this while still paying close attention to the stimulation of the clitoris.

The fifth and sixth stages, named pre-orgasm and orgasm respectively, encourage you to maintain the rhythm, tension and balance in order to bring your partner to orgasm. By keeping the pressure and rhythm heightened, you will allow her to achieve climax!

If you need to know more about rhythm, tension and escalation in order to establish the right techniques and methods for coreplay, then read on to the next chapter, where we will explore these matters in further detail.

MOREPLAY

Moreplay is a fairly new term that has been developed by sex therapists to describe further activities resulting in your partner climaxing after intercourse has transpired. After a man has reached orgasm, it is generally the case that he wants to turn over and start snoring. This is a natural sensation, which takes place while the blood begins to flow away from the penis.

The mistake arrives in the assumption that women feel the same way. From a biological perspective, the women's genitals are still engorged with blood and fully aroused. This allows for the perfect opportunity for enticing more pleasure out of her.

WHY USE MOREPLAY?

There is the obvious advantage in remaining emotionally connected to your partner. As their state is heightened they more often than not feel completely disconnected after the male orgasm has been reached. It provides them with enough evidence that you are concerned with her enjoyment and fulfilment. Most couples who indulge in foreplay will find that it evokes sexual intercourse all over again.

This leads me on to the second advantage. If your partner did not reach an orgasm during foreplay or intercourse, or simply wants more than one, then moreplay is the best way to achieve this. If you did elicit an orgasm out of her, you will find her much easier to stimulate the second or third time around. Remember that the clitoris is still very sensitive after foreplay and intercourse, so you want to take as much time with moreplay as you do with foreplay.

HOW DOES MOREPLAY WORK?

The basic principle of moreplay is focusing all of your attention on your partner to ensure that she reaches sexual satisfaction. After intercourse, it is important not to dive out of bed to watch the football, fix yourself something to eat or turn over and slip into the land of nod. Take the time to keep her warm and comfortable; talk to her and make eye contact. When you both feel you are ready to start again, take some of the elements of the foreplay genre and start from there. Avoid touching the genital area and clitoris for at least five minutes; although she is still aroused, this area will still be too sensitive to the touch. Start by kissing and cuddling, light touching and take things at a steady pace from there.

If you know your partner well, you will recognise the signals she gives when she is ready for manual stimulation in the genital area. If you are in a relatively new relationship or it is your first sexual experience, you will find that women will squirm away from your touch or move your hand away from their genitalia. This is a signal that they are not quite ready for further stimulation, as the sensitivity level is too high.

Moreplay is a great way to have an all-out, intense, passionate and emotionally charged sex session. It will mean a lot to your partner as it shows that you are devoted to her receiving sexual gratification time and time again, sometimes at the expense of your own. And the pleasure that you will feel from knowing that she has been given the best sexual experience ever will keep you walking tall for many a day.

So You Now Know About Foreplay, Coreplay and Moreplay

If you think about it, sex can be compared to a book or a play – that is to say it effectively has a beginning, middle and an end. In this way, you can consider the three "parts" of foreplay, coreplay and moreplay as the beginning, middle and end of the sexual process. Each part has its own role to play and is crucial in pleasuring your partner to the extreme.

By learning all about the different activities, techniques and methods used for each of the categories, you can ensure you are perfectly equipped to satisfy your partner emotionally, psychologically and most importantly, physically.

If you have any medical issues such as erectile dysfunction or premature ejaculation, I would urge you to find out as much as you can about employing the right techniques that can help you. Using foreplay, coreplay and moreplay can help relieve the tension, pressure and stress that are apparent with these conditions. You will become more relaxed and focused in the right way to help your partner climax and to help you concentrate on holding off your own orgasm.

Actions

If you have been in a relationship with your partner some time, it is likely that things have become a bit routine and quite frankly, stale. It is now time to enhance your sexual activities in terms of foreplay, coreplay and moreplay. Not only will you feel more turned on and confident in your own ability, but you will be able to please her more than ever before!

Find Some New and Exciting Foreplay Activities

The first thing I want you to do is make a list of the usual foreplay activities that you and your partner currently practice. Next, think back to when your relationship first started – were there any foreplay activities that you did then that you both enjoyed that have faded into non-existence in the bedroom? Make a list of any that you would like to re-introduce to your sex life. It is also the time to find new and exciting foreplay activities to add to your experiences and add a bit of spice back into your sex lives! Research the Internet for some more ideas. It may be worth discussing these choices with your partner to see which ones she would like to experiment with.

The Tongue Twister

As coreplay is essentially about pleasuring your partner with your tongue, I'm sure she won't mind you practicing and brushing up on your technique on a regular basis! If cunnilingus is something that is completely new to you, you can find information and tips in the "Exercise, Methods and Tips" chapter of this section. It is important to have the right technique in order to pleasure her effectively.

This will require some communication, a lot of time and complete focus. Using the tips and the knowledge you now have, start performing oral sex on your partner when you are in an erotic frame of mind. Communicate with her to find out what does and does not work.

Make Time for Moreplay

Moreplay may be a completely alien concept to you due to the assumption that women return to "normal" the same way men do after intercourse. It is worth including moreplay into your sexual repertoire.

After intercourse, take time to have a conversation with your partner. Remain affectionate after you have achieved an orgasm. Kiss some of her erogenous zones while leading up to her clitoral network. Remember, read the signals so that you know when she is ready for more clitoral stimulation. The moreplay part of the session does not have to lead to full intercourse again if neither of you are up for it. The main focus should be on pleasuring her to make sure that she is completely sated.

SEX, CHAPTER 4:
RHYTHM: TENSION AND ESCALATION

When it comes to pleasing your partner the processes of rhythm, tension and escalation have to be just right. But why do they matter and how do you achieve the perfect techniques to deliver the most pleasure? Read on to learn more about these three stages of the sexual process.

It is quite common to think that sex does not involve much thought in terms of establishing rhythm, tension and escalation. However, these are an integral part of the process and if they are not mastered and concentrated, you may just end up having one of the most unsatisfying sexual experiences ever. And you can bet your bottom dollar that if you have not enjoyed the experience, it is highly unlikely that your partner has.

We learned all about coreplay in the previous chapter and established that cunnilingus is an integral part of this process. Rhythm, tension and escalation can all be employed during cunnilingus to make sure your partner has the most excessive orgasm ever. These parts can be intermingled into the latter stages of the six parts of coreplay to help maintain the stimulation of the clitoral network and to create the perfect platform for complete satisfaction.

GETTING INTO THE GROOVE

Establishing the right rhythm is very much like learning to dance. We aren't all born with the innate capacity to do the Tango; neither are some of us able to identify the perfect rhythm during sex. It is a learning curve, but once established it should be committed to memory and used again and again.

The key to rhythm when performing cunnilingus is to take your time. It is also important to resist the temptation to dive straight in with your tongue. There has to be a balance between movement and rhythm; only when this is achieved will you be able to lead onto tension.

To get into the right rhythm you have to perfect the technique of breaking off contact from her clitoral network. Take it slowly at first and keep your tongue flat and your strokes light. The general rule of thumb is to ensure that each lick has the chance to be fully appreciated by your partner. Each stoke should be counted and allowed to linger! Once the tongue stroke has been fully appreciated you can then move onto the next lick and so on. The aim of establishing this rhythm at the start is to help build your partner's tension level, which helps to lead to her climaxing. Once you have established a pattern of tongue strokes and breaking contact, you can start again with some light strokes.

It is important to note that there is not a great amount of attention being paid to the glans at this stage; this helps in building up the tension in your partner and escalating her desire for you to move onto this particular area. So how long are you supposed to do this for? Well, how long is a piece of string? Experts suggest around the 3 minute mark but everyone is unique and your partner may want to continue for longer.

Because you have specifically avoided the glans area of the network, your partner's body will be awakened to the fact that there is a rhythm occurring. The clitoris will now be seeking your tongue out to receive some stimulation. Practiced cunnilinguists will note that the clitoris will pop out from under the clitoral hood to see why it is missing out! At this time you can start to vary the rhythm and then start to give the clitoris some deserved attention.

Remember to still pay attention to the other areas too. Essentially you want to add to the areas you are giving attention to, not remove any.

Keep the rhythm going and incorporate your tongue movements to include the clitoris. Apply only light pressure as you are still at the stage of teasing.

BUILDING THE TENSION

The concept of tension is to start to introduce your fingers into the equation. You should start off just by using one finger as this helps to escalate more tension for your partner. There has to be an aspect of teasing and anticipation, which will serve to make her more aroused and aching for sensuality. Which finger you choose is entirely up to you but most men begin with the index finger. It is crucial that you do not dive in with three or four digits, as this will just break the rhythm that you have already built up as well as eradicating the tension. It will also mean that your partner's pelvic muscles will be called into action.

Whilst still applying your tongue strokes and breaking off the contact, start to use your finger to explore the whole of the genital area of your partner. You can lightly trace around her outer lips (the labia minora) and give them a light pinch. Many women also like you to use the finger to rub the commissure area. If you haven't done your homework, this is the part that lies above the clitoral head and glans. It is smooth to the touch and incredibly sensitive. You can then insert your finger into her vagina but do not push it all the way in. You should be able to feel her internal clitoral network lightly throbbing and the vaginal wall should start to close in around your finger.

You can also employ your thumb to do a bit of work whilst you are using your tongue and your finger. Gently massage her perineum (the area of skin between her vaginal entrance and her anus). All the while you should still be maintaining the rhythm you have established and keeping the teasing very light. This may all seem like hard work but once you get into the swing of things it is relatively simple to maintain. And look at it this way – if you are paying so much attention to her you can be sure she is enjoying the process! It also means that you are thinking less about your own gratification resulting in less chance of you reaching your peak too soon.

It is now time to complete the set and add your hand into the process. The hand can be a forgotten tool and should be used in an appreciative way to help build the tension even further. In fact, the use of your hand is quite important in the process as it helps you to keep your tongue strokes steady.

If you are right-handed, it is likely that you are using the finger from this hand for the stimulation and insertion. Place your free hand under her bottom and squeeze the cheeks together so that you can hold them both in your palm. Make sure that the position you adopt is comfortable for both of you. The advantage of using your hand under her bottom is that it helps to keep her body steady and in the correct position for the movements of your tongue (remember your finger should not be moving if it is inside her vaginal entrance!).

Once you have established your rhythm and the right amount of tension using the skills above, you can now step it up a gear! By now her clitoris will have had some of attention and she is feeling incredibly aroused. Begin to intensify the teasing by playing around with your tongue strokes. This means putting your finger and hand work on the back burner, but just for a little while. Let your tongue take the spotlight again.

The techniques used for building this stage of tension should mean that there is less or no breakage in the contact with the clitoral network. It also means that she will instinctively start to do some work of her own. The first technique you can try is to tilt your head to either the left or right. Now use the side of your tongue to diagonally lick from the bottom to the top of her genital area. You can incorporate some brushing strokes on the clitoris itself so that it does not feel totally left out again. You may find that this position can get uncomfortable for you if you hold it for too long; with this in mind, change the direction in which your head is tilting frequently to prevent your neck from becoming sore.

There is a movement known as the "cat lick" and it does exactly as the name suggests. If you have ever watched a cat clean its fur, you will notice that is concentrates on one area until it is completely satisfied that it is clean. You can use this method on your partner's genital area. Choose a spot, preferably one that you have established that she likes, and make small soft tongue licks, over and over again. Then just like a cat does when it finds a particularly grubby bit of fur, apply a bit more pressure and focus to that area.

One of the techniques you can use which has a double advantage is to let your tongue lie completely flat and still. Not only does it give you a chance to take a short breather, but it will encourage your partner to add a little bit of movement of her own. She will start to push herself against your tongue and work her own rhythm to keep the intensity and flow of the process. Not only does this intensify her pleasure but many women are self conscious about just lying there like a sack of spuds – this way she knows she is doing some of the work and helping you to help her achieve an orgasm.

Seasoned cunnilinguists employ some simple methods during this tension building period that have a wonderful affect and add variety to the state of play. Choose a letter of the alphabet (a capital "f" is usually a good place to start) and trace this letter over her clitoral area over and over again. Take it slow and vary the pressure at different parts of the letter.

All the way through the tension process, it is important to keep your focus and attention on the rhythm that you have established. If this is all new to you it may take a while to get it right, but don't worry, once you have this in the repertoire it is there for life.

TAKE THE ESCALATOR, NOT THE STAIRS

It is now time to move on to the escalation part of the process. This is where all of the tools you have, namely the tongue, fingers and hand come into play. The aim of escalation is to put the clitoris under some more pressure so that your partner can reach the pre-orgasm stage (we will look at this in the next chapter).

The advantage of employing all of the tools for this stage is that you do not have to use them all at once. You can use some manual stimulation with your fingers or use both your tongue and fingers at the same time. Remember that the hand is crucial and should be placed under her buttocks to help the process run smoothly.

I want to talk to you a little bit about the infamous "G-spot". This was a term that was created in 1944 and named after one Dr. Graffenberg who maintained that this was where a true orgasm stemmed from. The G-spot is basically an internal area, a spongy tissue that runs around the area of the urethra. Due to the proximity, many women may feel the urge to pee when this area is massaged or touched. You can still give a woman pleasure in this area but it should be recognised that you do not need to hunt for one particular part inside the vaginal wall. Remember, it is not a specific spot but rather a large area.

To begin to escalate the pleasure for your partner, you can insert your finger into the vagina and bend it up as if you were beckoning someone towards you. This is where the "G-spot" area is located and it is not hard to find, as it will be swollen and sensitive. You can then curl your finger to reach the top of her pubic bone and apply some pressure.

You may be worried about applying too much pressure on her vaginal wall and pelvic bone. As long as you can feel the spongy tissue, you will not hurt her. Remember, as there are less nerve endings in this area than the other more sensitive areas like the clitoris, you will need to adopt more pressure.

If you want to add another dimension to your work, include light and straight strokes of your tongue along the clitoris. If this feels too much like juggling or you end up in an awkward position, then just return to the insertion of your finger only.

Once you are comfortable with this stage, you can proceed to insert one or two more fingers into her vagina. These additional fingers should adopt the same position as the first i.e., as if you were beckoning to someone. You can then use all of your fingertips to apply the pressure to the spongy tissue on the vaginal wall. By using all of these digits you can ensure that you are reaching all of the parts on her "G-Spot".

This is now the perfect time to add that extra pressure to the clitoris. The pressure needs to be constant as this is the most effective way of helping your partner to reach her orgasm. Whilst still keeping your fingers inserted into her vagina, you can use your gum to apply pressure to the area just above the clitoris and the clitoral hood. This position still allows you to use your tongue for the strokes needed for that all important rhythm whilst adding some much needed pressure to the commissure. You have to make sure that the gum position is correct; to do this raise the top lip as if you were snarling at someone. You now have the perfect position and can move your gum into position.

If this is something that you cannot get to grips with, there is no need to panic! You can still apply pressure by using your thumb or a vibrator. Use these tools on the frenulum area of the genitals, not on the commissure (the frenulum is the soft area of skin just below the clitoris).

Whether you choose to approach from the top, namely the commissure area, or the bottom, the frenulum area, they will both create the resistance needed for your partner to generate friction to help her reach her orgasm.

PUTTING IT ALL TOGETHER

You now have all of the information required to get you through the stages of building rhythm and tension. You should be able to escalate the teasing to a stage where you can apply the right pressure for your partner to start reaching the point of orgasm. We will be looking at the next two stages of pre-orgasm and orgasm in the next chapter.

By using your tongue, hands and fingers, you will successfully take your partner closer to ecstasy than ever before. It may take a bit of practice, a lot of patience and some manual dexterity but it is certainly worth the effort. An important point to remember is that it should be comfortable for both of you throughout the whole period of establishing rhythm, tension and escalation.

Before you start the sex session that is going to include these stages, make sure that you have a fair idea of what positions you are going to adopt. This will prevent you from having to stop and move positions. Remember, particularly in the later stages, it is essential not to have a break in contact between you and your partner.

If you do need a time out then you can still maintain contact by keeping your fingers inside of her. It is likely that your partner will do some of the work too to keep the momentum going. She will move her pelvis around to put some pressure on your fingers and maintain the rhythm and tension.

ACTIONS

Don't Panic!

This can all seem like a daunting and tremulous set of activities to undertake! It is women who usually boast about being multi-skilled and being able to do more than one thing at a time; but just know that you have it in you to undertake all of the elements above and lead your partner to extreme heights of pleasure.

Remember to take your time. Rome wasn't built in a day and you are certainly not going to master all of these skills overnight. If it helps, break it down into the three stages and concentrate on one to start off with. Even if you only incorporate one of these stages into your actions, she will feel the difference.

Send the Right Message

Before reaching these coreplay stages, remember to provide ample time for foreplay. As I keep re-iterating, time should not be a factor. You have all night (or day) to take your partner to the heights of pleasure. Indulge in as much foreplay as you can and then move on to the coreplay activities. The same principles apply; this is a process that should not be rushed.

Take the time to reassure your partner that you enjoy doing this for her. Again, if you are a bit squiffy about taste and smell in the vaginal region, make a sensual shower or bath part of your foreplay. After the session has ended get some feedback from your partner about what worked for her and what didn't. This is the best way to learn how to improve your techniques.

Add to the Intensity

One of the biggest complaints that women have in the bedroom is that men are emotionally disconnected. Even though cunnilingus is a highly personal and intense experience, some women actually state that it makes them feel lonely! This could be the result of you being down there and out of visual contact.

There are things that you can do to break this feeling of loneliness. You can try placing a hand on her stomach or rubbing your hand across her stomach. If the positioning allows it you can gently place your penis on her inner thigh or rub her leg if you have adopted an end-of-the-bed position. Anything that you can do to make sure she knows that you realise she is still there, is worth doing.

Try connecting as much of your body to hers as possible. It may be difficult to start with, but in between the breaks of the tongue strokes, try speaking to her. It will help her feel less insular through the process.

Sex, Chapter 5:
The Pre-Orgasm and Orgasm Stages of Sexual Response

As you may be well aware by now, there are many stages that a woman goes through before she reaches an actual orgasm. We have covered all of the other processes in the preceding chapters and now it's time to turn our attention to the penultimate final stages. Pay close attention as perfecting these stages will mean that your partner will not only achieve a more intense and explosive orgasm, but she will also feel emotionally connected to you.

Pre-Orgasm

After a long and hopefully enjoyable journey, you have now reached the final furlong. Your partners' breathtaking orgasm is now just in reach. The first thing to do to identify that she has reached this pre-orgasm stage is to look out for the various signs of imminent orgasm.

Reading the Signs of Readiness

One of the easiest ways to tell that your partner has reached the pre-orgasm stage is to be aware of the different fluids in the vagina. Normally, the fluids can taste somewhat bitter but as a woman's body prepares for orgasm, they become a little bit sweeter. There may also be an increase in the warmth of the fluids.

Other signs to look out for include the swelling of the breast, an increased heart rate, her breathing deepening and quickening, her leg muscles tightening or her pelvis arching up. If you get any of these signs, it is time to move onto the next part of the pre-orgasm stage.

MAKE THE TRANSITION

In order to give her the optimum orgasm, you will need to change your position in order to bring her legs closer together. This is the most conducive way for her to continue on to the final stage of orgasm. All of the muscles in her genital area and vagina tighten, which makes the orgasm much more intense. It is still possible to access her clitoris and the surrounding area even though her legs are closer together. This is due to the fact that the clitoris is higher up on the outside of her body. If the legs are kept apart, there is a larger risk of her failing to reach an orgasm. You can keep your fingers inside of her vagina and use your free hand to move her legs closer together. You will then effectively need to lie on top of them, which will help keep them in position.

It is important that you maintain the rhythm that has been established through the former stages and that your partner keeps as still as she can. This helps the build up of the orgasm and allows you to concentrate on bringing her to climax. It is still essential not to rush. By changing the rhythm, reducing your focus or being tempted to speed things up; you are setting yourself up for an anti climax.

Keep your tongue strokes going and if possible make them a little lighter and shorter. This will keep your partner teetering on the edge for a bit longer and will intensify the orgasm when it arrives. Some women will respond well to you slowing your rhythm and tongue strokes down. Re-introducing a little bit of teasing with your tongue and fingers will also heighten the experience for your partner.

ENCOURAGING THE ORGASM

There are a few techniques you can employ with the tongue, which can help ease a woman into the latter stages of orgasm. One method is to replicate the method used by a frog when it sticks out its long tongue to catch prey. You will notice that the frog's tongue darts in and out of its mouth very quickly. By doing the same on the top of the glans area, you will help mount the tension needed to reach the point of orgasm.

Similarly, there is a technique known as the "Jackson Pollock", named after the famous artist. If you are unaware of his art, it looked like big abstract blobs all over the canvas. This may sound like a strange technique but it works very well. You need to employ your tongue as if it was an artist's paintbrush. Keep your tongue flat and start to work it in large and sweeping strokes all over the genital area. It can also be likened to the action many of us adopt when licking an ice cream cone. The important thing to remember about this technique is that you should be decisive about which areas you are targeting and stick to them.

Finally, we have the method that it likened to the art produced by Georges Seurat. This method involved the use of a small brush painting pictures by using a series of tiny dots. Using the very tip of your tongue, dot around the clitoris and on the head with small and sharp movements. The same pressure you have been using up until this stage should be maintained.

Well, with all of this hard work and focus under your belt, the time has almost arrived for your partner to experience that mind-blowing orgasm.

THE ORGASM STAGE

The rhythm has been well established, the tension has reached its ultimate peak and your partner is now on the brink of one of the best orgasms of her life – thanks to you! You can tell when her orgasm is imminent, as she will begin to shudder and tense all her muscles. She will experience spasms throughout her body on top of those in her genital region. You are likely to see tension and spasms in the areas of the neck, arms, legs, abdomen and her face.

Her breathing will increase and she will take short, shallow breaths on the immediate cusp of the first wave of pleasure. All women are different and some will either breathe through the orgasm itself or hold her breath until the initial contractions have passed. She is unlikely to scream at this point of orgasm as shown on porn movies. Just for the record, many women with children have this in-built mechanism that prevents them from making too much noise when they are coming, just in case they wake them up!

As we have discussed, you will notice her vaginal muscles contracting when she is reaching orgasm. If you are practicing cunnilingus you will be able to feel the pulsing throughout the whole of the clitoral network. So whether you have your tongue on her clitoris or your fingers inside sitting alongside her vaginal wall, you will still be able to determine whether she has experienced a genuine orgasm.

The number and strength of the contractions will vary from woman to woman and can also be affected by several other factors. Firstly, it can be down to the intensity of the actual orgasm itself, what kind of mood she is in and how aroused she was during the build up to the orgasm. Other factors such as worry, stress and tiredness can also affect the number of contractions per orgasm. In general, a woman will experience between five and eight contractions for a "middle-of-the-road" experience. Now imagine what you can achieve with all the tools you have now!

Your Role During the Orgasm

To truly give her the utmost pleasure, you have to maintain your position whilst she is going through the actual orgasm. It is far too tempting to remove your fingers or tongue once she has started to climax. Continue with some light stimulation on the clitoris whilst she is having her orgasm – but it is essential you keep this light. This will allow for a more intense feeling and may even draw out the orgasm for longer.

SO HOW DO I KNOW WHEN SHE IS FINISHED?

Just as there are signs of arousal and imminent orgasm, so there are signs to let you know when your partner has been fully sated and is coming back down from her climax.

Her body will become fully relaxed, almost floppy like. The contractions will have subsided and her breathing will slow right back down again. She will most likely push your head away from her genitals or manoeuvre her body away from you slightly. As stated, the clitoris will be incredibly sensitive after her orgasm. Her cheeks will be flushed and she will in all probability want some physical reassurance.

Remember; you cannot always rely on looking at genital area to see if she has finally squeezed out her breathtaking orgasm. This is because her genitals will still be engorged with blood. Having said this, some women can and do ejaculate a clear fluid during the process of climaxing. This however is the exception and not the rule.

WHAT IF SHE FAILS TO ORGASM?

There are times when try as you might, you are unable to help your partner achieve her orgasm. There are several factors that can result in this. On top of stress, anxiety and feeling tired, there are certain emotional and psychological factors, which may prevent a woman from reaching this state. Firstly, as there is so much emphasis placed on achieving orgasms by way of vaginal penetration, she may not feel comfortable enough to climax any other way.

She may also be conscious of your face near her genital area, which will prevent her from relaxing enough to cum. This is particularly common for women who release fluids when they reach an orgasm. Again, your reassurance of the enjoyment you receive will go a long way.

The most imperative thing is to remain positive if you are unable to bring her to climax. Practice, reassurance and instilling additional levels of comfort will set the tone for more successful endeavours.

FEED THE EMOTIONAL SIDE

After your partner has had an orgasm, it is important to take a little time to make sure she is emotionally nourished. This is where moreplay becomes essential. Spend a bit of time talking, cuddling, keeping her warm and assuring her that you love making love to her. In the long term she will be more receptive as her comfort levels will be appeased.

IT'S ALL TRANSFORMING

Let's be honest here, sexual satisfaction is an important part of any relationship. There are very few couples out there, content without it. Satisfaction should be about both partners getting what they want during sex whilst helping the other to achieve orgasm. This maintains the equality dynamic. It goes without saying that a healthy and selfless sex life will endow your relationship to many other significant highs.

A Brief Conclusion

When I say conclusion, I mean in terms of having helped your partner reach that first orgasm! There is no excuse not to continue on to moreplay and give your partner a few additional doses of pleasure. Cunnilingus is one of the most intense, intimate and satisfying sexual practices that a loving couple can indulge in. Once you have mastered all of the skills to take her through the necessary stages, you will feel an inordinate amount of confidence, which will result in less inhibition and more exploration.

Actions

If You Become Stuck

If your partner has failed to reach orgasm through cunnilingus, it is still necessary and imperative for you to continue through to the end. It is important to create the mindset that this is not going to disturb the other elements of enjoyment, which will aid future interactions.

One of the most gratifying positions in terms of female satisfaction is when she is on top of you. She is able to stimulate her clitoris against the bone at the base of your penis. She also determines the rhythm and timing as well as being able to control the pressure. This may be a perfect scenario for her to achieve that elusive orgasm.

If this still fails, you will need to communicate potential resolutions going forward. She may just be looking for some essential reassurance, which is easy enough to provide. Get all the psychological and emotional baggage out the way and you will almost certainly edge closer to the ultimate goal.

Add to the Length of the Orgasm

This is something that your partner can do to help make her orgasm last longer. Get her to move her pelvis around after the initial contractions. This will draw out the orgasm as well as creating more intensity though the climax.

The Orgasmic Fingerprint

This may not apply to all women but it is a useful tool nevertheless. The Orgasmic Fingerprint is the name for identifying the specific triggers that make a woman reach an orgasm. For some it may be clitoral stimulation only, your hand pressed down on her stomach or three fingers inserted into her vagina whilst licking her clitoris. There are many variations and the fingerprint is the pattern that can emerge when a woman is being brought to orgasm on a consistent basis.

You can make a note of some of the triggers within the first few sessions and see if this develops into an orgasmic fingerprint for your partner. It is worth discussing with your partner what points during the pre-orgasm stage brought her closer to climax. You can then make a mental note to use these time and again during your sessions.

Of course, there may be inconsistent patterns that emerge. The triggers could be dependent on her mood, mentality, hormones or physical factors such as tiredness or menstruation. It is still worth exploring the possibility of the orgasmic fingerprint as it can help you to tailor your future sessions to her needs and ensure that she is always satisfied.

SEX, CHAPTER 6:
TWO BECOME ONE!

Now that you have all the basics under your belt in helping your partner to achieve an orgasm, you may be turning your attention to the simultaneous experience. This is no mean feat and takes a lot of skill, concentration and practice. Let's explore this ultimate phenomenon in more detail and give you all of the facts you need. We will also look at strengthening the bond between you and your partner so that you feel connected during all of your sexual activities.

DON'T BELIEVE THE HYPE!

The adult entertainment industries along with most modern day rom coms are the biggest culprits in perpetuating the myth of the simultaneous orgasm. The truth is it is a rare occurrence, particularly if vaginal penetration is your main port of call. The anatomies of both sexes are not conducive to this experience as her clitoris is situated on the outside of her body. Remember, only 25% of women ever achieve an orgasm during sexual intercourse.

KEEP IT SIMPLE

There are two main ingredients in achieving simultaneous orgasms with your partner. Understanding each other's hotspots or triggers and being able to manipulate them is the first step. This is obviously easier to do if you are in a continuous relationship with someone.

Repetition and consistency are the other essential elements. They both lead to emotional security, which is paramount in achieving this state.

Reaching the state of simultaneous orgasms will not require you to swing from chandeliers in a leopard print thong. Simple and comfortable positions such as the missionary are more than sufficient in generating the necessary requirements for simultaneity.

So How Do We Do It?

There are a number of positions that you can adopt which are as effective as the other. Remember, it is all down to individuality and personal preference. The only way you are going to uncover this hidden gem is through continual perseverance and perspiration.

The CAT Technique

The Coital Alignment Technique (known as the CAT technique) was developed by psychotherapists in the late 1980's and has been the subject of numerous studies ever since. Essentially, it is a modified version of the missionary position. The idea is that the position allows the male to stimulate his partner's genitals whilst penetrating the vagina. The main differences are that the man penetrates and thrusts at a higher angle than the ordinary missionary position and the movements are more restricted. This is so that the focus is solely on stimulating the clitoris.

When starting the Coital Alignment Technique, make sure that both of you are suitably aroused. Then enter your partner as you would in the missionary position. You will then need to manoeuvre your body so that when you start to thrust, the base of your pubic bone and penis are in contact with her clitoris. This will allow for simultaneous stimulation. Your partner should then place her legs behind your thighs and rest her feet on your calves. The angle of her legs should be no more than 45 degrees or this position will be ineffective. At this point you should not be supporting your body by using your hands or elbows, as all of your weight should be on top of her.

The movements should be limited to the pelvic area only. You will find other movements restrictive in any case. It is your job to control the rhythm. She will have to move her pelvis upwards with enough force to push you back. You will then apply counter pressure, which will result in her clitoris being stimulated. You should generate a rocking motion as opposed to the traditional thrusting style that is associated with the missionary position.

WOMAN ON TOP

This is one of the most popular positions and with the right technique; it can help both of you to reach orgasms at the same time. It has numerous benefits for her as she has the ability to control thrust, pace and stimulation. Essentially, the best way to do this is to do the Coital Alignment Technique in reverse. This means that she kneels or sits in a position where she can still manage the 45 degree angle as well as wrapping her legs around your thighs. The bonus of this position is you do not have to worry about putting all your weight on your partner. Make sure that the clitoris is situated on your pubic bone and at the base of your penis. You can then start rocking back and forth until you both climax.

OTHER IDEAS

The Coital Alignment Technique and the woman on top technique are two of the best ways to achieve simultaneous orgasms. You may find other beneficial positions out there, perhaps in Kama Sutra manuals or Tantric Sex books. As these philosophies tend to focus on giving pleasure and arriving at the same place at the same time, you will benefit a great deal by employing their teachings.

If you are still unable to achieve your goal, I suggest employing the use of vibrator. It can be a massive turn on for men to watch and assist their partners in trying to stimulate themselves through the use of it. They work well as they are able stimulate the clitoris whilst also allowing for that feeling of penetration. Its introduction can be something that is fun and enjoyable for both of you.

Achieving simultaneity is also relatively easy when using a vibrator. You will have identified the patterns of orgasm as well being aware of when she is close to climaxing. It is essentially just about timing your experiences together. The other advantage is that it can also be achieved in a variety of positions.

My final piece of advice would be to utilize the 'bridge technique'. This is just moving from manually stimulating your partner to the brink of climax and then only engaging in intercourse. Your partner should be stimulated all the way up to pre-orgasm stage. Once she has reached this point, you can enjoy intercourse with the likelihood that a minimal amount of thrusting will be required to tip her over the edge. Make sure that minimal time lapses between manually stimulating her and intercourse. Bear in mind too, that frequently changing positions requires your partner to start her stimulation process all over again.

A SNEAKY TIP

If you are concerned about climaxing before your partner does than I have a little trick for you. Pull down on your testicles before you cum. This will hopefully prevent you from climaxing prematurely. You can also bend the penis downward at the base, though many men find this to be too uncomfortable.

GETTING RESULTS

The secret to simultaneous orgasm lies in the fact that it requires a lot of work from both of you. Don't become negative if it does not happen overnight. This is something that can only be achieved in a stress free environment, and it will involve some serious focus and concentration.

YOUR ACTIONS AFTER SEX

If you have embodied all the techniques I have mentioned, indulged in some moreplay and are finally physically unable to continue, turn your attention to communication. A common trait for a lot of men is to turn over, sleep, read or inappropriately exit the room. Remember that you have not fulfilled her yet and she is looking for emotional reassurance and connectivity. By engaging in conversation you are remaining in the moment, which is essential for women in terms of satisfaction.

ACTIONS

Test the Water

Talk to your partner and see how she feels about trying to achieve a simultaneous orgasm. Make sure that you give her all of the details about what is involved and that it may take a bit of time for you both to adjust to the rocking motions and positions required. Take the time to make a few preparations, at least mentally, about how you will be positioned.

Practice Makes Perfect

It is most likely the case that you have established what your particular triggers are for an orgasm when you have masturbated. It is also likely that you recognise these triggers when you are having sex. Remember that it is just as essential to find out exactly what hers are. This all comes down to effective communication between the two of you.

Another issue that can be encountered when trying to achieve a simultaneous orgasm is that she may need a lot longer than you to reach climax. If this is the case, you will need to figure out a few methods in delaying your ejaculation. One of the best ways to delay your orgasm is to slow down your rhythm. Control your breathing by taking long and calming inhalations. Focus your mind on becoming relaxed, which will help you gain control. If all else fails, pinching the perineum (you can get your partner to do this for you) can also help to slow down the onset of your orgasm.

SEX, CHAPTER 7:
KNOWING HER EROGENOUS ZONES INSIDE OUT

Do you know how many erogenous zones a woman has? It is essential not to underestimate the importance of these hot spots in nearing your partner to an orgasm. Many of them are overlooked in the sexual build up to pre-orgasm, which can result in the entire encounter being less sensual. Let's take a closer look at these precious little areas.

We are all experts when it comes to identifying the erogenous zones of women, aren't we? Of course we all know that women like their necks to be kissed, their nipples to be tweaked and their genitals to be rubbed. But giving a woman pleasure via her erogenous zones should be much more than this. Again, we seem to have this urgency about getting her aroused by touching a few core areas that we know will get her wet and then storming off to intercourse. Men rely much less on erogenous zones than women do, as they are easily aroused by sight and smell.

SO HOW MANY DID YOU KNOW EXISTED?

The number of erogenous zones that a woman has is actually twelve and we will look at these in more detail as we go through the chapter. Just for the record, a man has nine erogenous zones and you may wish to find out more about these too – so your partner can return the favour!

Going from head to toe and back again is one of the best ways to turn her on and get her stimulated enough for penetration. By mastering the skill of touching these different points in the right way, you can awaken a new erotic pleasure from your partner.

So Where Are The Erogenous Zones?

Most of us know the most obvious erogenous zones, namely the breasts, genitals and neck. These are the ones that we give most attention to when pleasuring our partner. Let's now take a look at some of these and others in more detail.

Hair and Scalp – This is one of the most sensual areas on a woman's body. By massaging your partner's scalp you can help stimulate the brain and release the endorphins ("feel good" chemicals) that we experience from exercise. Some women also enjoy their hair being pulled but always ensure you start off gently. Run your fingers through her hair and move back up to the roots. Make a loose fist and tug very, very gently.

Ears – A woman's ear and its surrounding areas are home to many sensitive nerve endings and they are very receptive to being touched. You can use your lips, tongue and fingers to give her a variety of wonderful experiences. For example, use your thumb and forefinger to gently squeeze or rub her earlobes.

You can also give her outer ear a sensual and light massage. Behind her ear lies a very sensitive and prominent area for arousal. Use light licks and long strokes with your tongue. Some women like this to be a gentle action, whereas others prefer a little bit of pressure.

Lips – It's all about sensuality and eroticism. Women have their own unique preferences where some are all about firmness and passion whist others are more comfortable with sensitivity and lightness. The only thing you really have to rule out excess drool, opening your mouth too wide and biting the tongue. Not rocket science after all.

Neck – this is one of the largest erogenous zones in terms of size and sensuality. It is essential that you include this in your outercourse and foreplay activities. Honestly, this is one of the best areas to arouse stimulation from your partner.

Shoulders and back – Men are incredibly negligent when it comes to arousing their partner in this area. It is also an incredibly sensitive hotspot. The shoulders and back are in truth the perfect areas to progress to, after you have given her neck some attention. You can lightly kiss them, lick them or give your partner a sensual massage. I cannot emphasise enough how important it is to explore this area repeatedly. Her spine is perhaps the most sensitive area here.

Breasts – This is a well known and obvious region for eliciting amorous feelings. One thing to remember is that the sides of the breast can be quite sensitive and many women are ticklish in this region.

Stomach – Some women are incredibly self-conscious when it comes to this area. Excess fat or even stretch marks may result in her not wanting you to spend time there. Again, this is a communication issue and one you will need to address. Running your fingertips lightly over her stomach can be a huge turn on, especially if your fingers tease the top of her monis pubis (the pubic hair region).

Genitals – we have discussed this in quite a bit of detail so I am not going to delve into much more here. You now know that all her orgasms stem from the clitoral network and specifically the clitoris itself. You also know that cunnilingus is the most effective method in stimulating this region.

Thighs and legs – Even though men generally tend to pay attention to the inner thighs, we seem to neglect the rest of her legs. The back of the knee is a particularly sensitive and erotic area for women. Breathing on it lightly, kissing softly and deft licking can all result in a serious amount of arousal. The back of the thigh, where it meets the buttock, is also a highly sensual area. Try using a silk scarf over this area to heighten her pleasure.

Feet – This is another area that tends to be forgotten about. Issues with smell and general lack of appeal can result it men staying away. But remember, her feet are incredibly sensitive, especially her toes and can send an electric charge throughout her body if tended to properly. If you are conscious of the smell then share a bath beforehand. Sucking, licking or lightly nibbling her toes will elicit her desired response.

I cannot emphasise enough how important stimulating these areas are before proceeding to intercourse. Not only on a physical level, contributing to lubricate her vagina, but also on an emotional level as your attention will result in a trusting connection between the two of you. This is an important box to tick off if you are looking to pleasure her.

THE BIGGEST EROGENOUS ZONE OF ALL

We have covered all of the erogenous zones that you can reach with your hand, fingers, penis or tongue, but there is one erogenous zone that is a bit trickier to reach – and that is a woman's brain. It is no doubt her greatest erogenous zone, the central nerve operator from which all messages are delivered.

If her brain is stimulated, there is a greater likelihood that she will be responsive to your sexual advances. It is the difference between being turned on and nonchalant. How do you engage the brain? You do this by communicating and generating sufficient comfort, for inhibitions not to be a consideration. Remember, she will have to be in the right frame of mind in order to respond effectively to the stimulus you are providing.

The less conscious you are able to make her, the more successful your endeavour will be. Make her feel at ease about all those imperfections. Let her know how beautiful she is to you and be vocal about wanting to please her from head to toe.

THE ORDER OF STIMULATION

It is not necessary to plot out a route as if you were following a map. Spontaneity and variety are important in maintaining an interesting and fulfilling sex life. What I would suggest though, is to leave the highly sensitive and receptive areas until last – namely the breasts and genitals. Concentrate on the lesser know areas first, building slowly but surely up to these more sensitive areas.

A NOTE ABOUT AGE

As we get older the sensitivity of the body begins to fade. It takes men and women much longer to get aroused. Bearing this in mind, take cognisance of the fact that it may require more effort if the woman in your life is mature.

HOW TO SET THE MOOD

The environment has to be right if you intend to elicit all these reactions from your partner. As many women seem to prefer "lights off" sex whilst men prefer "lights on" sex, learn to compromise. You could try candlelight instead as many women love this, especially if the candles are scented. Smells such as rose, lavender, vanilla and jasmine are the best for creating a relaxed yet sensual atmosphere.

Essential oils are a great addition to any massages that you have planned for the erogenous zones such as the shoulders, neck or thighs. The oils you use should be chosen carefully and if possible take your partner with when choosing.

Have all of the aids at hand if you intend on using them when discovering your partner's erogenous zones. Certain textures and materials can have different effects on these zones and can help heighten arousal. As mentioned, a silk scarf is a good prop as any. As you get more confident, you could even try ice cubes or food.

EVERYONE IS DIFFERENT

An important point to remember is that although all of these areas are highly sensitive and stimulating, they are not always pleasurable for every individual. It is a learning process and if your partner says that she does not like a certain zone being touched, then you should respect her wishes. By trying to force the issue because it is a universally identified erogenous zone, you are going to defeat the purpose of what I am teaching you.

ACTIONS

Identify Her Hotspots

Ask your partner to lie on her back and to withhold from making any movement or sound. Start to experiment with all her different zones using your hands, tongue, lips and whatever props you have decided to try out. Communicate with her throughout the process and ask her for her suggestions.

Dicing with Pleasure

Take a dice and make a list of six erogenous zones on a piece of paper. For example, allocate the number one to her neck, number two to her shoulders, number three to the ear and so on. Throw the dice and let fate decide which area you are going to work on each time. It may be beneficial to throw the dice six times in a row, as she will generally respond better without breaks in between.

Enhance the Experience for Her

Take away one your partners senses whilst you are exploring her erogenous zones. Lightly tie a blindfold or dark silk scarf over her eyes, and begin to explore her body from top to bottom. This will also help her alleviate any self conscious thoughts she may be experiencing by monitoring your reactions. She will also focus purely on what she is feeling, which will thus heighten the sensuality of the experience for her.

Sex, Chapter 8:
Exercises, Methods and Tips

No-one is perfect, not even Casanova himself and we all need a little bit of help and advice from time to time! This chapter gives you hints and tips as well as useful exercises to make sure that you are able to satisfy your partner successfully. You don't have to use of all of them; just pick and choose the ones that you are comfortable with.

Exercises for Single Men

Kegel exercises can be incredibly useful if you are single. These exercises strengthen the muscles that are used during intercourse. Firstly, you will need to locate the right muscles and the easiest way of doing this is by holding in your urine. Try contracting the muscle five to ten times, three sets per day. Remember not over do this as it may result in actually weakening the muscles.

As previously discussed, one of the preferred positions for women is when they are 'on top'. It increases the chances of her clitoris and genital area receiving stimulation from your pubic bone. By utilising your pelvic muscles, you will aid the creation of friction, which will stimulate her clitoris. But this can be tiring and you will need to get into shape to sustain this for a reasonable length of time.

Lie on the floor with your knees bent and your feet flat. Keep your arms and hands down by your sides. Now lift your bottom off the floor until it reaches the same height as your shoulders; effectively, your knees and shoulders should appear to be in a straight line. Hold this position for one or two seconds and slowly lower your bottom back to the floor. Try to do as many repetitions as you can in one go; take a fifteen second break between the sets and then start again.

TONGUE EXERCISES FOR CUNNILINGUS

The first exercise may sound silly but it really works. Try and touch the tip of your nose with your tongue and hold it for as long as possible. This is excellent for strengthening the muscles.

Secondly, try sticking your tongue out so that it is extended as far as it will possibly go. Remember to keep it flat. Now curl the tip of your tongue upwards and then back down to the flat position. You can also implement this exercise by moving your tongue from side to side. The most important aspect is to keep the shape of the tongue consistent.

Finally, loosen your jaw and stick your tongue out. Try to keep your tongue in contact with the top and bottom of your mouth at the same time. Once you manage to hold this position, move your tongue in and out whilst still maintaining contact with the roof and bottom of your mouth. It sounds tricky, but with a bit of practice you will get the hang of it.

EXERCISES FOR PREMATURE EJACULATION

Premature ejaculation can be incredibly frustrating in terms of not being able to satisfy your partner. But fear not, there are a number of exercises that may help.

Masturbate an hour before you have sex. This can sometimes help you go the distance and relieve any insecurity about coming too quickly. You can also take this a level further by just stopping yourself before climaxing; wait a few seconds and then start over again. Repeat the process three of four times. You should find that the length of time it takes to reach the point near ejaculation will increase with each attempt.

Doing regular exercise and working your pelvic floor muscles (usually known as Kegel exercises) can help to delay ejaculation too. The key is to remain calm and relax; if you are all stressed and anxious, you are more likely to lose control too soon.

EXERCISES FOR ERECTILE DYSFUNCTION

Erectile Dysfunction, also known as impotence, affects one in ten men in the UK. The condition means that men are not able to sustain an erection during sexual intercourse. It was once believed that erectile dysfunction was solely down to psychological factors such as stress, depression, sexual boredom and relationship problems. It has since been found that there are links between ED and other conditions such as diabetes, high cholesterol and kidney disorders.

The recommended exercises for erectile dysfunction centre on strength-ening the pelvic floor muscles and in particular the Pubococcygeus muscle (commonly known as the PC muscle). This muscle is present in both men and women and runs from your coccyx to your pubic bone. The Kegel exercises help to strengthen these muscles and improve the blood flow to the penis, which in turn helps to sustain the erection.

Studies have shown that men who exercise regularly throughout the week can ward off erectile dysfunction. If you can devote three or four hours a week or burn off 200 calories each day, you will cut the risk of suffering from this condition.

METHODS FOR CUNNILINGUS

Right, so by now you should be aware that cunnilingus remains one of the best methods in getting your partner to climax. We have already covered the 'cat lick', the 'diagonal stroke' as well as the basic stroke. Here are a few more methods to help keep things varied and interesting.

The majority of men will lick from top to bottom or vice versa in terms of their strokes. Try employing horizontal movements. Make the strokes light and pay particular attention to the clitoris. This method is useful in the latter stages of cunnilingus when all your emphasis should be on the clitoris. Some women like these strokes to be particularly sloppy as it intensifies the sensation for them.

There is a lot of focus on licking your partner's genitals but you can also employ some suction methods too! Place your lips around the glans and start a gentle sucking action. Remember that it must be gentle as the clitoris is a very sensitive area. By using a sucking technique her clitoris will swell and the blood flow will be increased. This will aid her in reaching an orgasm.

One great way to take a break but keep the momentum going is to place your tongue just inside of her vaginal entrance. This way you are still maintaining contact but can take a breather. Keep your tongue flat and still. If your partner is suitably aroused, she may start pushing herself against your tongue or rotating her pelvis.

One of the most effective techniques is known as the "Circling Tongue". This may appear to suggest that you move your tongue around in a circle but you'd be wrong! It involves keeping your tongue still and moving your chin, nose and lips in slow and gentle circles. This one may need a bit of focus and concentration – it's a bit like rubbing your head and patting your stomach at the same time!

A NOTE ON THE NO-NO'S

Whilst there are many techniques that work well with cunnilingus there are a few positions and techniques that you should avoid.

Firstly, the "69" is a terrible position to adopt for cunnilingus, even if the woman is on the bottom. For starters, you are both concentrating on pleasuring the other person whilst simultaneously trying to prevent yourself from becoming aroused and reaching climax. Secondly, this position is not one that can be sustained for an inordinate amount of time. And as you now know, comfort and the ability to go on and on are crucial. Finally, this position does not allow you to use your tongue, hands or fingers to their full potential. This is not to say that the "69" does not have its place; it is a great position for a bit of foreplay.

Similarly, adopting the position of you lying on your back and your partner kneeling over your head is not the best in terms of sensuality. She will also be using her back and leg muscles to maintain the kneeling position, which is not conducive to long sustainable periods. Again, save this position for foreplay.

 The final no-no position in terms of pleasure is you kneeling whilst your partner is positioned against a hard surface like a wall. Her pelvis is more than likely to be tilted in the wrong way and you will end up hurting your neck and being unable to maintain any rhythm.

THE RIGHT WAY UP

Okay, so you now know which positions to avoid. Let's look at some of the right ways. Firstly, your partner should lie in a comfortable position on her back. This can be on the edge of the bed or further up, whichever is going to be comfortable for the both of you for a substantial period of time. Her legs should be bent at the knee with her thighs facing outwards. It is recommended that she does not have her thighs flat against the bed. This can become uncomfortable to maintain for a long time and will also create tension in her leg muscles, which can lead to cramps. Her back should not be arched as this can restrict the flow of blood to the areas that you are trying to pleasure. You can also prop a pillow under her buttocks to help her achieve the correct position.

When it comes to positioning yourself, you need to have ample space to manoeuvre as well as feeling comfortable. Your position should compliment your partner's and you should virtually be in a straight line. Position your stimulating hand close to her genital area. You can use a pillow under your arms to keep yourself comfortable. There should be a free and fluid path of motion so that if you decide to cradle her buttocks or stroke her stomach, you have enough room to move to the chosen position. Make sure that your head is in the right position. Ideally, your upper lip should be situated around the upper part of her clitoral area, somewhere around the commissure and clitoral hood. Essentially, if you were to take a photograph you would see very little of her genitals and more of the back of your head.

SEX TIPS FOR CUNNILINGUS

The first thing I want to cover is a medical warning. It is crucial that you never blow air into your partner's vagina. This can cause a gas bubble to enter her bloodstream and possibly cause an embolism, which is potentially fatal.

If you are still doubtful about performing cunnilingus on your partner because of the smell and taste, then try using a flavoured lubricant. The water-based ones are the best as they are more sensitive to the skin.

Prop a pillow under the head and shoulders of your partner before you start any cunnilingus activities. This will allow her to adopt the right position with her back flat and her pelvis tilting slightly downward.

Sometimes the most effective position is for your partner to have her legs in the air. This requires a lot of flexibility but it exposes her genital area, particularly the perineum and the anus.

If you are both new to the art of cunnilingus it can be a daunting experience. Start off by practicing your licks and movements through her underwear. This will not only help to build confidence, but the material of the underwear will also aid the sensory aspect. Satin, silk and lace are particularly enjoyable.

A great lover's hands are never motionless. Whether it is a light touch on the shoulder, a sensual massage or manual stimulation of the clitoris, women like to be touched. It gives them a sense of connection with their partner and makes the entire experience more pleasurable.

When your partner has reached the pre-orgasm stage, it is time to move into the position where her legs are together. If you find it too difficult to combine moving her legs, manual stimulation and tongue stimulation, you can tie her legs together at the ankles. Make sure that you do this before the session starts or during one of your breathers. And always make sure that the bond is light and not uncomfortable for your partner.

If you have a beard or moustache, consider trimming it or shaving it off. The stubble can be harsh on this area. A beard may also be ticklish in certain areas of her clitoral network.

Periods! Some women's capacity to reach orgasm is heightened when she is menstruating. This is because the clitoris is even more sensitive than normal. Of course, you and your partner may not be willing to try this at all; nevertheless, I am here to tell you that it is perfectly acceptable! There is even a name for this activity – the Scarlet Kiss. Just make sure she has inserted a fresh tampon and the area is clean.

Similarly, many men worry about oral sex when a woman is pregnant. Again, the change in hormones can make her genital areas more sensitive and receptive to achieving an orgasm sooner. The only time you should avoid it is when you have been medically advised. Another important point to remember in terms of cunnilingus during pregnancy is that a woman who is in the second trimester (from 14 weeks to 26 weeks) should avoid lying on her back for prolonged periods of time. You can still perform oral sex as long as you prop a pillow under her back and tilt her body slightly to the side so that the blood flow is not being restricted.

ACTIONS

Do Some More Research

Do some research and investigate some other positions, techniques and exercises. No matter what you are looking for, you will find hundreds articles on the Internet to help you find new and exciting ways to please your partner.

Take a look at the Kama Sutra, which is the sex bible to many couples. Not only are there a myriad of positions intercourse itself, but there are also positions and techniques that can be adapted for giving great cunnilingus.

Do Some Exercise

Exercise is a key ingredient for maintaining stamina and endurance during your sexual escapades. Try get into a routine where you are doing some cardiovascular work at least three times per week. It will provide you with immeasurable support in trying to get your partner to climax.

Planning Activities

Although spontaneous sex is a wonderful experience, it doesn't hurt to do a little bit of planning. Have an idea in your head about which positions, techniques and methods you would like to try. Make sure you articulate these to your partner.

SEX, CHAPTER 9:
YOU ARE NOW A PERFECT LOVER!

Well, almost perfect – there really is no such thing as a perfect lover! It is now time to analyse all the skills that you have learned and find out how to put them into practice.

FORGETTING ABOUT THE PAST

The modern male has been brainwashed into believing that women are satisfied with intercourse and intercourse alone. And women are no better, believing that repeated insertions of the penis result in orgasms.

I want you to understand that the art of successful lovemaking is a selfless one in which your primary concern should be the fulfilment of your partner. Forget about the media, friends' banter and other superficial mechanisms through which you have achieved all your previous advice.

HOW WOMEN FEEL ABOUT SEX

For the majority of women, sex is not as important as other aspects of a relationship. Certainly in terms of their own sexual pleasure and achieving an orgasm, they like to take a back seat. Most women are natural born givers and would prefer to give you pleasure than to receive it themselves. This is partly down to the way they have been brought up and their portrayal as sex objects in the media.

Once they become aware of the importance you place on their attainment of pleasure, their mindset will shift and you will be in store for a more fulfilling sexual relationship. You need to restore the balance of equality within the bedroom, only then will you achieve the potential heights that sex can bring to both parties.

COMMUNICATION, COMMUNICATION, COMMUNICATION

In all areas of your relationship, communication is crucial and none more so than when it comes to sex. The subject of sex can still remain a taboo subject, even for couples who are very close. Women tend to discuss any issues with their girlfriends rather than us men. It is essential to break through this barrier and embrace the art of open, honest and sensitive communication.

Break with tradition and learn to communicate about all things sexual with her. It may feel embarrassing and awkward at first but this will soon fade away until you are both discovering the most essential aspects of pleasuring each other.

ALL OVER THE PLACE

You now know that women have a number of erogenous zones. Gone are the days of you exploring just her neck, breasts and genitals. The perfect and attentive lover will closely examine every inch of their partner, from top to bottom.

One of the largest complaints that women have is that their partners are too pre-occupied with going in for the kill. They remain in the triangle mentality – start with the left breast, move to the right and conclude with the vagina. You now possess all the knowledge to go beyond this limiting methodology and begin to take account of all those areas that have previously been ignored. Remember to take it slow and administer as much concentration on technique as possible.

KEY POINTS TO REMEMBER ABOUT CUNNILINGUS

The first step to giving your partner pleasure by way of cunnilingus is to remember that her sexual gratification needs to come first. Whether it takes five minutes or an hour, you need to delay your own pleasure so that she can have hers. Women are wired in a completely different way when it comes to arousal and stimulation. Once you respect and understand this, you will be able to unselfishly let her indulge in her own need to orgasm.

The second thing to remember is to take it slow. Find the right rhythm and try not to alter it too much. This is primarily in the latter stages of the coreplay process. Keep your tongue strokes light and apply more pressure, as your partner becomes more aroused.

One of the most crucial elements of cunnilingus is assuring your partner that this is something you want to do. She should know that her fulfilment is more important than your own pleasure. Keep the assurances coming before and throughout the activity. Communicate to her that you love her particular taste and smell and that performing oral sex is something that excites you.

Comfort can be a big issue when performing cunnilingus. It is important to adopt the right positions that will not leave you aching all over. You could be there for some time so prepare before hand with plenty of pillows, cushions and blankets. Being comfortable will allow you to concentrate purely on the essential elements in getting her aroused.

Make sure your tongue, fingers and hands work as a team in perfect harmony. Movements should be smooth and fluid not rough and ready. If for some reason she does not climax, remember that it is no-one's fault. It is sometimes just one of these things that you have to put down to experience. As long as you have perfected the techniques and skills I have mentioned, you can be confident that it will happen in the near future.

DUST YOURSELF OFF

Getting the hang of all these new skills and techniques isn't just going to happen overnight. Learning and utilising these techniques takes time. Communicate your intentions to your partner. Once she is aware of the new direction you are heading in terms of personal pleasure, she will be more than willing to support your efforts. As with all worthwhile things in life, if at first you don't succeed, try, try, and try again.

STAYING SAFE

Even if you have been with your partner for quite a while it still pays dividends to remain safe. In terms of anal activity, always remember to use a condom. It can be an erotic area to indulge in, but it remains essential be protect yourself and her from the nasty infections that can be passed on. If you are partaking in bondage, remember to avoid causing any pain. Make sure the binds are not too tight and remove them if they are causing too much discomfort to your partner. Respect is the key here.

STAY MOTIVATED

Motivation can be one of the hardest things to endure. We all get tired, restless and discontent when trying to adopt changes in our lives. But in terms of pleasuring your partner, it remains essential. Do not revert to old habits or self serving sexual techniques. Becoming an amazing lover will require you to bypass all of these limiting beliefs and stumbling blocks. Remember to discuss any anxieties or tensions that are resulting from your newly acquired intentions. Ask her for support and reassurance. You will soon both be awakening experiences that neither of you could previously have imagined.

Actions

Write Down "Routines"

I recommend drawing up a list of activities that you and your partner would like to explore, i.e. foreplay, coreplay, outercourse, intercourse and moreplay, as well as some of the more detailed routines of cunnilingus. This will also help out in the planning process and prevent any severe breaks which could result in your both losing momentum.

Always Ask for Feedback

Asking your partner how you performed may seem like a daunting idea but it does have numerous obvious benefits. After the first few sessions of introducing these new techniques, she will be more inclined to be honest with you. Remember to take all feedback as constructive criticism. This will be your greatest learning tool and one that will hold both of you in good stead for many an orgasm.

Take a Sneaky Peak

If you are still curious to know more about how the female mind works and their views on sex, I suggest taking a look at some of your partners' magazines. You are likely to learn far more from this than any other porn movie. They are filled with useful information regarding fantasies and other sexual tit bits that could be incredibly useful.

FINAL WORDS

Congratulations on completing this section on Sex. You are now equipped to indulge in all the mesmerising and truly satisfying areas of your sexual life. I hope you have taken on board all the essential elements of satisfying that special person in your life, and are ready to embark on a completely new and gratifying regime. Remember, that sex is about respecting your partner and yourself as well as breaking down the barriers of inhibition. I cannot highlight enough, the importance of creating an open and valuable medium for conversations and constructive feedback. This will endeavour you both to understanding each other's wants and catapult you to numerous sexual awakenings. Let's move onto the next section on relationships.

RELATIONSHIPS

RELATIONSHIPS

All too often us men are inclined to accept the inadequacy of incompatibility and continue to remain in the doldrums of an unfulfilled relationship. We become contently discontented without understanding or trying to implement mechanisms that can lead us away from this environment. There are numerous causes, from low self esteem right through to disparaging levels of communication, with the end result always remaining the same, an unhappy relationship.

This section on Relationships is about creating sufficient personal awareness and providing you with an alternative to displace this vicious cycle. We will analyse certain core issues in sufficient depth for you to understand and address some of these areas. Take your time to work through each and every chapter, at the end of which will be a few actions, which will help you to consolidate what you have learnt so far, and put this knowledge into practice.

Many men come from a background where they genuinely feel emotionally deflated and lacking in self-esteem, they become resolute to the fact that love and happy relationships are the reserve for other, far more fortunate people. But through intense research and an affinity for personal fulfilment, I will acquaint you with a blueprint through the mountains of research done, which in turn will hopefully lead you to a happy and harmonious relationship. Let's take a look at what we will be delving into.

In Relationships, Chapter 1, we're going to familiarise ourselves with some of the most common problems that occur in relationships. This will involve looking at issues ranging from an inability to adapt to a non-single lifestyle to the complexities of trust. We will also give considerable attention to the importance of communication.

We will then evaluate self-esteem and its importance in fulfilment. Finally, we will conclude with a short synopsis on the effects of alcohol and drugs, which have become prevalent and acceptable in the United Kingdom, with the unfortunate results remaining the demise of numerous relationships.

We're going to take this overview of self-esteem much further in Relationships, Chapter 2. The importance of developing genuine self-esteem will be imperative if you are to achieve a fulfilling relationship. This chapter is essentially going to assist you in achieving this with insight and essential actions.

The following two chapters are going to look into the different interpretations that each of the sexes have regarding love. Relationships, Chapter 3 has been sourced through the opinions of numerous women and has been included to highlight the essential mindsets of the fairer sex in terms of love. I am sure this will provide enough thoughtful insight for you to embark on immediate changes.

Relationships, Chapter 4 is going to take look from a man's perspective of this elusive and rewarding emotion. As men, we are often inclined to repress emotional awkwardness as a result of infantile social stereotypes. Finally, to take some of the sting out of the tail, we will conclude with some zestful actions. This is purely for some much deserved respite.

The most complained about and essential ingredient in relationships will then be considered in detail in Relationships, Chapter 5. I cannot express the importance of this enough and if there is one chapter that will need your continual review, it is this. The underlying core principle that resonates in all my research comes down to a single point. No one is ever right or wrong: they are just unheard. We will then conclude with some useful actions, designed to help you communicate more effectively.

In Relationships, Chapter 6, we will identify why we choose certain types of people when it comes to relationships. This is a fascinating insight and I am sure you will be in for a few surprises.

Relationships, Chapter 7, consolidates all that we have learnt so far and embraces the actions required for you to start making positive changes. These will include your appearance, hidden agendas, the concept of negativity and your diet, which believe it or not, has a profound impact on the value you bestow upon yourself.

By now we would have made significant progress into the core principles behind achieving a more fulfilling and lasting relationship. Chapter 8 will provide some insight into the essential alternatives available to you if your relationship is to prosper.

Relationships, Chapter 9 will discuss a few alternatives for you to embark on a more successful relationship. We will discuss types of behaviours as well as assessing whether your partner is right for you.

Relationships, Chapter 10, is the grand finale to this section where we will contemplate the possibilities and probabilities of your successful future. We will envisage the realisation of you embracing success with current or potential relationships.

At this point I would like to congratulate you on your intent in achieving more in terms of your relationship. This personal ambition will, no doubt, bring you closer to fulfilment and understanding. You are the master and commander of this vessel called 'Your Life' and we are about to embark on an insightful journey. Good luck!

MEN NEED HELP TOO?

We are too familiar with the multiple sources of support for women when it comes to addressing relationship concerns. The masses of articles and columns on feminine advice are in abundance, yet there is less insight for the male perspective. I believe this mindset will change as more and more men are gratefully looking for viable educational alternatives in aspects of life where there was little or no tutorial. This chapter is such and I believe it will go a long way to addressing various relationship issues that men find themselves navigating through.

My belief is that you have sufficient self-awareness to understand the need for a resource to have a positive and influential impact on your relationship. I also maintain that varying levels of diminished self-esteem have equated to an unfulfilling union of you and your partner, preventing suitable contentment and resounding successes. The nature of a relationship itself is that its birth resonates excitement, spontaneity and communal feelings of well-being. Unfortunately time is a relationships mistress and more often than not lends itself to a diminished level of romance and heightened annoyances. This chapter accentuates the normality of this predicament and will guide you towards being aware of the fundamental elements that can be addressed in the pursuit of a happier relationship.

READY TO TAKE SOME ACTION?

Let's get started. We've established why you are reading this and should be aware of the structure we are about to pursue. Let's take the proverbial bull by the horns and establish a solidified base for yourself and current or future relationships. I will request that you allow yourself the luxury of sufficient self-analysis to allow for competent development. You have already taken the most difficult step by acknowledging the need for help. Now let's embrace this courageous act by taking it a few steps further.

WHAT CAN SECTION 2: RELATIONSHIPS - DO FOR YOU?

This is of course completely dependent on your level of engagement with the content and actions that are provided. If you only give 50%, do not expect to reap the full potential that is on offer. It genuinely is as facile as that.

I have endeavoured to remain contemporary throughout this chapter as well as regarding you as sufficiently intelligent enough to absorb the advice on offer. The chapters in section 2 are designed to guide you one step at a time through the essential elements towards embarking on a successful and fulfilling relationship. It is essential that you fully comprehend each one before moving onto the next. Make every effort to involve yourself in the actions as they are there for you to digest important aspects of tutorial. I have also included some light-hearted activities to instigate some enjoyment and keep your motivations strong. Just before we get going, I want you to spend a moment thinking about your impetus for engaging in this section and what you are hoping to derive from it.

WHAT ARE YOU LOOKING FOR?

Obviously you are aware that some guidance is required in terms of creating a more harmonious relationship. But delve a little deeper. Write down all the reasons you feel past or current relationships have failed. Be completely honest and list as many elements as you can think of. In the next chapter you will get the opportunity to compare what you have written with some of the common pitfalls that arise in relationships.

I would then like you to think how you could administer these negative outcomes into positive ones. Much of this will be common sense but nevertheless essential. I also anticipate that this will be the start of heightening some deeper issues aligned within your subconscious, moulded through decades and decades of reinforcement with the consequences being the development of discernible self-esteem and an avoidance of trust. Understand that you have had limited control in deciphering your current destination and that remorse, although important, is inconsequential at this point.

RELATIONSHIPS, CHAPTER 1:
COMMON RELATIONSHIP PITFALLS

It is probably fair to state that most individuals have contributed to some type of destructive behaviour prevalent in problematic relationships. It is not something to judge, but rather to evaluate and resolve so further disengaging habits may eventually subside. This chapter will look at some of the more common types of adverse behaviours in an attempt to help you identify and overcome potential warning areas.

The concept of having a relationship can be a frightening prospect for a number of men. The imaginary baggage associated with commitment and trust often lead to reclusive and insular ideologies. The added premise of lost freedom reinforces this. Being accustomed to the independent lifestyle leads to a predisposition, which embodies statements like:

'It's too much hard work'
'I don't want to give up my freedom'
'I won't be told what to do'

It can be incredibly difficult to incorporate someone else into your life when independence remains an essential ideology. This is where the concept of interdependence becomes essential which maintains secular lifestyles whilst still remaining in a partnership.

INDEPENDENCE VS. INTERDEPENDENCE

The modern lifestyle attributes to a mindset of self-gratifying behaviours like multiple sexual partners, short-term relationships and essentially the pursuance of complete independence. This mindset is not isolated to single people and often occurs midway through long-term relationships. The misplaced thought of having missed out on an element of youth, fun or individuality as a result of the responsibilities that embody the modern relationship is common. Newly formed relationships are also susceptible to this adherence with complications arising out of the sudden impact of having someone around you all the time, sharing your bed, administering duties and other communal activities. This readjustment can be difficult when entertaining the idea of a long-term commitment. Enter the realm of interdependence as opposed to independence.

The value of independence lies in autonomy and self-reliance, with the individual remaining unable to absorb the concept of growing together. It results in communication breakdown and the inability to commit. Essentially, independence prevents the relationship from growing by continually negating all the essential elements in terms of developing trust. In terms of relationship development, it is harmful and destructive.

Interdependence is what every couple should be gearing towards. It entertains the necessary levels of independence, allowing for individuality, and the capacity to rely and depend on each other. The bottom line is simple. You grow as individuals but remain there to support each other. How you decide to draw this up amongst yourselves is completely subjective and will involve boundaries being set by both of you. But the essential elements remain the same. You grow as individuals but remain available to each other through support and commitment.

COMMUNICATION

As I have previously mentioned, communication is one of the two more essential ingredients in a healthy relationship, the other being trust. And it is not necessarily only the level of communication that can cause issues, but also the type. This is where conflicting cultures and upbringings can cause riot. Let's get the initial stating the obvious out of the way. You need to make your partner aware of concerns or anxieties through sensitive communication. You cannot find fulfilment if you are beset with hidden agendas and are unable to vocally commit to them.

The unfortunate result is that you elicit your anxieties, not through constructive communication, but via mannerisms, which exude frustration and discontentment. They create a loss of understanding and inevitably trust, as your partner is unaware of your genuine intentions or concerns. Let me give you an example; your wife comes home late one night and you have an irrational fear that she is having an affair. Your inability to share this fear results in you making sarcastic comments about her appearance in the hope of eliciting a reaction, which could potentially lead to the eradication of your anxiety. Well guess what, it does not. It creates an additional breakdown and you are left no clearer on understanding whether she is being faithful or not. What is the solution? Straight and sensitive communication!

Q: Honey, I am feeling a little anxious about you working so late all the time and wanted to know if you are having an affair?
A (1): No darling, I am sorry but I have just been under severe pressure at work and needed to finish off these deadlines.
A (2): Yes, I am seeing someone else.

The resulting response is not important in terms of the communication itself. Only that it has taken place and there are no hidden agendas from either party. This allows for sincere movement in whichever direction you choose.

Differing personality types also develop differing methods of communicating. Where one party may be passionate and vocal the other could favour being reserved and processing his or her thoughts with more deliberation. It is crucial to understand which category you and your partner fit into and to create boundaries to accommodate this. In the previous example this could result in you taking a time out while she processes your question. Remember, there are no right or wrong types, only different types requiring different methods of approach.

Communication is a joint responsibility and one that requires both of your time. But I need to highlight this point again. Ensure it is always sensitive and resonating from a place that is respectful. If you are caught up in the heat of the moment, insist on taking a break and reviewing the discussion later on.

LOW SELF-ESTEEM

So many relationships are condemned to failure as a result of one or both parties not being able to love themselves. The mindsets of inferiority complexes result in continual antagonism with the intent of making the other person feel ill equipped. These irrational living and breathing role-plays are devastating, with both parties often feeling emotionally dishevelled. It's simple. You cannot expect someone to love you unless you are able to offer it to yourself first. If you are predisposed to having a low self-esteem I suggest Cognitive Behaviour Therapy (CBT) as a treatment. The key here is learning to understand that you are thoroughly deserved of a happy, loving and fulfilling relationship, irrespective of past indiscretions or experiences. I'll come back to this in more detail later on.

HIDDEN AGENDAS

Hidden agendas do not work in relationships. They are a manifestation of an inability to express and will always result in the breakdown of trust. Trying to elicit a response from your partner through provocative behaviour is both pointless and reckless. It's a conscious decision to test your partner to see if they will acknowledge you. The cause, more often than not, stems from some form of insecurity regarding:

- The level of commitment held by a partner
- The anxiety of a partner cheating on him or her
- Various levels of inadequacy in terms of not being good enough

Again, the key to avoiding this cycle is developing self-esteem and sufficient interdependence allowing for personal development.

COMPROMISE

If you cannot learn to compromise you might as well set sail for emotional solitary confinement now! Successful long-term relationships cannot succeed unless both parties are willing to adapt to certain changes. Think about it in terms of this. Two people are brought up with entirely different methodologies, core beliefs, reinforcements and varying levels of awareness. Notwithstanding their similarities, they exist on different plains. Now throw them together with the intent of spending their remaining days in unison. It's not difficult to comprehend how little they will achieve without the ability to compromise.

Remember, it is inconsequential who is right or wrong. The importance lies in the capacity to follow through with something you would normally be opposed to as a result of your partner. This involves a sufficient need of selflessness and empathy. This also needs to be offered on an equal basis. If one person constantly compromises for the other, he or she will feel undervalued and unable to grow within the relationship.

TRUST

This is the priority of maintaining the best interests of the relationship at heart. Honesty, communication and genuine concern for the success of the relationship are always prevalent. A breakdown of trust in a relationship almost inevitably leads to its demise. The only way to maintain it is through honest communication and basing your actions on that.

The past also has a role to play here. Almost everyone will have experienced an infidelity or some manner of deception resulting in the incapacity to believe your partners intentions. The important realisation to make is that every relationship is unique with no individual being the same. There is no rationality behind the following logic:

- My ex cheated on me so it will happen again
- Women can't be trusted
- I am not right for long term relationships

Irrespective of the severity of your own disposition towards trust, CBT can provide useful insight in coming to terms with past breakdowns. It is also important to remember the following: The breakdown of mistrust in the relationship will subside in time as long as both parties are interested in its success.

Mistrust is kryptonite when it comes to the health and well being of a relationship and it is certainly common. So don't feel you are unique in terms of struggling with it. By elevating your expression along with your self esteem, you will go a long way to genuinely being able to forge meaningful and trustworthy relationships. When you are able to discuss these issues openly and honestly with your partner, there are a number of mechanisms to make you feel safe. An example is drawing up boundaries of what is appropriate in terms of feeling secure.

ALCOHOL OR DRUG DEPENDENCY

This is a serious and common issue in the UK, so I found myself intent on having to mention it. If you are dependent on alcohol or drugs, your relationship exists with the dependency and not with your partner. The results are normally always catastrophic with the destruction of trust and honesty being the first symptoms.

I am not going to stand on a moral high ground when it comes to substance abuse. What I will say is this. The problem exists in the breakdown of the individuals character itself. Aggression, confrontation, violence and paranoia are just some of the symptoms that result from the abuse of drugs and alcohol. Bottom line! If you have dependency issues, fulfilling relationships are highly improbable. Get help and get clean!

So, in this chapter we have taken a brief look at some of the more common problems that contribute to the breakdown of relationships. It is more than likely that you are guilty of one or more of these traits and it is nothing to be ashamed of. The complexities of human nature make them conducive for adornment. But it is essential for your personal development that you become aware of the consequences and make intentional decisions to move forward.

I also want to highlight another common issue that seems prevalent in the UK culture, namely, the belief that emotional exploration should be a feminine characteristic. These social stereotypes have existed for centuries resulting in women being the primary participants when it comes to self-exploration. Addressing this and throwing out any dated predispositions to chauvinism are going to be paramount when it comes to the success of your relationship. Before we move on to the next chapter, there are a couple of concepts that I want you to mull over.

ACTIONS

Throughout this book, you will be given the opportunity to put what you are learning into practice. This allows you to consolidate what we have gone through as well as enabling you to engage on a more practical level. My primary aim is to allow you to envisage yourself and determine what aspects of your persona are preventing you from sustaining or engaging in a long-term relationship. The intensity of the process is entirely up to you but I want you to remember one thing. Your discoveries are communal and there is nothing unique about the negative traits you will find.

Assessing Your Partner's Opinion of You

Irrespective of the length of your relationship, few couples actually cite and verbalise their opinions of each other. It is an essential activity in terms of transforming partnerships and can provide unique insight. This action is going to be adapted as if you are in a long term relationship, but can be used irrespective of this.

Long-term Relationships

This is formulated in such a manner for you to be able to recognise the positive and attractive traits at your disposal. Many people with low self-esteem negate their own attributes and fixate on their downside.

Write down all the qualities you feel your partner sees in you. Be completely immodest, remembering that you are not going to share this list with anyone else. Compile this list of traits on the left hand side of your piece of paper, as you will be using the other side for the next part of this activity.

Now, I want you to write down all of the traits of your character that you feel have caused problems in your relationship on the right hand side. This could be an inability to communicate or an activity in which you were self serving.

Importantly, if your right hand list is longer than the left hand side, you have a partner who loves you very much. Be grateful. The purpose of this exercise is to generate some awareness. You don't have to perform any further actions as long as you have stimulated sufficient thought to both sets of traits.

Single

I still want you to participate in this activity. Follow the activity as it is laid out above but this time collectively consider the negative and positive traits of your character, which you remember receiving feedback on from past relationships. What personality traits did people seem to be drawn to and which ones did they find particularly hard to deal with?

Stop Playing Games

This is one action I want you to take on board immediately. The rewards are far too great to ignore and it is essential for your personal development and that of your relationship. Whenever your partner seeks counsel or opinion, your only objective is to protect her feelings with your response. No sarcasm, no humour, no intentional emotional traps and no negative connotations. It's easy; so don't even think about talking your way out of it. Even if she is annoying and insistent on irritating you, stick to the activity. This is a process and I want you to start implementing these simple actions as if your life depended on it.

Relationships, Chapter 2:
Self-Esteem: Learning To Love Yourself

Self-esteem is how we view ourselves. It's the genuine value you place on yourself; underneath all the social predispositions you lend yourself towards. It is your real acceptation and the one you will find yourself questioning more often than not. It is your own personal sense of worth and affects your ability to love and be loved.

Your self-esteem becomes evident through a variety of mannerisms. Eye contact, a calm demeanour and tonality of your voice are just a few of the gages. These outward manifestations give out your true feelings and the value of worth you bestow upon yourself.

What Defines Our Level Of Self-Esteem!

Your past experiences define your personal inner value. The nurturing you received in your formative years, the relationships you developed and lost, your interaction with peers and the meaning you placed on events and actions in your past. I want to talk a little about the concept of meaning.

Imagine two people with identical horrific upbringings, physical and emotional abuse being rampant. These two people with identical experiences go onto to lead two completely different lives; one being a success and the other being dependent on alcohol and drugs. What's the difference? They were both physically abused, they were both victims to psychological abuse – surely they should either both be successful or both be committed to substance abuse.

The difference in their development comes down to the meaning they attached to the events themselves. This is critical to understand. The events in your life do not define you, but rather the meaning that you have given them. That is why some of the least suspecting people, adorned with some of the most severe atrocities are still able to place an enormous amount of value on themselves.

So let's assume you have been subjected to discouragement and it has been sustained for a long period of time. You then consider this to be true and you diminish your personal value. You then project your low self-esteem on others through numerous manifestations because you have decided that all of the negative reinforcement is correct. What you fail to realise is that the people who have administered the discouragement, are identical in terms of their own diminished self-esteem. Someone discouraged him or her, and those before him or her and on and on and on. By understanding his or her motivations, not condoning, you can begin to break away from the cycle.

THE EFFECTS OF LOW SELF-ESTEEM

The most obvious effect is the inability to feel that you are worthy of love. You feel your partner is too good for you and the necessary equality that needs to exist in the relationship disappears. If there is an imbalance on this level, your partnership is headed for troubled waters. Many individuals with low self-esteem sabotage their relationships in order to justify their own diminished personal opinion of themselves. Outward symptoms can be having affairs, leading people on, substance abuse or the inability to express or communicate. Bottom line, if either partner has a diminished level of self-esteem, the relationship will suffer.

DEVELOPING SELF-ESTEEM

There is unfortunately no overnight pill for the development of self-esteem. But there are a number of genuine actions and thought processes that can help you to elevate the value you place on yourself. The male predisposition is to accept that this is his definition and to engage in relationships despondently and destructively. You are ahead of the game and need to appreciate yourself a little more for this personal insight.

Firstly, you need to comprehend that your past does not define who you are. Your actions remain responsible for this and when you embrace the concept that personal history is nothing other than an interpretation, you can begin to move forward. Now I am not saying forget. What I am pointing to is the idea that for you to develop self-esteem, personal responsibility will have to be embraced. This means accepting events as they were and making the concerted decision that they are not your potential definition.

Secondly, you are going to need to develop assertive qualities when interacting with people. Assertive behaviour is engaged when the concept of equality is understood as the prevalent quality when engaging in decisions. It embodies respect and a willingness to avoid control. In simple terms, it requires you to become active in the choices you make. This means embracing your opinions, decisions and desires and making them apparent to those around you. Not in an aggressive or domineering manner, but rather in a sensitive and engaging one. There is no point in agreeing to something your partner has requested, with the intent of harbouring resentment and fulfilling your obligation with animosity. You may very well make the decision to compromise in her requested action, but make sure your opinion is voiced with respect and sensitivity so there are no hidden emotional agendas at your disposal. It is not about a winning or losing outcome but rather the meeting of two minds with the single intent of benefiting both parties.

To Love Oneself Opens The Door To Loving Another!

By accepting your faults and embracing your qualities, you will learn to forge a loving relationship with yourself. This is a necessary credential for your relationship to prosper. Understand that you are a unique individual, embodying characteristics that people will be drawn towards. Further, opinions that you have allowed to define you are nothing more than expressions of others dealing with identical diminished levels of self-esteem. Everybody is worthy of loving and being loved. That includes you too.

We're going to move on to the Actions at this point and I'm hoping that the steps I have set out for you will help encourage you in developing your self-esteem.

Actions

At this point I want you to embrace the following beliefs. Your historical experiences are not going to define you from this point forward. Secondly, no one is more worthy of love than yourself. Whatever unique transgressions and tribulations you have, irrespective of their severity; this is your starting point.

The Worthy of Love Story – Written by You

I want you to write a love story from the perspective of a character that has fallen hopelessly head over heels for you. Write about the moment she first saw you. Think of it along the lines of 'her' writing in a diary about every unique and remarkable quality you possess. Make sure you allocate at least thirty minutes for this exercise.

Dismissing Those Negative Thoughts

I want you to deliver a positive though to every negative assumption you absorb. This is actually a lot easier than you think. Let me give you a few examples.

a) Negative: This breakup is devastating and I am never going to find someone to love again

Positive: This is an opportunity for me to learn from this setback and make sure I don't make the same mistakes when I love someone again.

b) Negative: I never speak up for myself

Positive: I understand why I have not done this in the past and am working towards becoming more assertive

Rating Your Days

I want you to start recording a day diary, recording how you felt at the end of each day, whether you were assertive, whether you carried any hidden agendas, whether you were selfless etc

The purpose of this is to generate a measuring stick for you to accelerate to higher grades as time goes by. Don't be annoyed if you slip back into old routines; remember that life is about 70:30 and not 100. Use the following scale:

A= A truly excellent day where you have felt confident and interacted in a constructive and assertive manner.

B= All-in-all a good day. You felt reasonably confident and socialised with most people.

C= A rather average day. There may have been times where you felt confident but there were also some awkward periods where you felt a little diminished.

D= Not a good day. Decidedly lacking in confidence and compelled not to interact with others.

E= Akin to agoraphobia in that you felt inclined to isolate yourself from every one. Very low self-esteem and not a day you want to repeat in a hurry.

RELATIONSHIPS, CHAPTER 3:
DEFINING LOVE: A FEMALE PERSPECTIVE

Although the feeling of love is a universal concept with both men and women experiencing similar understandings, there are still a number of differing expectations that we need to be aware of. They exist through the differing social values and stereotypes that have been present for centuries. Fortunately the modern era has aligned us more closely with equality but it is important to understand some of the concepts experienced through the eyes of a woman.

EQUALITY

It is a false belief that women are more prone to falling in love than men. Marriage and the conception of children have been their watermark through most of our history with their underlying status being determined by whether or not they wore a wedding ring. The modern world has changed a lot and this mould is incongruent with reality. There is more equality in the workplace, although this is still incredibly chauvinistic, with more opportunities being made available to women. Many of them have shifted priorities to include a successful career and embody the joys of independence before committing to a long-term partner and the concept of love.

That is not to say there are not woman who exude intensity and a willingness to develop love before its natural time. But this is more often than not an individual disposition and not gender related. That said, core beliefs and past experiences influence our behaviour and the journey of the female gender has been different to men. I believe in the common mindset that women mature faster than their counterparts, resulting in having to deal with the more juvenile acts associated with slower development. The resulting consequences are commitment concerns and thus when the right individual is accepted, there can be a genuine intensity for the relationship to develop before its time.

Men have been conditioned into being protectors, providers and intent on deciphering solutions. Women have been more akin to sensitivity, gentility and a reliance on the former. This mindset has become dated and the critical element to remember is that women are looking for a partner who views them as an equal. This incorporates acceptance and the capacity for empathy. Flowers, chocolates and prized dinners are always welcome but it is essential to understand that this does not elevate your status in terms of equality. If anything it should be a manifestation of the belief that you have found someone proportionate.

So what other expectations are in store for men? Stability and the capacity to listen are predominant on her wish list. Where men embattle to find a solution to every obstacle, women are more aligned to share the experience rather than pursue its clarification. This differential mindset can be the cause of multiple arguments and annoyances, so take on board the importance of lending an ear without the need for being vocal.

SO WHAT DO WOMEN TRULY WANT FROM A RELATIONSHIP?

The million-dollar question! There is obviously no simple answer to this and it would be infantile to assume that a hard and fast generalisation existed for an entire gender. We are all individuals with unique insights, interpretations and inconsistent desires. But there are few key admissions to take notice of when it comes to understanding her needs in a relationship.

As I have previously mentioned, acceptance is paramount in her fulfilment. The comparison to air brushed models, actresses and ex-partners is counterproductive and condemns her to feelings of inadequacy. Her desire is to remain secure in the knowledge that you are comfortable with her ideas, values and opinions. Taken a step further, that you respect her and the core set of beliefs that she accompanies.

Support is the prerequisite for maintaining this healthy bond. Irrespective of action or consequence, the level of empathy you direct towards her is indicative of being in a worthy partnership. Deep and meaningful love is synonymous with these qualities and more often than not, pertains to long-term success. There is of course the natural instinct of wanting children one day and developing a partnership that either steers away or directly towards their parental authorities. But this is something that develops as a result of the former boxes being ticked.

REMAINING CONSISTENT WITH YOUR TRUE SELF

I want to tap into this briefly and even though it is not particular to the female gender, it certainly affects them as it does you. Trying to embody the characteristics of someone who you think your partner will find attractive is short term and leads to inconsistency. If you fall prey to accommodating and embodying these varying interests, not only will you misunderstand the demise of the relationship, but you will also be left with a sense of confusion in terms of your true self. Let me be very clear here. You cannot be someone you are not, even if that false self encourages reciprocation. You will encounter indifference through continual modes of trying to convince yourself that this is right. The downside is severe. You will remain with the wrong person aspiring to be something you are not and inevitably prevent yourself from meeting someone who is compatible with your unmasked self.

THE POTENTIAL FOR LOVE

Women think about the potential of a partner rather than his current predisposition. If the future is presentable and the possibilities entail happiness, the foreground is open for a long term and genuine emotional bond. Characteristics that embody emotional intelligence necessary to indulge in a meaningful future will hasten this journey. It also goes without saying that we are affected by our understanding of love, which was formulated in youth. What do I mean by this?

Let's say your parents were argumentative and confrontational. Your understanding of love is that it embodies conflict. This has been created on a subconscious level and unknowingly you may employ this characteristic in your current relationship. To your partner it demonstrates disregard and contempt, where in fact, you are projecting your idea of love. Again this is prevalent to both genders and may require CBT to develop enough insight to maintain a healthy perspective.

UNDERSTANDING LOVE

What is the true identity of love? It is of course complex and manifests itself through varying stages in a relationship. There is the 'in love' stage where he or she is elevated to a pedestal, with all of his or her faults regarded as cute idiosyncrasies. This however diminishes in time to a more meaningful and realistic stage, where those once charming habits now reside in annoyances. The affinity for acceptance and compromise are at the fore, with psychological support leading the way. Is it any different for women?

As a result of heightened emotional awareness, women can be more adept in dealing with the diminishment of the 'in love' stage. Their capacity to embody the prospect of a relationship and not its current status make them more akin to moving from one phase to the next. This can sometimes result in the more devastating approach when dealing with incompatibility and relationship breakdowns. This is, however, not completely accurate. Many men struggle to deal with the emotional aspect of pain as a result of the social expectations of remaining strong and in control. The result of a lack of personal exploration can lead to severe meltdowns. That said, women are more often than not, able to adjust to the complexities of love with more agility than men.

COMPROMISE

I have already noted the importance of this concept, but I want to look at it from a female perspective. Imagine having to fight for equality through most spheres of life before entertaining the idea of an equal partnership. The right to vote, the right to command equal salary, the right to participate in equal events, the right to enter the same venues and the right to communicate opinions free of ridicule or harassment. It is something many men are unable to relate to as these experiences have eluded them. Just as being kicked in the groin is unique and indescribable to women. Crude example, but the point is made.

Compromise can remain a difficult quality to adorn for many women. Their entire journey has been one of overcoming the inequality that previously existed and in many respects still exists. Now I am not asking you to sign up to a left wing feminist group. What I am alluding to is the difficulty many female partners face when negotiating with the concept of compromise. This is normally something that occurs at the beginning of a relationship and subsides with time. Be prepared to negotiate and empathise during this stage of the relationship, it will steer you clear of unnecessary disagreements.

COMMUNICATION IS MORE THAN JUST IDLE CHAT

At this point of the chapter, you should have taken on board the importance of being able to express genuine feelings in a respectful and sensitive manner. I will be investigating the importance of communication in a lot more detail later on, but let's take a brief look at it from the feminine perspective.

Woman utter on average about 30 000 words per day in comparison with a man's meagre 10 000. It's not hard to deduce from this their ability to communicate in a more predominant fashion. What is less clear is the dysfunctional nature of assumption, which often stems from a man's inability to express genuine wants. Whereas men are often akin to actions without expression, women are more likely to communicate their way into a mindset that allows for a specific action to take place. A simple analogy; in the same way as men prefer to avoid trying on clothes when shopping, women will spend hours negotiating their way through an abundance of attire before purchasing anything. This is because the resulting action needs to be thought through, contemplated, consolidated and eventually agreed upon on an internal level. Thus, even in their minds they are performing a monologue to aid the decision making process. What becomes evident are two completely antagonistic approaches to expression. The solution is simple and again involves the quality to compromise. Learn to express decision-making thoughts in a sensitive and respectful manner.

Another mindful aspect to remember is that women are curious as to the development of your character. Seemingly unnecessary questions are not inconsequential. She is gathering information about you, likes, dislikes, beliefs, annoyances etc. So when the conversation seems meaningless in terms of providing resolution to a particular obstacle, remember that this is how men are geared in terms of problem solving, and not women. Remain attentive and engaged.

The final short point I want to make in terms of communication is the capacity to listen attentively. What this involves is directing complete and utter focus to what she is commenting on. I honestly could have written another book dealing solely with the number of complaints women have about men not listening. Turn the television off, put the newspaper down and learn to contribute.

ACTIONS

Become Attentive for the Evening

I want you to mark an evening out on your calendar and invite your wife, girlfriend or friend around for some dinner. The purpose of the evening is for you to engage in the art of listening. Make his or her company the focus of your attention and remain steadfast in generating insight from him or her. Find out how their day was, what annoyed them, what made them smile, who they like, dislike, what they had for lunch, would they eat there again etc. Your agenda is to make that person the centre of the vocal communicative experience with you providing the supportive metaphorical ear.

What's Love Got to do With It

The next action involves you being more expressive and attentive to the qualities, which endear you to your partner. Explain to her that you want to spend an hour discussing the qualities that drew you to each other. Talk about the first time you met, what you found attractive about her, which quality you were drawn to first, mannerisms which make you smile etc and don't spare any detail. Do this for fifteen minutes and request her to return the favour. If you are single, perform the exercise with a close friend. This activity will reinforce a number of essential foundations on a conscious and subconscious level.

The Compatibility Check List

It is important to understand that sometimes love is not enough for a relationship to survive. Conflicting goals, beliefs, characteristics and ambitions can lead to the antithesis of longevity. So I want you to address this now. List down twelve of the most important characteristics you want in your partner. This can include political beliefs, spirituality, socialising, travel, money, career, sex etc. Prioritise these in order of importance and give them each a rating out of ten; most compatible being 10 and least compatible being 0. Remember to place more importance on the prioritised characteristics. If there are genuine incompatibility concerns, express them to your partner.

RELATIONSHIPS, CHAPTER 4:
DEFINING LOVE: THE MALE PERSPECTIVE

Forging an understanding between love and being particularly fond of someone can be complex and confusing. What pertains is the underlying predisposition for compatibility and not love. What I mean by that is simple. We become accustomed to the knowing, and continue with the partnership for that reason rather than love. Men can be more indifferent than women in terms of their emotional sincerity and what often develops is an unhealthy and unloving relationship.

In terms of the susceptibility and expression of love, are men really any different to women? Past exploration would lead me to say yes. As we were the providers and equality was not a popular mindset, we tended to care less about sentimentality or the assertion of how we felt. There remained more reservation, irrespective of the level of commitment we felt for our female counterpart. Fortunately this has changed with time, and men have become more encouraged to analyse and decipher much of the self, including the awareness of feelings. But we still remain infinite years behind the opposite sex.

WHAT IS LOVE

Let's first discuss some symptoms of love and differentiate between the initial 'in love' phase and the more meaningful juncture. We begin with the intense physical attraction, constant affection, intense communication and the need to be present with this person. After approximately 18 months these symptoms fade and the relationship either ends or develops into a more meaningful state. The latter embodies empathy, respect, honesty, emotional intimacy, companionship, friendship and acceptance and is more complicated to sustain.

As with women, we need to be able to accept the transition with the understanding that this is a more advanced domicile, which does not equate to the loss of love, but rather its development. With our less enthusiastic nature to develop self-awareness and the exploration of seemingly feminine interests, men often misinterpret the transition with the loss of love.

THE FORMATIVE EXPERIENCE

A large number of men will more often than not have encountered differing parental expectations than woman. A single generation gap incorporates much more discrepancy than one thinks. The male figure was the patriarch who worked to provide, while the female was disposed to raising children and maintaining balance within the home. Thus, the formative reinforcement was different with intense scrutiny being placed on men to succeed in order for them to provide. This is not particular only to men, but it is certainly more common. The resulting consequences were numerous.

Intense pressure, through the self or parental figure, led to beliefs that that academic and sporting success was a definition. I am certainly not deflating their importance, just highlighting the effect of the intense scrutiny. The concept of the Alpha Male – the leading stock – was to be aspired towards, exuding control with the incapacity to exude emotional discomfort. Childhood novelties remained guns, knives and exaggerated muscled figurines, which embodied aggression with the tacit implication that winning, resulted in the ultimate male. Media, politics, core beliefs etc all had their part to play in designing the male into a provider and not a communicator. The ultimate symptom remained the belief that masculine traits did not embody the expression of love.

This modern male mindset is evolving into an equilibrium, which remains healthier and more forgiving when it comes to the health and well being of relationships. Men are being encouraged to get in touch with their feelings and express themselves in or a more vulnerable and honest state, void of hidden agendas. But the reinforcement that was attributable to our lack of understanding and expression must never be ignored; rather it must be accepted and investigated until we are able to overcome the meanings we placed on it.

HOW DO I KNOW WHEN I AM IN LOVE?

With the resulting lack of importance being placed on men exploring self-expression and love, they are often left confused and fluctuating when conflicting emotional states are achieved. Romantic dispositions of 'I can't live without her', 'She is perfect for me', 'She completes me' are all dangerous and false. The correct mindset should always remain that life will almost certainly go on without her, but you choose for this not to be the case because it remains a want rather than a need.

Love as opposed to lust, is a choice rather than an infliction. It is certainly based on evaluation and psychological investigation, but it is a choice nevertheless. When it comes to deciphering the emotional impact a particular person will have on you, its resolution remains in your hands. The active decision is made to support, commit and compromise because that particular person embodies characteristics, which you believe will endear you towards happiness.

What this means is that the onus of responsibility lies within you and not Aphrodites or Cupid. Now I am not saying that you can walk out the door, grab the first person that walks past and choose to love them. There are most definitely certain pre-requisites for every individual before the active choice can be made. But the responsibility of the success or lack thereof is determined by you.

Finally, I just want to highlight a particular point, which is all too common in modern fixations with the concept of love. Many men reach the deeper meaningful phase, become discontent with the sterility of the dynamic and make acceptations of loving another. For the most part this is false as the belief is based on an ideal that does not exist. It is a human preoccupation to imagine other realities as healthier, happier, more meaningful and consumed with the 'in love' phase. Understand that this resonates in a fictional part of the mind and that no matter whom you choose to love, there will always remain inconsistency and the need for realistic compromise and work.

AM I READY FOR LOVE?

I maintain that the choice to love and be loved remains a responsibility, which embodies the capacity to commit, compromise, communicate and create the necessary environment to prosper. It also requires sufficient levels of self-awareness and self-esteem to prosper. The reality of having a relative stranger in your world, in terms of your entire life cycle, is not an easy manifestation to deal with.

There needs to be an awakening to the realisation that individuals are more similar than unique and that interdependence is a healthy and viable option for you to grow. The divorce rate in the United Kingdom and most of the western world is prolific. The romance and ideal of love is prosperous without consideration as to the effort that is entailed in making it reciprocal. The question is difficult and there will never be a clarifying right or wrong answer. But ask yourself the following:

- Do I love myself enough to allow someone else to love me?
- Do I have sufficient self-awareness to answer the above?
- Do my personal interests become secondary?
- Am I able to embody the necessary commitment, compromise and communication for love to remain consistent?

If you are able to consider the above and establish a healthy response, chances are you are ready to absorb and distribute love. A number of horrific breakdowns, separations and heartbreaks occur due to the individual not being able to embody these responsibilities. But it is also essential to remember this. The development of the psyche is never a destination, but rather a journey and there are no certainties when it comes to entertaining the idea of love. But what I wish to get across to you is that love is a gift and one that should be administered with great respect and understanding.

CAN LOVE DEVELOP?

The answer is yes. Many friendships develop into deep, meaningful and loving relationships. Initial symptoms of attraction and immediate interest are not necessary for the development of this emotion. In time, the awareness of initially unknown or unimportant characteristics of a person can lead an individual to a state of longing. Does this mean that you can learn to love someone who you are not attracted to?

Yes, but that initial lack of attraction will develop into attraction. You will form alliances with personal attributes, which were previously ignored or not regarded as important. Let's use an example. When younger, the physical attributes of an individual may have been high on your list of necessary credentials. You will only allow yourself to develop intimacy and trust with someone who embodies this qualification. Later on in life these credentials become less important and you reprioritise with qualities like understanding, acceptance, sense of humour, intelligence or communication. With these changing needs, so does your capacity to develop attraction and love.

With this said, you cannot force yourself to love someone if they do not demonstrate certain attributes which you qualify as lovable. It is completely subjective and dependent on the individuals themselves. It also has a unique metabolism, incongruent with any general timeline.

I am going to keep the actions in this chapter relatively light hearted, so we can enjoy a bit of relief at this point.

ACTIONS

We are going to compare our partners and rate them accordingly. If you are single, do this exercise by using an ex partner or friend. Right, let's have some fun.

The Stepford Wife Test

I want you to imagine the perfect partner or wife, namely 'The Stepford Wife'. Now we are going to see how lucky or unlucky your choice in partner has been.

Allocate a score of between 1-5 for your partner, based on the following questions and use a zero where they do not apply:

1. Does your partner do most of the cleaning?
2. Does your partner find you funny and laugh at your jokes when you are alone together or in a social environment?
3. Is your partner sexy?
4. How amenable is your partner to sex when you want it?
5. Is your partner agreeable?
6. Does your partner appear to be listening to you all of the time?
7. Has your partner become more attractive since the birth of your relationship?
8. Is your partner well tempered?
9. Is your partner sexually exploratory?
10. Does your partner cook for you?

If you score anywhere above 35 on the Stepford Scale, you have 70% to be grateful for. Remember, this is just for fun, so don't go banging down her door because she failed 'The Stepford Wife' test.

THE LOVE SCALE

As you should be aware, there varying degrees of companionship, so I thought it might be a good idea provide you with some food for thought. Remember, this is a very basic yardstick and all I want you to do is develop a little thought. If you are single, again, use one of your past relationships. Decide which of the categories your past or current partnership falls into:

1. Convenience

The relationship has no realistic chance of longevity and you are both completely aware of the fact that you are only together for convenience. There would be no denying that if something better came along, for either of you, the relationship would end and you would both separate. One night stands also feature in this category.

2. A level of fondness but no real commitment

You do or did feel something towards this person, but at the end of the day, you have no intention of remaining with her in the long run. You defend them in conversations, but that's as far as it goes.

3. Definite fondness

You hold this person in high regard. You are aware of the fact that you have feelings for her and you would be sorry if the relationship were to end. But you will not negotiate or compromise when it comes to the decision making process and having your own life is imperative when it comes to your happiness.

4. In-Love

You are on top of the world. You can't stop calling her, talking to your friends about her, you just want to have sex and spend all your time with her. She has no genuine faults; they are just endearing little habits and make you want her even more. You just want time to stop when you are together.

5. Deeper Love

The initial lustful attraction has subsided but you want this person to be involved in your life through to the very end. She has become your friend, confidant and lover and you are committed to the relationship 100%. Again, no analysis required, just a bit of personal observation.

Relationships, Chapter 5: Communication Is Key

Communication is a skill that has to be learnt if a relationship is going to survive. Numerous partnerships break down, not because of diminished love, but because one party feels he or she is not being heard. Conflicting styles resulting from varying pre-dispositions can cause confusion, instability and numerous hidden agendas. I can promise you one thing, if you are brushing things under the carpet and failing to address concerns, there is only one inevitable destination and it does not involve a happy union.

You should be aware at this point that is more common for men to struggle with personal expression. Through varying forms of reinforcement, which I have discussed, their predominance lies in keeping a 'stiff upper lip' and remaining in control. It is essential that communication becomes an equal responsibility for both parties, resulting in the alleviation of misunderstandings or misconstrued insinuations. Bottom line, if you want the relationship to work you are going to have to open up!

The Importance of Communication

The inability to actively listen is a common complaint. Many couples talk over each other, often agreeing on similar principles, yet unable to hear the meaning behind the others expression. The result is a conversation with personal inner monologues and a failure to process your partners concerns.

Being able to decipher emotions and deliver their true meaning (what they mean to you) is the essence of good communication. Bottling up thoughts, intentions, fears or personal truths is short term and manifests itself through anger, rage, frustration and active mannerisms. The debilitating conclusion is a cumulative build up of unresolved issues, much like a pressure cooker waiting to implode, which ultimately results in passive-aggressive styled behaviour. Breakdowns result, not from dramatic acts of indifference, but rather small seemingly inconsequential build ups that can be best defined as 'the straw that broke the camel's back'.

The inability to negotiate, encourage or express your feelings through verbal or non verbal mechanisms is going to leave you both dissatisfied and seeking acknowledgment elsewhere. Both parties need to feel active in this process and the only way for this to happen is through joint participation.

Healthy communication allows for a medium to convey not only grievances, but also praise. It is exceptionally difficult for partners to feel fulfilled when their positive actions are met with a lack of acknowledgement. In many long-term relationships there seems to be a familiarity and comfort with critical feedback and an avoidance of assurances. No one wants a negative reviewer as a partner; it diminishes their sense of worth and results in a destructive mindset. Make sure adulation is more important than harsh critique.

Let me make this clear. Communication is about reinforcing the security blanket surrounding your relationship. It is about creating awareness so that both parties are under no illusion as to the truths of each other's intent. It involves the eradication of intentional hidden meanings and results in the capacity for trust to develop. You cannot embody a successful relationship without it!

If you had to knock down every psychologist's door in the world and ask them what the single most important attribute in every healthy and loving relationship was, they would say the same thing. COMMUNICATION. It ensures no unresolved agendas become misplaced and keeps the sincerity of motives prevalent. It is the underlying quality that leads to contentment and a successful future together.

How to Communicate Effectively?

Initially this is going to seem like an incredibly difficult hurdle, you are attempting to overcome the habit of a lifetime. But it will also be the most rewarding, in terms of your relationships and your own personal development.

Listening

This embodies taking time out to remain attentive to her concerns as well as the more mundane aspects of her expression. What this entails is to stop what you are doing and to engage in the process itself. NOT while you are reading a paper, watching sport or some other activity that would require some semblance of your attention. Women are aware of our inability to multitask, so don't try pitching it. It involves creating a free and uninhabited space for her to voice whatever she wants. It will also require you to encourage her to elaborate on matters.

Become Alert

This involves being susceptible to picking up signals from your partner that indicates her particular frame of mind. It's remaining attentive to her mannerisms and body language as well as supporting the inner messages she is trying to convey. If she comes home from work and exudes exhaustion, excuse her from dinner with your friends.

Expression

Learn to express genuine feelings no matter how vulnerable you may perceive this act to be. Be real and remember to embody respect and sensitivity when anger is prevalent. Remember, the expression of both positive aspects as well as annoyances, remains imperative. The act of expression is a giving one and should be regarded as such by your partner.

Compromise

Find solutions to obstacles by meeting in the middle. In every relationship there comes a point where one party makes an offer that shifts the dynamic. But remember, the span of a healthy relationship is a long one and the favour is always returned. You must always try to create a win-win situation.

THE BIGGER PICTURE

There are going to be situations where you perceive yourself to be in the right and refuse to back down. The concept of right or wrong is a blurry one and too subjective to ever remain factual. Irrespective, what I implore you to do is to look at the bigger picture.

Minor victories will often result in major catastrophes. It can be more rewarding to remain selfless and concede, than to remain perched on a pedestal. The act itself will not remain unnoticed and irrespective of the initial anxiety involved in giving up your 'right to be right', you will be engaging yourself in one of the more fulfilling and rewarding acts of love. Let it go, move on and understand that love is not a destination, but rather a journey. One which will involve you both needing to look at the bigger picture from time to time.

You've had a lot to take onboard in this chapter so I am going to put some of the aspects we've looked at into practice.

ACTIONS

Start Communicating Properly

Earlier on we engaged in the activity of listening. Now I want you to spend the next few days remaining attentive to all the other qualities that I mentioned in terms of successful communication, namely, becoming attentive, expressive and willing to compromise. Pay attention to your partners' body language as well as her mannerisms and try to be more accommodating. Share something with her that you have never told anyone else before. Agree to do the cooking for the entire week. These are simple yet effective starting blocks to help you understand the more subtle aspects of communication.

Thinking Time

This is geared towards all you guys on there with the tendency to fly off the handle every time a breakdown in communication takes place. Understand that although anger has its place in stipulating boundaries, disrespect and insensitivity do not. You will find that most of the irrational fears causing you to become heated will dissipate with time and thought. Welcome to thinking time and the concept of taking a 'Time Out'.

Remember that once actions are set in place, it becomes much harder to reverse the process. This includes saying things you do not mean. What I want you to do is familiarise yourself with taking time out to think. When you feel an argument escalating to an uncomfortable level, tell you partner you need a time out. Go for a walk, collect your thoughts and have some breathing space. Come back to the issue when you have evaluated what is rational and irrational in terms of your feelings. Put things into context by keeping the bigger picture in mind.

RELATIONSHIPS, CHAPTER 6:
WHO YOU CHOOSE

I want to briefly look at why we choose our particular partners or what we become drawn towards. There are their obvious characteristics and traits which we become attracted to, but why are those qualities so important? Our past plays such an important role here. Understanding the reasons behind your choices will direct you to more enlightenment in determining what is good or bad for you.

It is most likely that your subconscious steers you towards or away from people as a result of formative reinforcement. In many cases partners recreate a particular dynamic that was prevalent in their childhood. The obvious affects can be dangerous and lead to patterns of behaviours that may encourage excessive conflict or becoming withdrawn. Let's take a look at some of these subconscious choices.

TOWARDS

You find qualities in a partner similar to those of your more influential parental figure. If your mother was expressive or emotional, you become drawn to women who embody the same characteristics. In the same token, if she was aggressive or outlandish you form alliances with women who embody these characteristics. What you are attempting to do is recreate an identity of love that may or may not be healthy.

REVERSE

You find qualities in a partner that are completely contrasting from your influential parental figure. In essence, you become attracted to the opposite of your mother or father. Thus, if your mother had a dependency on substance abuse, you would be drawn to people who abstained from alcohol or drugs.

REPLICATE

You yourself adorn qualities of the influential parental figure. Your mother could have embodied victim like characteristics, in need of attention and continual emotional support. You would thus embody this trait and be drawn towards people who offer attention and excessive emotional support.

COMPLETE

This is where you are driven towards a partner with the need to complete yourself. You look for qualities and characteristics that you admire but have failed to embody yourself. This type of behaviour is congruent with low self-esteem. The resulting problem is a lack of equality in the relationship, which is a pre-requisite for its health and wellbeing.

Successful relationships are based on choice and not need. You make an active choice to be with that person because they embody certain characteristics and you enjoy the freedom and responsibility of that determination. You are fully conscious that you would survive and prosper without that person by your side, but you choose this not be the case because you love and respect him or her.

ACTIONS

Why are you attracted to Your Partner?

Take some time to think about the potential subconscious reasons you have chosen to be with your partner. Do you or your partner fall into any of the categories listed above and are there any resulting needs.

If you are single, do this exercise using a past relationship. You don't have to write anything down, just spend ten to fifteen minutes thinking about it.

RELATIONSHIPS, CHAPTER 7:
CHANGE FOR THE BETTER

Too many relationships are inconsistent as a result of partners suffering from self-esteem issues. They become comfortable in the discomfort of the relationship and fail to take any progressive actions in personal development. Hopefully, at this point in the book, you will have developed some awareness regarding destructive patterns of behaviour that either you or your partner have fallen prey to. Now I want to spend some time discussing a few basic actions that are going to help you develop some more self esteem.

It is true to say that women are more likely to make developmental changes when it comes to relationships and personal growth. We find comfort and solace in our inability to peer outside the box, mostly because we think we have never needed to. But by now, you should know that this mindset is congruent with unhappiness and a lack of fulfilment.

'Insanity is doing the same thing over and over again and expecting different results' Albert Einstein

AVOID NEGATIVITY

Negative thoughts result in negative actions. They feed off each other and stimulate irrational set type behaviours resulting in dysfunctional mindsets and animations. Your mind can be trained to perceive a more positive outlook on events that take place, no matter how traumatic and earth shattering they may seem. Remaining defensive is the antithesis of protecting oneself. Freedom is born out of acceptance. So I would like you to start emphasizing empathy in your thought processes. Refrain from judging your partner, as this is an insular activity, which personifies

186

diminished self-esteem. Embody the concept of acceptance, remaining grateful for the fact that we are all unique individuals with our own particular strengths and weaknesses. Remember, right or wrong is a perception and not a reality. It does not exist outside of opinion.

LOOK THE PART

It is a common occurrence for men to reach their thirties or forties and give up on maintaining an attractive appearance. They put on excessive weight, indulge in unhealthy habits and become content with the idea that they do not need to look after themselves. The mindset can relate to the fact that they already have a partner, so effort on this front is not required. But in terms of self-esteem and developing a healthy respect for oneself, it is essential, and the effects on your relationship will be ground breaking.

Make an effort when it comes to style and the anticipated superficial elements of looking good. You may be right, it may be social stereotypes and society reinforcing beliefs, but the results remain positive in terms of self-esteem. Acceptance, positive reinforcement and acknowledgement from partners, friends and colleagues will create a healthier internal view of yourself. Make an effort when it comes to attire and purchase garments that make you feel comfortable and confident. Make an appointment with the hairdresser and bypass the barber. If you are balding, embrace this, as it is a reflection of your worldly experiences. Pay attention to your weight and get into the habit of going for walks, runs, swims, cycles etc; anything that will get your blood pressure up and give you a healthy cardiovascular workout.

MAINTAINING YOUR HEALTHY DIET

The benefits of maintaining your healthy diet are immeasurable. Not only will it give you more energy and a definitive high level of self-esteem, but it will also substantially decrease your chances of developing those potentially fatal diseases we discuss in Chapter 4. I am going to repeat a few of the essential lessons from that chapter.

- ✓ Cut out as many saturated fats and trans-fatty acids as you can. Replace these with far higher level of monounsaturated and polyunsaturated fats. Try to make sure that you get a good supply of the omega oils.
- ✓ If you are a definite meat eater and unwilling to eliminate this from your diet completely, cut down on your intake of red meat and replace this wherever possible with white meat or even fish.
- ✓ Watch your intake of dairy foods. These are not as good for you as this industry would have you believe and they can even be harmful to the body. Be especially vigilant with cheese and butter, which are particularly high in saturated fats and certain dangerous fatty acids.
- ✓ Watch your intake of alcohol. It is a proven fact that if you aim to stick to the recommended daily allowance (28 units per week); this is actually beneficial to the body. It is when you exceed this limit that your health is at risk.
- ✓ Watch your consumption of sugary snacks and junk food. These are empty calories and they will never satisfy your body for more than a couple of hours at a time. These empty calories will also make you feel lethargic and depressed and they are known to lower your level of self-esteem.
- ✓ Eat plenty of fibre rich foods. Although the body finds it hard to digest these, they work exceptionally well in cleansing your gastrointestinal system.

✓ Your whole body relies on a constant supply of protein for cell renewal and countless other functions. It is therefore imperative that you eat foods that are high in protein.

✓ Avoid eating exaggerated meals where your plate is piled high. Instead, eat smaller portions and more often. This in turn will increase your metabolism and overall level of energy.

✓ Eat at least 5 portions of fruit and vegetables every day and make sure that these portions come from varied sources.

THE CUMULATIVE EFFECT

If you embrace the psychological and physiological aspects of development into your lifestyle, you are en route to personal fulfilment. The obvious benefits of a healthy esteem are numerous and in terms of your relationship, it is essential to give the above serious consideration. If you are single, a developed self-esteem will direct you towards partners who are more likely to contribute to your happiness.

ACTIONS

As this chapter has all been about generating more self-esteem, it is only fitting that the Actions follow suit. The following activities are designed to help you register the beneficial effects of implementing the above advice.

P.M.A.

We have already implemented an action pertaining to a Positive Mental Attitude earlier on in the book. But it is essential you learn to embody this characteristic so we are going to repeat the exercise. List three personal annoying events that you have experienced in the last week. Now write three positive effects that resulted from this experience. Example:

Event: My Manager embarrassed me in front of colleagues.
Positive Effects: I made an active decision to be more assertive next time; I remained calm and respectful throughout; I did not let it affect me in terms of productivity.

Get Dressed for Success

I want you to go shopping for some clothes and pick out something that accentuates your qualities and hides your flaws. If you need help, ask your partner, friend or store assistant for advice. Remember to pick a style that is suitable for your age and body type.

Eat Properly

I cannot emphasise enough the importance of a healthy diet. The benefits are vast and in terms of looking and feeling good, it is the foundation. Make an active decision if you are not eating well to do something about it.

RELATIONSHIPS, CHAPTER 8:
KEEPING THAT SPARK GLOWING

Let's cut to the chase. Relationships require work and a serious level of commitment. The 'happily ever after' mindset is an illusion that will constantly keep you disappointed if it is an expectation. Most couples will have had to overcome seemingly insurmountable hurdles at some point in their partnership and no doubt yours is going to be no different. You can take solace in the fact that it is common and your relationship is not particular to problems.

Monogamy can be a difficult concept to appreciate and come to terms with. When the in-love phase of a relationship begins to delve into the more complex and intrinsic nature of compromise, many men feel frustrated with the abandonment of these short term effects. Sexual chemistry is not once what it was, butterflies in the stomach are a thing of the past and routine seems to be the order of the day. Your relationship is going to change, you will both develop in your own particular way and it is something that needs to be appreciated and accepted rather than doubted. This chapter is going to look at overcoming these obstacles so you can learn to appreciate what you already have.

THE GRASS IS NEVER GREENER ON THE OTHER SIDE

It is human nature to look into the windows of other lives and imagine a more fulfilling existence. Why? Because we are introduced to fragments of their existence, which are actively designed to express all the highs and none of the lows. When you meet someone, rarely will they express all that is wrong in their life. Instead, they will embark on the positive aspects in the hope of finding acceptance and acknowledgement. They will paint a fictitious picture of multiple rewards, joys and accomplishments without entertaining the less stimulating truths of hardship, failures, and insecurities. Yes time and time again, we convince ourselves that some-one else is more suitable, compatible and loving; embodying all the characteristics our current partner lacks.

The truth always remains the same when we act on these fictitious beliefs. We wake up one day to the realisation that it is often more work and less fulfilling. We reminisce over lost loves and fuel our demeanour with more and more regret. Understand that every relationship will embody highs and lows, arguments and feelings of inadequacy and that the existence of one without these characteristics is as real as the ending of a 'Hollywood Romantic Comedy.' Acting on a mindset that is based on fiction will lead you towards regret and continual disappointment.

FIDELITY

If you are with someone, remain committed to him or her. If you want to act on a thought, which involves having an affair or cheating on your partner, remove yourself from the relationship. Again, it comes down to the responsibility of choice. It makes the decision-making process more real when you anticipate the symptoms of integrity. You cannot have someone committed to you, if you are not willing to offer the same. The other imperative lesson here is to respect other partnerships. Treat them with the same level of appreciation and understanding that you would want yours to be. Look, the bottom line is this. If you are cheating on your partner and he or she is unaware of your actions, you are no doubt embodying self-esteem issues and need to break this cycle. You will cause more self-harm by not addressing this and the likelihood of ever being able to enjoy a functional relationship is slim to none.

LEARN TO APPRECIATE

Another common characteristic of the modern relationship is to forget what we enjoy in our partner. In time we become obsessed with what we fail to have and take for granted the luxury that has been by our side year after year. We take on board new worries, embody new ambitions and set new expectations without allocating any time for reward or reflection. This is a human characteristic and prevalent in most relationships; so don't give yourself a walloping. Instead, make a concerted effort each and every day to remark on how your life has been elevated as a result of having your partner in your life. Along with dismissive splendour of water out of a tap, heat or light at the switch of a button and shelter at the end of each day; so do we escape the wonders and joys of having a unique and committed individual in our lives beset on loving us along with all our inadequacies.

SOCIAL DEVOTION, POSITIVE REINFORCEMENT & COMMUNICATION

Devote quality time to your relationship by doing things that involve you being social whilst escaping the monotony and repetition of life. Share interests beyond conversation and embark on actions that contribute to both of you being involved. Cook together, hit the tennis courts in tandem, entertain a book reading with friends or learn the tango in unison. This needs to be initiated and maintained by both of you on an equal basis. Now I am not maintaining that separate identities are not essential, they are. What I am lending towards in the growth of the relationship as an entity unto its own – requiring the intent of both parties.

You cannot do enough to elevate her level of self-esteem. As the relationship develops and hidden agendas become apparent, more men escape the value and importance of positive selfless expression. Stop neglecting this responsibility and learn to vocalise the aspects of her personality or physique that you appreciate. If she has bought a new dress, tell her she looks exquisite. Get the digital camera out, take a photo, get it framed and set next to your bedside table. This is not rocket science. People respond to positive reinforcement and withdraw with criticism. Make an active choice to contribute to the cycle you want your partner to embody.

Finally, get the communication back on track. By now you should be well aware of the importance of genuine expression and the role it has to play in a healthy relationship. Identify areas where you remain unvoiced and take sincere actions in developing them. By learning to embody success-ful communication skills you will develop a resource for overcoming conflicts and creating more positive outcomes.

SEXUAL RE-IGNITION

Reigniting some of the passion in the bedroom is going to go a long way in generating some much needed fulfilment. When relationships hit rocky patches, one of the first areas to be neglected is sex. Time also becomes a culprit to this plight and in many cases, couples who become bored and stagnated with their sex life, seek gratification elsewhere. So there are two things I want you pay attention to.

- ✓ Sexual experimentation is useful in avoiding mundane and ritualistic experiences.
- ✓ Realign your sexual priorities so that her pleasure is equal to yours. In other words, your orgasm should not be the highlight of the experience.

There are a number of exploits that you can adopt to spark the intensity and passion in your relationship. Embarking on a bit of romance should be a consideration as the emotional connection to the act itself is as important as the physical for women. When it comes to making love, understand the concepts of foreplay, coreplay and moreplay. They embody a more rewarding experience for women. The critical element here is not to be concerned with the destination, but rather the excursion.

WELL WORTH THE EFFORT

The rewards of the deeper and meaningful relationship are vast, with fulfilment developing on many levels. The self becomes more acknowledged and the capacity to give, provides more delight than not. It does not require an exceptional amount of insight to understand this. We are social beings with a predisposition for being adorned, cared for, thought of, depended upon and provided for. It is a symbiotic relationship, which leads to open and meaningful revelations, as we grow older.

The importance of companionship draws itself on many levels:

- ✓ It provides meaning to our expression
- ✓ It creates perspective
- ✓ It embodies impartiality

ACTIONS

At this point you should realise that relationships require attentive work and that the natural progression for the spark to fade is as normal as biting into an apple. So the next few actions are going to involve you and your partner having some fun.

Fun Activities Together

Find an activity or pursuit that you both enjoy and start committing to it together. This could be a dance class, a card game, a communal sport etc. The importance here is not the activity itself, but rather than mutual enjoyment of it.

Date Night

Allocate one night a week to each other, irrespective of other commitments, in the form of a date. Go out for dinner, a movie, a theatre performance etc. Remain incredibly stubborn when it comes to enforcing this evening together once every week.

Do some Research

Do some research on foreplay, coreplay and moreplay.

RELATIONSHIPS, CHAPTER 9: ANYTHING ELSE?

There are a few other important ingredients I want to talk about in terms of maintaining a healthy relationship. Getting your head around these concepts will help you understand personal dispositions and hopefully create awareness for further possibilities. There are a number of characteristics that are attainable through personal development and contribute towards alleviating obstacles. The objective of this book is to stimulate sufficient thought and impetus for you to move in the right direction.

COGNITIVE BEHAVIOUR THERAPY (C.B.T.)

We've already discussed this option earlier in the book, but as there may be some significant and damaging underlying reasons for your self-esteem remaining low, it might be necessary for you to seek this type of treatment. You need to remember that there is absolutely no stigma attached in pursuing psychological assistance in areas you want to improve. If anything it is a testament to your willingness to excel. The vast majority of people, who use CBT, do so because they have finally accepted that there are underlying issues preventing them from moving forward.

Cognitive behaviour therapy evaluates thought processes and mechanisms we have in place when it comes to dealing with issues. The reality exists that we can retrain our brains and the associated meanings attached. Many traumatic experiences in our childhood manifest themselves in our behaviour when we become adults, with disastrous effects on relationships and our opinion of ourselves. By adopting its methodologies, individuals are able to ascertain more rational meanings behind actions and experiences.

Neuro Linguistic Programming (N.L.P.)

NLP is another method used by Psychologists to reprogramme the subconscious mind enabling you to communicate more effectively, overcome limiting behaviours and learn to excel in whichever area you choose. It is sometimes regarding as 'a user manual for the brain' and looks to identify important questions such as:

- ✓ How do we know what we know?
- ✓ How do we do what we do?

NLP can give you give you set skills to help you manage your thoughts, moods or behaviours more effectively. It can be an incredibly useful tool in terms of the development of yourself and your relationships.

Behavioural Types

Our particular type of behaviour incorporates the thoughts, actions and methods we adopt in approaching situations. It is dependant to a large degree on your level of self-esteem and can be directly proportional to how well you fair in a relationship. It is more than likely employed as a survival technique with its development being born and reinforced throughout your formative years.

Approval

You are more often than not compliant and agreeable in the hope of gaining acceptance. It embodies submissive qualities and a fear of confrontation.

NEED TO BE RIGHT

You like to get your own way. It embodies a need to dominate and often results in hostile and aggressive forms of behaviour. In essence, you feel the need to be in control.

PRETENCE

You like to appear to embody a carefree demeanour but in truth this is just a façade and you're often beset with holding grudges. You world is one of pretence and you embody a cynical nature.

ASSERTIVE

You react towards others in the same way you would want them to act towards you. It embodies honesty, sincerity and respect. If you disagree with something you are able to communicate it in a non-threatening and understanding manner. There is less of a need to seek approval.

There is more often than not a combination of these different types of behaviour in individuals. We are of course incredibly complex and single patterns rarely define us. But what you should be looking to embody is a sincere level of assertiveness in your personal mainframe where equality and empathy are the benchmark. Your understanding of control is that it rarely exists and even when it does, it is not a prerequisite for happiness. You are more concerned with sharing thoughts and opinions and placing equal value on what others have to offer. Interactions are about both parties succeeding and developing the idea of win-win. You are not concerned with domination or the exertion of power. Here is a list of key elements to remember when maintaining an assertive type of behaviour.

- ✓ Fair play and respect should be your mantra.
- ✓ Competent communication is required void of hidden agendas.
- ✓ Mistakes should be regarded as learning curves and available to both yourself and those around you. There is a lack of cynical judgment in your perspective on events.
- ✓ Everyone, including yourself, deserves respect.
- ✓ We are all equal.
- ✓ The expression of thoughts and opinions are valued highly.
- ✓ You are entitled to say no as are others.
- ✓ You have the right to fulfil your ambitions

IS SHE RIGHT FOR ME

Earlier on we looked at you taking a brief compatibility test with your partner. Now don't freak out if you have identified a number of core beliefs that are different, the capacity to compromise will come into play here. If you are both willing to put the relationship first whist agreeing to disagree on political or social beliefs, you will be fine. It is all dependant on whether you or her are willing to negotiate or not. That said, the initial desire of 'just wanting to be together' will not suffice if you are both completely incompatible. Differences need to be addressed early on for the relationship to prosper through difficult times. Remember, most couples do not separate or divorce because they are not in love; they do so because certain core beliefs are unable to be negotiated. Compromise on issues like having children or financial management become unattainable. There definitely does need to be an overlap of certain priorities in the ambitions of the relationship as well as personal interests.

Differences on a social and cultural level also need to be noted. As I have said, remaining poles apart does not necessarily mean the end of your relationship. No one wants to date a clone of themselves; they would probably have too many personal issues. What you need to realise is that if there are big discrepancies in your core values and ambitions, you will need to embody empathy, communication, acceptance and understanding with far more diligence.

ANGER

Many people believe that anger is a negative emotion and one that should not be synonymous with a healthy relationship. I disagree. Distinguishing anger from hostility and threatening types of behaviour is important. The latter two predispose themselves to negative consequences and embody aggression. That is certainly not what I am talking about here. Being angry whist remaining assertive, embodying respect and equality, is an essential method of communicating disapproval of certain behaviours. It does not lend itself to violence. It is useful in terms of dispute resolution and should not be frowned upon. But always remember to indulge in its deliverance as you would expect to receive it.

BREAKING UP

Successful relationships have cycles and just because you and you partner decided to go your separate ways, does not mean the partnership itself was not successful. It just means its course has been run and it's time to move on. Remember, the relationship should be based on 'a want' and not 'a need'. Your need for survival and prosperity has nothing to do with who you are with. When love, respect, honesty and the ability to compromise have become too difficult to maintain, it can be a sign that it is time to reconsider both of your commitments to the relationship.

I maintain that it is far healthier to be single and aspiring towards developing the self, than remaining with someone who prevents or even diminishes personal levels of self-esteem. When the environment becomes congruent with self-depreciation and continual conflict, it may be better for both of you to move on. Ultimately there is always a sense of doubt, a feeling of failure. But this is only a result of the stereotypical nature of society, which places no essential value on the 'best interests' of both parties. The most important conclusion to reach is not one of failure, but rather of intrepid experience with the result being insight and wisdom to engage in future relationships.

I believe it is an important aspect and process in the development of the self. When it comes to remaining friends, I maintain that this is always a suitable option. Why would you not want someone who shared such a large part of your life not to be involved in your future? But remember. This can only be successfully achieved in time and a clear break should be the immediate consideration. Unless the break is completely unanimous from both sides, a rare phenomenon, time apart to develop and come to terms with the separation remains essential.

ACTIONS

Your actions for this chapter are going to revolve around investigating some developmental methodologies as well as trying to assign your most common type of behaviour.

CBT & NLP

I want you to do some research on Cognitive Behavioural Therapy and Neuro Linguistic Programming. The Internet has a plethora of insightful articles on these subjects. Make sure you have a clear understanding of their benefits and what type of impact they could have on your personal development and that of your relationship.

Your Behavioural Type

I want you to look at the list of behaviour types I mentioned earlier on in the chapter and decided which one is most congruent with you. Remember, more likely than not, you will embody the characteristics of a few of them. But one will should stand out and remain more aligned with you as a whole. Make some notes on the potential effects your type of behaviour has and identify a possible solution. For example:

Type: I am agreeable when my partner asks me to do things.
Effect: I often get angry with myself for not speaking my thoughts.
Solution: I am going to be more assertive the next time she asks me to something I don't want to do.

RELATIONSHIPS, CHAPTER 10:
A LOVING AND LASTING RELATIONSHIP

We have been on a relatively short but insightful journey together and again, I congratulate you on your desire for personal development and that of your relationship. Men are the more likely gender to avoid this type of augmentation or psychological appraisal. But it becomes imperative in the pursuit of a healthy and loving relationship.

A sign of strength is the ability to recognise inconsistencies within oneself and to make distinct and attentive commitments to overcoming them. You have begun this journey and it will only become more enlightening. Let's take a look at some of the important aspects for your continual review whist allowing you to embark on a healthier and more loving relationship with your partner.

RELATIONSHIPS GOING WRONG

At this point you should be able to take stock of your current relationship and identify some traits that either you or your partner have embodied which have either led to its success or enhanced complications. A word of warning! Do not embrace a particular piece of knowledge and endeavour to highlight all the issues your partner has. This book is about your self-development and encourages you to define personal responsibility. The definition of your actions remains a responsibility of yours, with empathy and consideration being at the forefront.

If you are single, this section should have highlighted a number of issues in past relationships, which could have resulted in its demise. It is important to understand them and develop on a personal level, so that the same mistakes are not made again. Again, remember that this is just your starting point and if you want to maintain a healthy and realistic perspective, work is always going to be needed. Follow through with the actions and remain diligent with the advice that has been given to you. If there are severe traumatic issues, seek counsel from someone who has experiences in CBT or NLP.

"Nobody can go back and start a new beginning, but anyone can start today and create a new ending" Maria Robinson

Self analysis can sometimes remain painful and frustrating, but always remember that it is not something to judge. Your past will not define you, your future will. Make today exceptional by embracing the concept of changing derelict behaviours that have provided little or no personal fulfilment.

Work on your communication and continually strive to embody all the varying aspects of it. Expression is a right; a freedom bestowed on each and every one of us and should be enjoyed as such. Incorporate respect, empathy and understanding into conversations and give up the need to be right or look good. You will learn more about yourself by adopting these qualities. You will also become engaging and enlightening resulting in more intentional interest being sought after.

Learn to love yourself. Understand that we are all bound together by past indiscretions and regrets. There is nothing unique in your history that defines you as better or worse than anyone else. Remember that you are your own harshest critic and the interpretation you provide for yourself is nothing more than a story. Learn to be immodest with your attributes without lending yourself to arrogance. There are particular reasons why someone has chosen to love you, have faith in her decision and embrace the idea that you are worthy of being loved.

AIMING FOR THAT ULTIMATE GOAL

Everyone is deserving of love, irrespective of transgression or tribulation. But as with anything worthwhile, it is a responsibility that should not be regarded lightly. Human beings are social and require the attentive qualities of companionship. With this endeavour comes immense reward as well as impartial duty. Make sure you are able and willing to offer what you expect in return.

Developing esteem, communication skills and behavioural patterns congruent with success is determined with time and constant endeavour. It is not something that happens overnight. Do not condemn yourself to failure when you find yourself set in old habits. Employ the 70:30 rule. Strive towards employing the positive patterns 70% of the time and realise that 30% of your efforts will not resonate with success. Continually work at improving this whilst remaining cognisant of the fact that this is a journey and not a destination.

I also suggest your keep this by your bedside table and continue to review it from time to time. You will most certainly need reminding of the essential patterns of behaviour that elicit harmony and contentment. Your work has in truth just begun.

A MORE SUCCESSFUL RELATIONSHIP

What I do guarantee is that by employing a number of the teachings, you will embark on a more prosperous relationship with yourself and those you love. You will begin to develop the necessary insight into understanding disengaging behaviours whilst doing something about it. Follow through with the actions and your partner will endear herself towards not only the intent, but the symptoms as well. Your ability to adapt and transform will remain an infectious quality and steer you towards more successes than just your relationship.

ACTIONS

As we have reached the conclusion of this chapter, your actions will allow you to put your newly acquired knowledge into practice.

THE RELATIONSHIP INVENTORY

I want you to go through the following inventory to identify areas that may require some work in your relationship. I have posed a few questions in varying categories where you will be able to assess particular domains, which will require your attention. Remember to remain genuine and connected in your responses.

Your Communication Skills

For the questions below, I want you to allocate a score of between 1 (least applicable) and 5 (most applicable).

1. Have you had an argument with your partner that resulted from a clear lack of communication on your part?

2. Has your lack of communication ever been commented on?

3. Do you feel inclined to brush issues under the carpet and avoid confrontation?

4. Does the thought of apologising make you feel vulnerable?

5. Do you mask personal agendas?

You will have a score between 0 and 25. Check your score against the following scale:

A (0-4) Your communication skills are very good - well done! Keep this up as you're definitely implementing the right level of skill here.

B (5-11) Your communication skills are average. There are a few areas you may need to keep a close eye on.

C (12-17) It is time to take action. You're communication skills are not at the level they should be to maintain a healthy relationship.

D (18-23) Very poor communication skills. Immediate and determined effort needs to be made.

E (24+) Congratulations for being so honest. However, your communication skills are non-existent. CBT or NLP are strongly recommended.

Your Self-Esteem

As above please, with the score of 1(the lowest) to 5 (the highest) for the following questions:

1. How do you feel about yourself right now?

2. Do you maintain a healthy diet?

3. Do you express concerns?

4. Do you partake in any form of exercise?

5. Do your express your successes?

Five simple questions, but they should help to ascertain your level of self-esteem. Use the following scale to determine what action is required:

A (22+) You are doing very well! You clearly feel confident and have more the sufficient levels of self-esteem

B (17-21) Very good – The occasional blunders may occur but you are still on top of things.

C (13-16) Average level of self-esteem. Take some active steps in developing this.

D (8-12) Revisit the chapter that is devoted to self-esteem. Identify areas that need to be worked on and take necessary steps.

E (0-7) Immediate action is required. You have a low opinion of yourself and should look into CBT and NLP.

How 'Loved Up' Are You?

Let's take a look at your current relationship. Maintain scores of 1(the lowest) to 5 (the highest) for the following questions:

1. Are you able to express concerns with your partner?

2. Do you feel supported by her?

3. Do you enjoy spending time together?

4. Does she encourage you?

5. Can you imagine spending the rest of your life with her?

A (21+) You are absolutely in love and she is good for you.

B (16-20) Your love life is definitely something to look forward to.

C (12-15) Your relationship is ok but could be better. Take some time to work out why you are more fulfilled.

E (11 and below) Your relationship is in trouble. Immediate action is required. Go through the section with your partner and discuss potential areas to work on.

DATING

DATING

This section on dating is about social attraction and getting that special woman to say yes. It will teach you the basics of attracting women, and how to deal with inner confidence issues that might have prevented you from connecting with women in the past. After this section, you will be able to approach with confidence and increase the likelihood of setting a date with a woman you've just met.

We will look into various psychological aspects of the dating game as well your male agendas that, more often than not, sabotage successful connections with women.

But first, a request... To be able to maximise the lessons from this chapter, you must be willing to do the simple actions I have prepared for you. Also...

OPEN your mind to change.

Old-fashioned beliefs do not work in the current game. Nice guys, who hesitate, do not succeed with women. The guys who do get the beautiful women are those who are open to improving themselves using strategies that are designed to push them out of their comfort zone.

If you are looking for a 'magic pill' to solve all your dating problems, you are going to be disappointed. You have to learn the basics of attraction from the ground up to be able to build a solid foundation that will gear you towards attracting more women. This is what I will endeavour to do for you and by following the actions, you will start to create habits that will lead to more successful interactions with the opposite sex.

What you will get here is straight talk on how to date a woman through highlighting the very best version of yourself. Section 3 is about getting your social life back on track and getting that girl to say YES!

This is a journey of enlightenment and action, one that will take you from an insular lifestyle to a more social one. The entire aim of this section is to get you confident in your ability to attract as well being able to accept the negative traits with the positive ones. Through this level of self-awareness you will develop rapport with whomever you choose. Let's quickly review what we are going to be delving into over the next few chapters.

In Dating, Chapter 1, Mirror Mirror on the Wall, we are going to evaluate where you are right now in terms of accepting yourself. We will then discuss the aspects of fear, sabotage and your true self in some detail concluding with a few actions in getting your social life back on track.

In Dating, Chapter 2, Get the Basics Right, we will address confidence and assertiveness and the role they play in generating interest. We will then get rid of a few irrational anxieties and discuss the necessary requirements in projecting confidence.

In Dating, Chapter 3, Conquer Approach Anxiety, we will look at developing your social skills and investigate the fear factor when it comes to approaching women. By the end of this chapter you will have a much clearer understanding of the debilitating effects of irrational thoughts.

In Dating, Chapter 4, The Power of Your Mind, we delve into the power of thoughts and their relationship to habits. We will take it one step further by addressing your past and transforming your current mindset into a more positive and attractive one.

In Dating, Chapter 5, Attraction, we look into the characteristics that women are attracted to. This will include presence, demeanour, potential and confidence. We will also take a quick look at common personality types that seem to attract the fairer sex.

In Dating, Chapter 6, Rapport Basics, we are going to build your approach confidence by developing rapport skills.

In Dating, Chapter 7, Conversation Topics, we are going to get your sparking her curiosity with some essential advice when it comes to communication.

We will conclude with Dating, Chapter 8, Emotional Connection, where you will learn to develop attraction by mirroring certain behaviours whist always keeping it real.

So now that you know what's in store, let's get started.

Dating, Chapter 1:
Mirror Mirror on the Wall

This chapter is about taking an honest look at yourself, your personality and the underlying factors that affected your psyche. Read through the insights and do the actions to increase your awareness of where you stand right now as a person and as a man who wants to attract women. When you finish with this chapter, you will have a better idea of what you can do to increase your self-esteem and develop your personality. Moreover, you will be able to answer this question honestly "What about me is attractive?"

Who You Are Right Now

Whether you have just started dating or not, you've most certainly been interacting with people around you. At work, you talk to your colleagues about random things. You introduce yourself to people and start conversations. In essence, you already know what it takes to talk to people on different levels. Now, what I want you to do is to think back to a time when you have had to reply to this statement: "tell me about yourself."

People will always be asking this question. If it's your would-be boss and you're in your job interview, you might have listed a few characteristics that you think will land you the job. If it's someone you just met, you might have revealed some superficial information that doesn't tell much about who you really are. Women continuously run this mantra in their head and the bottom line is you need an answer.

Woman will be sizing you up and reading you through revelations about your personality and your individual status in life. Whenever you enter into a conversation, your body language, tone, inflections and resonance are designing a portrait in the minds of your avid listeners. The million pound question? – What do you really think of yourself?

Instinctively, you might have started thinking about your achievements (I am a doctor, a lawyer, a university graduate; I bought a car when I was 18, etc). Or you might have gone deeper and begun listing the traits you know you possess (e.g. I have a sense of humour, a generous nature, I am sympathetic). You might describe your usual mood (crabby, carefree, and fun), your reactions to various stimuli, or things that you dislike.

Here's the first thing you should know before you start dating: a large part of being sociable is knowing exactly who you are and what you're capable of doing. Self-awareness leads to self-acceptance, which in turn leads to better interaction with everyone. If you don't know what you're about, you are subconsciously giving people the wrong impression.

The women you will meet will ask you about yourself, with questions varying from likes, dislikes, reasons for choosing your career path, and even your views on relationships. My point is this. You need to have an answer and the only way for you to have a connected response, is by having a firm grasp of who you are and what you stand for.

This means embracing the aspects of your personality that are uniquely yours and making sure you are aware and comfortable before you open yourself up. I am going to get a little simplistic here to try get some questions answered. What makes you, UNIQUE?

- ✓ Your reactions to things, people and situations that evoke feelings of anger, pleasure, sadness and confusion.
- ✓ Your response to stress through fight or flight
- ✓ Your choices and motives behind decisions
- ✓ Are you introvert, ambivert or extrovert

✓ Your capacity to be comfortable in your own body
✓ Your generosity and empathy toward others.
✓ The way you rise to challenges and deal with adversity
✓ The things that excite or bore you to death
✓ Your motives for wanting to pursue certain activities
✓ Your capacity to learn from mistakes

These 'personality traits' originate from years and years of reinforcement in the environment you were raised in, or the way you interacted with other people during your formative period. Acquiring these traits and your current mindset was a natural process, and truth be told, you didn't have much control over these factors that influenced the development of your personality. However, and you need to get this. You do have control over the direction you're heading, and that is your responsibility. When you embrace this, you will know what you're about and in turn, you will know what you can offer someone else.

LOVING YOURSELF

Simply put... you need to ACCEPT and LOVE yourself. Now, that does not mean there are not traits, which annoy you and you would like to change at the drop of a penny. What it entails is accepting that you are who you are, which incorporates the good with the bad. If you want to transform, if you want to achieve your goals in life ... your journey starts here.

I am stating the obvious by saying self-awareness plays an important role in building your confidence. But let's take it a step further. Self-acceptance plays the leading role in creating your self-image, which is a pre-requisite for genuine unaffected confidence. Once you start loving yourself, you will be more willing to explore passions and talents you probably are not even aware of. The people who have committed to loving themselves are the ones who try to exceed expectations. Now tell me, is that an attractive quality? You better believe it!

LET'S LOOK AT SELF-ACCEPTANCE SPECIFICALLY IN DATING TERMS:

1. If you don't accept who you are, how the hell is anyone else supposed to!

JUDGMENT is a scary thing, and it's something that can control the way we think, act and speak. The other interesting aspect of this kind of feedback is that your reaction to criticism or praise depends entirely on who said it. If it's from someone you respect, you feel humbled. If it's from someone you acquaint with little regard, you feel contempt. So... what about a judgment from someone you want to date?

That's right. The most heart wrenching of them all, and more often than not, unjust and prejudiced.

Now I want to get this clear. Women are not cruel, but the nature of the dating game means men open themselves up for criticism, and there will always be a small number who will try to knock you down just because they are in the perfect position to take a swing. They know you're interested, and because of that that, they feel powerful. This is not a problem if you have accepted the good, the bad and the ugly of yours truly. However, if you don't love yourself and emotionally expose yourself, you inadvertently turn yourself into the perfect sitting duck for a small section of the opposite sex's ego trip.

Remember, these scenarios are as real as you make them. 99% of the time, they have absolutely nothing to do with you or what you are about. You cannot change her and I certainly suggest you don't even try. Hold on to what you know best, your self-awareness, and get the hell out of there.

2. The more you love yourself, the better you feel and ultimately, look.

Every guy has something he hates about his personal appearance, and you're no exception. Maybe your eyes are squint, maybe you you're overweight or there could be a certain facial feature that annoys you. The fact that most people have an aspect of 'self depreciation' is not going to win any awareness awards. The great thing about attraction is it does not matter at all.

Some of you are in denial. Buying the clothes that don't fit because you are trying to bulk up a bit or wearing that loose shirt on the beach because you are worried about your moobs. The answer is simple. Do something about it or get comfortable with not doing something about it. There is no alternative. But remember, you are doing this for your own personal self-esteem and again, I reiterate, it matters little in terms of attracting the opposite sex.

What I can guarantee you though, is that a huge part of being attractive is learning to love yourself. Understanding and accepting that you are as you are and being aware that this superficial element contributes very little to what women find attractive. Attraction is about confidence and inner comfort, and when you exude that, there is nothing that can undermine you. Think about it. How many times have you seen unattractive men with gorgeous women, and you're kidding yourself if you assume it's always about security.

I want to drive this home – so pay attention. Looks and money aren't the only things that attract women. Your personality and sense of worth will determine the level of attraction women will feel for you. Added to this, no woman wants to be with a man who flies off the handle whenever someone cracks a joke about his appearance. They want men who are comfortable inside their own skin, and this my friends, is what self-awareness and self-belief is all about.

3. If you love yourself, you are able to express yourself.

Self-Esteem can be built through constant exposure to new experiences and people. It's the process of growing, getting out of your comfort zone and opening yourself up to a different way of thinking or being. Through this exposure, you learn to rise above challenges and when you do that– you learn to love yourself and begin to find expression as a useful ally.

Through this expression comes conviction, which you are going to need when standing your ground. And there are going to be plenty times in the dating circuit when this will be required. At the end of the day you will be communicating from a place that has no hidden agendas. You will also learn how to appreciate the opinions of other people, without being threatened. This will keep you centred, calm and proficient in appeal.

The fact is your opinion; life story or belief system carries more weight that anyone else's out there. Its value is neither exceeded nor diminished through social status or your current account balance. It's there to negotiate, interact, flirt, humour, concur and opinionate. The interaction allows you to empathise with the other person, or discuss things from a point of view you were unaware of five minutes earlier. The key here is simple. Men with a healthy self-esteem never concern themselves with the notion of being right. It is about the interaction and sharing of opinions and this kind of self-acceptance is infectious and humbling. Get this right – and you will attract.

Ditch the FEAR

Fear can be debilitating. It can completely define your actions, which is a terrifying thought. Think about it. Through a simple thought pattern, you can either achieve greatness or sink into oblivion. You can either walk up to the most attractive girl in the park, or walk away justifying your lack of action with a less than compelling reason. This cocktail of emotion leads to aggravation, anxiety and doubt. There are two kinds of fear: the constructive type and the destructive type. The constructive type alerts you to imminent danger and can be your best ally. The destructive type is based on fiction and will send you to the pits of loner-hood with little or no success with women.

Needless to say, the destructive type of fear must be dealt with now. So I want you to think about this. When is the last time a fear of yours entered your reality? It's a difficult one for you. Why? Because as soon as the reality set in that the fear was not valid, you forgot about it. I can harp on here for pages and it will come down to the same conclusion. If you live your life with the aim of overcoming and not succumbing to your fears, you will succeed.

'Everything you want is on the other side of fear' George Addair

How does FEAR debilitate your actions with women? You get locked inside your inhibitions. What is it about approaching women that makes you panic? It's the fear of being ridiculed, rejected or hurt. You might also be thinking about offending her with something you say, or about not being good enough. If you let this type of fear grip you when you're approaching women, you're history. Here's what you need to do: commit to taking the action, regardless of the fear.

I can tell you this in all honesty, the men who look like they can make girls say yes at the drop of the hat, feel anxiety right before they approach, but they approach anyway. Why? They are not dictated to by their fears. They see it as an opportunity to overcome and not hide.

Fear will always be there whenever you think you have something to lose, but you can turn that fear into something positive just by interpreting it as 'excitement'. So when you start thinking "I'm too scared to approach her", turn things around by telling yourself "I'm really excited right now"... then approach. There is no guy in the planet that approaches a girl he likes, absolute of fear. It's in all of us. If we like something, we want it and there is an innate reaction, which links us to loss or rejection. There is one simple solution to it all. Do it anyway.

Are you still worried?

You might have convinced yourself that you're totally free of the dreaded "Approach Anxiety" but if you still worrying about rejection, humiliation and spinning off every pre and post approach scenario, that will 99% of the time never happen, you haven't got it yet. Worrying is a habit. And habits are as easy to break as they are to create. They exist because of the unknown. In essence, worrying is a manifestation of fears that you have not conquered yet. So, how do you get over this fear? You try, fail, change and then try again until you conquer. Do this until your actions are dictated by choice, and not anxiety.

The things you worry about always fall into one of two categories: things you can't control and things you CAN control. Examples of the former include a girl's reaction to your appearance, her mood, her friends' reaction to your approach and the presence or absence of a boyfriend. What you can control, however, is the first impression you make and your confidence level when you approach her.

Here's the thing, if you have no or little control over the situation, why worry about it? You can't change what you can't influence directly, and worrying about it will only lead to more frustration and unnecessary guilt. What will happen, will happen... you just have to roll with it. Worrying about her reactions won't make a difference to the end result. This anxiety will only add to your fears and prevent you from dealing with the things you can control. The other problem with fear is that it often leads to a self-fulfilling prophecy which in turn leads to failure.

So, you know how futile fear and worry actually are. You know you will experience various levels of excitement when approaching a girl you like. You know you can't control all the variables. And you know if you want to get the girl, this is the price you pay for complete and utter intoxication of having someone special like you back.

Self-Sabotage

That's an interesting term there... "Self fulfilling prophecy of Failure". Think about the quintessential clichéd sports story. An athletics coach with a no-nonsense approach in tolerating anything negative. One of those uncompromising type figures whose results with his athletes are second to none, pushing them harder and faster than they could ever have imagined. The day arrives, the most important track event of the year...he turns to his star athlete and asks, "Do you think you will win?" "I'm not sure' is the response, "A Top three finish would be nice." The coach laughs, hands the sports bag to his star athlete and takes him home. "If you don't think you can win, you've already lost."

Clichéd yes, but remember, clichés exist because they originate from an obvious truth.

Winning is not a conclusion, it comes before that. You've heard the saying, "Seeing is believing". Well I'm here to tell you it's not true. " Believing is seeing".

You see, there are so many ways you can sabotage all the groundwork and it boils down to the same thing, 'I am not good enough'. Maybe it's true; in all honesty it does not matter and no one really cares. The fact is that if you allow this thought pattern to dictate your mindset, you are going to get caught up in a cycle of mediocrity for the rest of your life.

Let me ask you if any of the following ring a bell when you see a girl you like:

- ✓ "If only…"
- ✓ "She looks like a bitch…"
- ✓ "I'm not in the right space…"
- ✓ "I like being single…"
- ✓ "She must have a boyfriend…"

Negativity will turn all your preparation into dust. The fact is that most men think that looks and money are of paramount importance when it comes to women. Now, I am not saying there aren't Gold Diggers out there, but we don't give a toss about them, and you certainly don't want to attract that kind of attention. The women you really do want, the ones that are not superficial, are attracted to the guy with the positive attitude who embodies the potential for success.

Remember that positive emotions attract people, while negative ones have the obvious opposite effect. When you approach women with a positive frame of mind, she feels reassured and safe. If you approach her with a nervous attitude, she will think you've got something to hide.

The best thing you can do is show a fun, friendly attitude towards women without thinking of the outcome. This is important. Have fun and interact freely without dreading the outcome.

YOUR TRUE SELF

There's another line that could lead to failure... "If only". You might find yourself thinking 'if only things didn't happen the way they did, I would have become a more confident person', but before you start in that direction let me tell you this: no matter what happened in the past, you will always have the rest of your life to develop yourself. It is likely and reasonable to place yourself in a position where future ambition and not past reality become your shaping mechanism. The key here is acceptance. Once you achieve this state, the world becomes your oyster and your true self begins to emerge.

Your true self lies underneath all the years of bad habits, false fears and the behaviours associated with these thoughts. It is your best version and lies underneath all your insecurities and inhibitions.

WHAT YOU TELL OTHERS VS. WHAT THEY KNOW ABOUT YOU

Introducing yourself to someone new means opening yourself up to potential judgment. The more you talk to that person, the more she will grasp what you're about, irrespective of the level of detail you go into.

Intuition allows for a greater degree of understanding among men and women. No one can guess what you're thinking or feeling, but everyone has the capacity to perceive. You may not say 'I am insecure', but you will manifest it in your body language or through your tonality.

The way you speak is a fundamental part of your identity, and women are likely to brand you just by the way you talk. It tells of your background (what region you were brought up in), your status in life (well-spoken and educated) and it conveys what you think about yourself. The key to making a lasting impression on someone is being in complete control of what you reveal.

ACTIONS

The Woman you Want.

The first action assignment today is about getting a clear picture of the kind of woman you want in your life. I want you to take 15 minutes to sketch out her personality, looks, height, habits, favourite movies, anything and everything you can think of. This is not a lottery, it is the science of attraction and you are going to start becoming proactive. If you don't know who she is, she won't.

My Qualities

Secondly, write down 10 of YOUR most important qualities and put a score beside it (10 being the highest, 1 being the lowest). In the column next to your thoughts, I want you to write the score you think your friends, family or acquaintances would give you. You must be completely honest throughout this. The purpose of this exercise is to start becoming aware of what you have to offer as well ascertaining whether you communicate these qualities. Take a look at the example below.

Qualities	*What You Think*	*What You Think Others Think*
Sense of Humour	7	3
Honesty	6	8
Sensitivity	5	2
Confidence	1	4
Sense of Romance	7	8
Generosity	8	3
Compassion	5	5
Audacity	6	4
Considerate	5	6
Attentive	8	8

DATING, CHAPTER 2:
GET THE BASICS RIGHT

This chapter will teach you how to speak with confidence. You will learn the skills you need to effectively talk to women, and how you can deal with the fear of expressing your opinions.

CONFIDENCE AND ASSERTIVENESS

Confidence will get you through a lot. During your job interview, one of the first traits an employer looks for is confidence. It conveys the capacity to deal with pressure and encourage personal responsibility. Dating is no different.

Needless to say, inner comfort and security become aligned when you are confident in your work environment. You inspire trust in others; you accomplish more in less time; and you are less anxious regarding the future. You will also be able to assess and attract opportunities without hesitation. Assertiveness is the bi-product of confidence. It allows you to have conviction, belief and the capacity to overcome.

Do you know a person who embodies this level of assertiveness? Think about that person now. This could be someone in your work environment, family or even a character on a TV series. In your mind's eye, that person embodies all the characteristics you admire and wish to transcend upon yourself.

As human beings we are attracted to confidence and assertiveness; it's about control and the ability to protect. What I want you to do is simple. Emulate the people you admire on an internal level. Take a characteristic out of their portfolio and start wearing it. This can be whatever you want, carefree, cheeky, diligent, concentrated etc. This can be a lot of fun and incredibly interesting in terms of self-exploration. Let me give you an example of a generic assertive personality.

Watch How a Good Public Speaker Delivers a Speech

They personify boldness and composure, something you're going to be looking for in your own life. Pay attention to what they say and how they say it. Watch their body language closely. Observing people who have the characteristics you want to harness will become the quickest way for you to develop it yourself.

"COMMUNICATION CONFIDENCE"

The true test of confidence is public speaking. Effective public speakers personify the core abilities required to deal with other people, including the women you want to interact with. These skills can be applied across the board. Once you've developed the confidence to stand in front of people and speak your mind, the seemingly impossible task of turning a stranger into a date becomes less daunting.

Are people scared of speaking in public? The answer is YES. Even the people who do this daily find themselves nauseous at the thought. You could have labelled yourself as 'too shy' or 'introverted' to communicate to a wider audience, the fear of judgement remains constant. That is...until you begin, until those first words come out of your mouth and the irrational fears that were manifested through the imagination become fictional.

What you need to realise is that this fear directly relates to unexplored social skills and an irrational fear of being judged. The quickest and easiest way to address this is to understand a simple thought. Everyone is afraid of talking in public, just as everyone is afraid of taking their first step towards the gorgeous blonde at the bar. The feeling is normal and you are not unique in this regard. But in the game, as in with life, you are judged not on your thoughts, but by your actions. Overcoming the fear and doing it anyway, is what defines you and you will more often than not, find that fear disappear once you have committed to the action.

Your fear of talking in public stems from the same insecurities that are keeping you from socialising with women. Considering this, we can assume that if you increase your communication confidence, the way you socialise will also improve. How exactly can we do this? We can start by dealing with the issues that crop up inside your head when the notion of facing a crowd occurs to you. I am going to reference public speaking here for a few pages, think of it with an audience of three or three hundred people, it matters not. The principles and fears associated with this are identical to that of communicating with the fairer sex. Get these principles under your belt and you will exude a greater confidence when approaching a woman you are attracted to.

1. FEAR OF SAYING SOMETHING IDIOTIC

Your mind is racing and your heart is in your throat. You wish you were somewhere else. The main reason behind this is the fear of ridicule. The thought of being laughed at becomes an overbearing anxiety. So how do we address this source of anxiety?

Talk About Something Familiar

First rule when talking to people: do not fake expertise. If you're not familiar with a topic, do not claim to be a guru or an expert. Instead, express interest in the topic and encourage discussion. This way, you won't feel self-conscious about your lack of knowledge. To be able to speak with conviction, you must be completely familiar with your topic. You must also be able to articulate the main point by looking at it from different angles.

Broaden your knowledge about current events and things that interest you so that you have something to bring to the table when your friends (or your potential date) brings up a topic that you're not too familiar with.

Use Humour Wisely

You most certainly have heard that you should 'break the ice' when giving a speech or talking to women. However, before you start cracking jokes, you should first make the other person or the group comfortable. Smile, introduce yourself and talk in a relaxing manner before you crank up the humour. Self depreciation is always well received, but be sure to make it funny and not sad.

2. LOSING FOCUS

When you stray too far from your original topic, you will find yourself at a loss of things to say next. This is the time when 'conversation fillers' such as uuhhm and errm start to invade your speech. The more you use these random sounds, the more you will lose your focus. Here's what you need to do to avoid this blunder:

Practice

The proper way to practice a speech is to simply pretend you're talking to one person. Some speakers get so caught up in fretting about the memorised script that they forget the most important part of talking to a group of people: a speech is essentially conversation between you and your audience. Only, you get to talk first, so they can ask questions later.

3. FEAR OF BEING CRITICISED

Being aggressive is also a sign that you lack communication confidence. You secretly fear that people will criticize you on your opinions, so you talk in a way that exudes aggression. Remember, it's a conversation and thus its success depends on the level of interaction.

Be Assertive, Not Argumentative

Don't bully people into accepting your opinion. Instead, encourage them to respond to what you're saying by asking questions and debating the subject with you. Real communication confidence comes when you can discuss a topic in a healthy manner, regardless of how heated the discussion becomes. Being aggressive and unyielding will highlight your lack of knowledge or your need to be right, and will diminish the point you are trying to get across.

Get Your Audience Involved

A 20-minute uninterrupted monologue is BORING. Pause every once in a while to allow feedback from your listeners, and encourage interaction. Pauses will also help you emphasise your main point and are more often than not, the most poignant part of engagement. If you avoid them because you're afraid of sounding unsure, your audience will find it difficult to follow your train of thought.

4. PHYSICAL DISCOMFORT

If your knees feel weak, your stomach feels funny, you can't breathe or you feel dizzy during a public conversation or a chat up with the blonde, try doing the following:

Breathe from the Diaphragm

Breathing correctly is a simple trick you can do when you're feeling anxious. When talking, your flow of breath must be constant for you to speak continually without panting. Moreover, proper breathing will ensure that oxygen-containing blood will flow better, making you more alert and able to think on your feet.

Actors and singers learn this trick to optimise their voice and get rid of stage fright instantly. Take a deep breath and control the flow of air from the diaphragm (located under the lungs). You know you're doing it right when your diaphragm contracts as you breathe in, and relaxes as you breathe out. Speaking from the diaphragm makes your laughter resonate and your tonality more flexible. It will also prevent your voice from breaking.

If you've somehow forgotten to breathe from your diaphragm when you talk to a girl, there's still a simple solution to making your speech better. Clear your throat unobtrusively and take a deep breath.

Achieving a better Posture

Align your head, your shoulders and your hips while standing with your feet approximately two inches apart. If you do this right, you will instantly feel your breathing improve and your back relax. Your spine should look like a slightly curved line (S-shaped).

Posture matters when you're the centre of attention. Don't worry about puffing your chest out for now and concentrate on easing your back in a position that doesn't feel uncomfortable. As long as your posture is fine, your feelings of self-assurance will supply the rest of the body language signals you need to exude.

Projecting your Voice

The ideal voice is slow, calm and assured. Surveys suggest the sexiest voice on our planet belongs to an old Bond actor, Sean Connery. Your voice needs to sound assured so you can pronounce words easily. Learn to enunciate your words to maximum effect. Remember, people who talk fast or babble are obviously very nervous; and the jittery demeanour associated with this will distract your audience. Don't be afraid to use pauses to your benefit. Pauses add a sense of drama to your speech and get the audience excited about what you'll say next.

If you speak fast, you will come off as uncertain and tense. You will also have less time to think about the ideas you're spouting. Simply put, you are more likely to say something stupid if you can't slow down to analyse what you're actually saying.

Speak with the suitable volume. There's a big difference between being loud and speaking assertively. If you're confident, your voice should stand out and make people take notice. After all, you want to be heard, not disregarded.

5. SHYNESS

Shyness is not the same as having low self-esteem. Many shy people have a very positive image of themselves, but they lack boldness. These people can ordinarily talk all day if they're relaxed and in the company of familiar people, but they turn beet red when speaking in front of strangers. Introverts tend to be the most creative people out there, so the assumption that dating is an activity for extroverts alone is a fallacy. I will touch on this later. Let's first look at a few ways we can deal with shyness.

Visualization

If you're shy, you can visualize that you're talking to close friends instead of the sexy bombshell in front of you. Pretend that you've known her your entire life or that she is incredibly unattractive. Remember, in the dating world an attractive woman is inundated with pseudo alpha extroverts, so the unique opportunity to offer her something which is real and unobtrusive can be refreshing. You are peacocking, standing out from the crowd, whether intentional or not. This is an attractive quality.

Exposure

Visualization is a good way to remedy shyness, but the long-term solution to this is exposure. Go out and meet other people in coffee shops, parks, the library and in clubs. When you get used to interacting with strangers, the shyness becomes secondary until it eventually disappears. Think about this in terms of any other learning process. Once acquired, you rarely think about what you are doing. You just do it.

Your Inhibitions

The feeling of being self-conscious comes when you realise just how visible you are to everyone you're talking to. Even if you're ultra confident about your speech or the way you talk, the feeling of being ogled at like a fish inside a glass bowl can be intimidating.

Most of the time, this feeling is associated with shyness or the inability of fully expressing your emotions because of inhibitions. Your strong anxiety about intruding into other people's personal space or disturbing others thoughts contribute to this. Shy people usually speak robotically, and with very little enthusiasm. So, what do we do to get you less timid and even enjoy yourself while you interact with other people?

"FAKE IT 'TIL YOU MAKE IT"

You can feign self-confidence to increase your confidence without anyone noticing it's a put on. Actors live and breathe this principle when delving into character portrayals. You need to do this to improve your mood and to control your emotions before you speak. Faking it is the best way to deal with the feeling of being flustered. For instance, someone made fun of you while you're talking and you were unsure of a response. You can use your little act to cover your annoyance until you regain composure.

Feigning bravado initially can jumpstart confidence. Faking enthusiasm at the onset will make sure you start right with minimal awkwardness. After a few minutes of this, your audience (or the woman you're talking to) will respond to you; making it easier to genuinely feel confident and enthusiastic.

Regardless of what others say, 'faking' confidence isn't a bad thing. It helps you project a better image when you're really not feeling it. What most people don't realise is that your emotions can change in a flash depending on the situation and the people you're interacting with. For instance, during your speech, the audience applauds. How would you feel? You would feel elated and renewed, making you drop the act and start feeling genuine confidence.

The quickest way to project self-assurance is to alter your body language. Lean back to look relaxed. Smile widely and gesture with your hands. Uncross your arms and tilt your head slightly to one side.

Adopting a body language that contradicts your real mood can be tricky, so if you use this tool, make sure you commit to it. What I mean by that is go all the way, exaggerate the movements until they look normal.

Take my advice and sit in a coffee shop and spend an hour or two watching people. Think of it as research on body language. People feign confidence as soon as they get out of bed. It's one of our many masks. See if you can spot the genuine article or someone who is projecting another image. The lesson here is simple. Act confident when you need to feel confident and hold the act until you've gained genuine belief.

Do the Necessary Prep Work

Acting confident is a great way to start feeling self-assured, but to be able to sustain this for a long time, you need to prepare. Your clothes and your over-all appearance will have to align with your projection of confidence. What I am saying is simple – dress the part. If you go on a date wearing a vest and sneakers, don't anticipate a carefree enjoyable evening.

The game starts as soon as you get out of the shower. Wear something, which is congruent with the impression you are trying to create. Only when you have looked in the mirror and aligned yourself with what you are going to be about, will any of the above work.

Carefree is good, but not in the same vain as 'I don't give a shit. Even if you manage to convince yourself of this through the pre-date preparations, you will most certainly become aware and insecure when you see her. The key here is to feel confident. And looking the part is going to go a long way towards acting the part.

Plan for Contingencies

If I had a nickel for every time I had forgotten to plan for a contingency in my youth. Let's agree on this basic premise. Intense anxiety happens when you're forced to deal with a situation that you did not plan for.

Let's suppose you spoke to a group of girls, and one seriously attractive woman wants some one on one time. You know what could happen and you're extremely pleased that someone's hitting on you, but you find yourself mumbling an excuse because you don't have enough money on you.

Think of scenarios that could happen if everything goes well. Bring enough money, shave well, put on aftershave, cut your nails, trim your bush and wear your best underwear. Don't forget the mints. Trust me; you don't want to feel self-conscious just when things are starting to look good.

ACTIONS

I have discussed the phobias and fears one has when speaking in public, as it is an experience we have all faced at some point. The association between this activity and approaching someone you have never met before elicit similar fears, emotions and internal mantras with the solution for both activities remaining communal. The analogy is used as I want you to remember this the next time you are watching someone in the office deliver a presentation, a colleague talking to potential new suppliers or a graduate being interviewed for a new job. The point is we elevate the action of approaching an attractive woman to a pedestal it does not deserve. We experience and overcome the same obstacles faced in the dating game in everyday activities, even if we are unaware of them. If you can do that, there is no reason you can't do the other.

Two Minute Speech

I want you to prepare a two-minute speech that you are going to give yourself in front of the mirror. Make sure your topic is something you are familiar with. I also want you to imagine you are talking to a group of girls at the pub and your only job is to keep them hanging on everything you say. Use all the tips I have provided and after perfecting it – don't worry, there is no such thing – get your flatmate or friend to take a look at your deliverance. This is supposed to be a lot of fun – so make sure you enjoy it.

DATING, CHAPTER 3:
CONQUER APPROACH ANXIETY

Approach Anxiety is a frame of mind you enter when you let fear prevent you from developing the most fundamental social skills and from obtaining the level of confidence needed to mingle with strangers. This chapter will give you unconventional advice on talking to women and losing your social phobia.

Getting rid of approach anxiety is not only for socially awkward guys who want to learn how to strike up conversations with women. Any guy who has trouble opening up to people and getting them to listen, be it friend, family or foe needs to address approach anxiety. If you deal with it, you can increase your social value and interact with pretty much anyone out there.

We are designed as social beings. Interaction is ingrained in our genetic makeup. It's only through years of negative social reinforcement that we begin to question the validity of walking up to a complete stranger and trying to get her number. Understand that this is a false thought pattern and one that prevents you from growth.

PERSONAL DEVELOPMENT

Before we get to the core of what's causing approach anxiety, the symptoms and the ways to get over it, let's first address the issue of "not being interesting". If the main thing that's holding you back from getting to know more people is your fear that you don't have enough to offer or are not compelling enough, I am here to provide you with a reality check. I have never met anyone that did not fascinate me! Let's say you regard yourself as uninteresting, lacking in social skills or unadventurous.

There are THREE things you need to do to transform this mindset...

1. Develop the Initiative to improve your Social Skills

The fact that you're reading this and committing to living your life to the fullest by interacting with others means you're on your way to developing your True Self... or that version of you that can effectively interact with anyone at any time on your terms.

While most guys are happily enjoying their solitude playing online games or thinking that socialising is drinking twenty pints in a pub every Friday night, you're here refusing to stay immersed in fear and learning how to become more social. Whether that be from an introvert or extrovert perspective, remains irrelevant. Pat yourself on the back right now because your wheels are already in motion in developing your social personality.

Socialising opens your mind as you pick up on habits, interests and thoughts of people with different beliefs and unique idiosyncrasies. This creates personal exploration, which in turn creates the capacity for empathy. Try discussing the meaning of life with the next lady making your Americano, or question a photographer in the park about what compels him or her to take pictures. You will learn more about yourself by being in the company of others.

2. Control Your Emotions

Controlling your emotions entails doing the positive version of what you usually do when you're faced with a difficult situation. Remember flying off the handle the last time someone annoyed you, and then 48hrs later you were replaying the event in your head with the more desired outcome. How you handle stress is a perfect gage of how emotionally in control you are. I'm not asking you to suppress anything. Passion is an important trait, but losing control is unattractive. It portrays a childlike need to be noticed, to be heard and is the antithesis of rapport. You will learn later how important this is in terms of attracting the opposite sex.

Emotional stability is an important aspect of personal excellence and attraction. Understanding that the goal is in the interaction itself and not the result creates a disregard for being right or wrong, which enables two people to make a connection.

3. Sense of Adventure

The curiosity to find out what's around the next corner is paramount in developing yourself. Being intrigued about your capacity to achieve and having that burning desire to push your limits will create interest in the type of person you want to be. This is the key here and will be talked about later. Women are attracted to the potential of men, and not their current status. If you can push personal boundaries and explore options you would normally avoid, you become interesting. Plain and simple.

The most interesting and absorbing people I have met in my life continue to challenge themselves. Whether this be cycling from London to Paris, trekking the Himalayas or taking a Salsa dance class, the principle remains the same. They continue to look for a challenge, irrespective of the scale, and make a commitment to overcoming their fear of doing it. Their hunger for emotional knowledge and a "desire to enquire" separates them from the herd.

The best way to develop your Sense of Adventure is to just go for it!

Every day, list down something you want to learn. It can be a foreign language or a musical instrument. Meet with someone who swam the channel. It honestly does not matter. What is essential is that you attempt to do something you have never done before. Try some of the following:

- ✓ Interview your favourite coffee attendant when she's not too busy.
- ✓ Watch a Meringue video tutorial, download a Britney Spears dance track and practice. Show your mates.
- ✓ Cook one exotic Asian dish every weekend for a month.
- ✓ Visit specialty cuisine shops or restaurants twice a week. Close your eyes, point at a dish on the menu and eat it.

Now that I have got you thinking, let's delve a little deeper into Approach Anxiety. Believe me, even if you're totally in control of your emotions, you've developed an incredible sense of adventure and you have an encyclopaedia of topics at your disposal, you might still feel the following symptoms when you're face-to-face with a woman you like.

Symptoms of Approach Anxiety

I want to let you in on a true story. I know this guy who fell head over heels for a girl who seemed way out of his reach. She was head girl, degreed in International Politics and modelled her way across the globe on shoots for a variety of huge brands. She was almost 10 years younger than him and at first sight; she looked way out of his league. Did he encounter approach anxiety when he asked her out? Yes. Did he do it anyway, yes! In fact, the first time he tried to kiss her she turned her head away and he was so embarrassed he had to ask her to leave his room for a few minutes so his skin colour could return to its' natural pigmentation. What transpired from overcoming his fears? She moved in on their second date and wedding vows were exchanged three months later.

When approach anxiety hits you, you feel out of breath, tense and nauseous. It's all about the fear of rejection. Although cognitively there is a very good chance that the other person will respond positively, you choose to dwell on the opposite. That negative thought affects your demeanour; body language and all your attractive qualities disappear into oblivion.

Your shoulders slump, your face loses colour, your hands tremble and you fidget uncontrollably. You look dejected, freaked out and disengaged – and the sad fact of the matter is that the physiological change does not bode well for attraction. So, how do you deal with it? You go through with it. You experience the supposed trauma, which results in an action. The reaction is never as we imagined it and more often than not, it becomes a pleasant experience. You do this again and again, until your brain begins to identify that this entire experience is safer than you initially imagined. What ensues is a more rational physiological experience through the power of habit. In a nutshell, practice makes close to perfect.

If shy, lonely, socially introverted men…and I have met quite a few…can get over the psychological and emotional issues preventing them from social interaction, then so can you! Books like the Game and Rules of the Game by Neil Strauss are all about these introvert, so called socially inept men conquering their fears and dating the most gorgeous women alive.

WHAT ARE THE CAUSES OF APPROACH ANXIETY?

I've met a lot of men who don't approach women because they didn't know what to say, doubted their ability to strike up an interesting conversation or assumed the women already had boyfriends and wouldn't appreciate being approached.

The fact is, your brain will acknowledge whatever fear absorbs you. It's a sensation called fight or flight, and in the past you have more often than not picked up a set of wings. When you're in this state, your mind will spout out excuses like a machine, and it will try to convince the rest of your senses that you're not good enough to get this woman's number. Even if you've memorised line upon line of witty pick up phrases, the fact remains, if you can't get rid of this fear, you will not follow through and approach her.

I am going to bridge a few common issues that normally complicate the approach and can end up turning a perfectly good attempt into a nightmare.

1. Friends

Let's agree for arguments sake that the majority of social events you are going to go to are alongside mates. Now, this is beneficial in many respects, as women tend to feel less uncertain of a bloke when he has friends. I suppose it rules out the loner categorisation. But these mates, wingmen, advisors…whatever you want to call them, can be more debilitating in terms of getting you your date. What I am asking you to avoid is their coaching, pressure, methodology and set of beliefs. If they provide moral support, great…but the aim of this section is to get you to absorb the responsibility of being proactive and making decisions for yourself.

The other factor is the pressure cooker scenario. You tell your mate you like her, he applies the pressure and you end up approaching for the wrong reason, the outcome. As I said earlier, at this stage the outcome has nothing to do with the success or failure of the objective. If you get her number great, if not, also great…as you are developing yourself into someone who is not afraid of getting what he wants. This journey is about approach development and not bragging rights.

What I am also trying to get you to do is develop your own unique style of approaching. Don't let anyone tell you that their techniques are the 'best'. There is no such thing. Remember, you and your friends have different personalities, with a variety of unique attributes and so your affect on women will differ greatly. While cracking jokes or saying crude opening remarks might have worked for Boris, these might not work for you because your disposition is different.

Let me drive this home. An opener that worked for a mate might not work for you. It's dependant on timing, mood, even her body language which varies from minute to minute. . It's never the line.... There are dating development programmes out there that will give you sixty guaranteed one-liners to get her into the sack. It's garbage! A girl who seems sullen or bored might not react well to a cheesy joke, but she might respond positively to a smiling "hello" and a sincere "how are you feeling".

Trying to memorise witty openers that your friends claim are 'fail-proof' will only make you more tense when you approach women because you have to deal with two issues: getting the joke right and worrying that she might not get it. So get this out of the system now, it is one less thing you have to worry about.

2. "What if"

Ninety nine percent of the time, your mind is going to roll out a worst case scenario, and this small clip of you failing to catch the girl's attention will drive you nuts before you even get to her. Free your mind from the worry brought about by the "what if" scenario and give yourself the chance to find out whether or not you can develop some attraction with her.

Before you utter "what if" again, think about this: you don't know for sure that she will dislike you, and there's a very good chance that she might like you. You will never know what she is genuinely thinking when you approach unless she tells you. Worrying and not approaching because you've already decided that she won't like you is all about you wanting to stay comfortable and safe. And as I said earlier, that is not good enough. It's fear based and congruent with further failure. The key here is to mentally come from a different place. Imagine 'what if' in a positive frame. What if we hit it off and she really likes me? What if there is serious attraction and she wants to meet up again? What if this is the start of an awesome relationship? The next time you are running your worst-case scenario through your head as you are about to approach, I want you to think about this quote.

'The most drastic and effective remedy for fear is direct action" William Burnham

Always bear in mind that women, especially the gorgeous ones, are almost always in conversation with men or their friends in a crowded place. Considering this, you should know better than to pass up the chance to talk to a girl who's currently not busy talking to someone else just because you're second guessing yourself. Feel the fear, and then overcome it through your action.

3. Limiting Self Beliefs

Belief systems stem from inherent childhood experiences that crop up when you're faced with a similar situation. Let me illustrate this with an example. Let's suppose you've always been emotionally bullied by girls because of your height, disposition or inability to take control …and you never learned how to handle it. Now, you're in front of a beautiful woman and you base your approach with her on your past experiences with pretty girls. This assumption is incorrect. It is purely down to the reinforcement you have provided for yourself. Think about it. She knows nothing about you, your past or your psychological disposition. And truth be told, at this stage, she does not care. Her interest is aligned completely with where you are going, what your ambitions are and the potential you possess.

Some of the self-limiting scripts that you play inside your head

- ✓ "She will think I am an idiot"
- ✓ "My mates will abuse me when this all goes wrong"
- ✓ "She probably has a boyfriend"
- ✓ "She is too hot for me"
- ✓ "She is not hot enough for me"
- ✓ "I like being single"

This inner voice is a reaction to the fear you're feeling, and effectively your inhibitions are doing the talking. It is essential for you to understand that this has nothing to do with who you are. You are defined by your actions, not your thoughts.

What is the cause of the limiting belief? It is the inability to take responsibility, wanting to be right and wanting to look good. Give these notions up and acknowledge that you will make mistakes but you will learn to laugh at yourself and who knows...maybe even make her laugh in the process.

THE FIRST STEP TO GETTING OVER APPROACH ANXIETY

Before you can start putting you social life in order, you must commit to making it a priority.

This means you have to go out, invest time in making new friends and trying new activities (even those that you normally wouldn't try). This can be simple for those who are frequently exposed to socialisation, such as those in sales who constantly talk to people, albeit about business. However, for someone who has never tried striking up a conversation with a stranger, it can feel difficult.

How do I know? I've had numerous friends there. The quintessential loners... guys who didn't place much value on social interaction. Even when everyone around them was partying and celebrating the start or end of a school/university or calendar year, they never felt the need to join in. Needless to say, that kind of imbalance solidified and embedded itself deep into their subconscious.

The fact that they didn't see mingling with people as a healthy thing isolated them from the rest of the world. They had friends, sure, but they were people with whom they interacted with on a regular basis and never tried making new ones by going out of their way to experience new things.

The simple fact remains that being open to new experiences and straying from your comfort zone will improve your social life drastically, and this is the first step you need to take if you want to get rid of Approach Anxiety....

COMMIT TO BEING SOCIAL

You don't need to spend your weeknights going out, but you can...

- Take the occasional dance class
- Go to a book reading,
- Start a conversation with a waitress serving you coffee in your favourite Starbucks

These are simple baby steps you can take to bust Approach Anxiety. You need to actually approach people to improve your communication skills, and consequently, your social skills.

Being more social means you need to begin spending time where most people hang out. Ditch the broadband for a day or so and go strolling around a market. Spending all your time alone will not help you if you want to overcome your fear of meeting women. In the modern multichannel world we live in, technology has actually made us more insular and less social. Think about it like this. In terms of communication, seven percent is conveyed through words, thirty eight percent through vocal elements like tonality and fifty five percent through non verbal elements like facial expressions, gestures or posture. Yet we have defined communication in the modern era as an email, a status update or a text message. We have become less social and rely on technology as an alternative which flatters to deceive. So when I talk about committing to being social, it does not mean signing up to a dating website. It means getting out there, seeing a pretty woman in the flesh, approaching her and engaging through face to face communication.

HOW TO GET RID OF APPROACH ANXIETY ONCE AND FOR ALL

"My life has been full of terrible misfortunes most of which never happened" - Michel de Montaigne

To get rid of Approach anxiety, you need to acknowledge that your inner voice is incorrect and avoid self-sabotaging your actions. Accept that you are going to feel nervous and that it's ok to be nervous as long as you take the first step towards meeting her.

Another trick:

When you imagine the negative scenario in your head, speed it up, make it comical, and put someone else in the lead. Create your own internal version of the movie and imagine you're watching a comedy where the guy in the lead role approaches a woman who obviously loves him and is terrified of making a fool of herself. Make it funny, laugh out loud and see how ridiculous the fear really is when the shoe is on the other foot.

Forget about the outcome and learn how to really interact with women so that the fear of approaching won't touch you. The victory is being in the game.

Don't place too much value on what onlookers think or say. This is the best way to deal with rejection. Don't take it to heart and simply look at the situation objectively. You're a stranger to her and she's a stranger to you. She might have misjudged you, and you don't know her enough to explain yourself thoroughly, so move on.

Learn to treat rejection as a form of feedback. When you get rejected, it simply means you have to improve your engagement style more. Lastly, do not rehearse negatives scenarios in your head. These self-limiting scripts will only demotivate you.

ACTIONS

Negative to Positive

Write down three negative things that have happened to you in the past 10 days. Now I want you to replay them over and over in your head, in different genres. Examples can include Western, German porno, War, Foreign Film with Subtitles, Kung Fu. Again, this is something I want you to have fun with.

Rational Response

Write down all the things you are afraid of happening to you by talking to a girl, then write down a rational way of dealing with them.

DATING, CHAPTER 4:
THE POWER OF YOUR MIND

This chapter will jump start your ability to think positively about yourself and forget your fears. After all, no one is more qualified to change the way you think (and consequently, the way you act) than you.

WHO AM I – THE POWER OF THE MIND

Every day we react to situations by responding to prompts silently within the recesses of our minds. Notice the way you replied "no thanks, I'm full" when someone offered a bite of their sandwich, when you really wanted to say, "Can I have two?" The way we react to things and scenarios outwardly may or may not reflect the thoughts brewing inside our brains. There's a huge difference between what we show people (The Mask), what we really think and ultimately someone else's interpretation of who we are.

Now, I am going to ask you to listen closely to your thoughts when reading through the following statements:

- A friend who is always nice to you, but gossips about everyone else.
- A family member who continues to make disparaging remarks at your expense.
- Co-workers who always go out for drinks, but never ask you.
- Activities that you wanted to take part in but never did.
- The concepts of extrovert and introvert
- Socialising yearly at the company Christmas party
- Your circle of friends who loved you but will never be interested romantically or sexually in you
- A lifestyle you wish you lived

The thoughts that you have developed are reflections on how you view several aspects of your life and people around you. If you've become indifferent then stop. This is the perfect time to tag your thoughts as negative, positive, or neutral. Now, let's suppose you're with another person as you silently react to a situation in front of you. Would that person be able to gage what's going on inside your head?

There's an obvious link between what you think and what people observe. Usually, they can sense something is either positive or negative even if you say the opposite. That is the mask begins to crack. This comes down to basic intuition and projection. People project their thoughts and feelings constantly, which are often completely incongruent with what they are saying. The point is simple. Your mind dictates what you personify. And no matter how hard you try to avoid projecting it, it can become visible. Not through what you say, but how you say it and through body language.

THOUGHTS ARE THE MOST POWERFUL THINGS IN THE WORLD.

"Believing is seeing"

Thoughts affect everything. The way you view things and your general attitude towards any issue and projects onto virtually every essential aspect of your demeanour.

Actors and actresses use the power of thought to enter into the minds of characters they play. They do this by manipulating the images in their head to be more aligned with a particular personality they are trying to personify. That is how they become connected and it's the difference between a believable performance and a wooden outward performance. The bottom line is this. In order to genuinely alter your state; you will need to realign your thought patterns.

THOUGHTS LEAD TO HABITS

Some courses on body language will teach you how to control your body language regardless of your feelings, but if you're already reading this part of the chapter, you should know that this is all about transforming your self-destructive thoughts patterns into positive ones. As we mentioned in Chapter 3, you can only "fake it 'til you make it" for a short period of time; your next step must be to use your thoughts to direct your actions towards your goal.

Thoughts don't occur to you just once, they become repetitive and habitual.

If you have convinced yourself that you don't like a particular activity (for example, socialising at parties), and your initial thought when asked to go with friends is "no thanks, I don't like partying", you will continue to think that way each and every time you are faced with the option to choose whether or not to go out and socialise.

If your thoughts have derailed your attempts at achieving more in life, your only option is to alter them or ignore them. It again comes down to actions determining your own outcome. Either way, once the ball is in motion and you begin to realign your thoughts with more positive outcomes, the new habit will begin to form.

THOUGHT ALIGNMENT PROCESS

Turn Negative Thoughts into Positive Thoughts Using the Power of Your Mind

Events in life do not determine the outcome of any given situation. Your thoughts associated with the event will dictate the end result. This is why

254

some people achieve greatness through adversity and others fall away into oblivion. The power to control any situation falls directly onto you and your interpretation. This means anything and everything is possible, dependant on the thought you choose to associate to it.

Positive thoughts, like negative thoughts, are infectious. The girl you're talking to will rely on you to supply the prompts that will allow her to be more open and relaxed. This is the start of the rapport process. In order to be successful, you will need to align your thought pattern with a positive outcome.

Here's how you can turn your negative thoughts into positive ones: list down all the things you dislike and beside each one, write the opposite.

Example: I don't want to mingle → I want to socialise. Or, I feel lazy today → I feel so energetic today.

Just reading through the things you've written will make you feel the glaring difference between the moods you create using negative and positive thoughts. Now the next step is to stick with the thought that creates and maintains your positive mood.

If you make this 'thought' process a habit, you will be able to change limiting beliefs into achievable aspirations. Moreover, you will learn how to create positive emotions that will directly lift your morale. You know those people that walk into a room and create a buzz, a rapport with anyone and everyone around them. This is the mantra they use to create attraction and interest.

A POSITIVE ATTITUDE ATTRACTS PEOPLE

A positive mindset is attractive, while a negative one has the opposite effect. When you're around people who are fun to be with, you have fun.

The same thing happens when you put a plant in a dark room with only one light source. The plant will grow towards the light source because it wants to be nourished. Think about becoming that light source.

People will shy away from you if you let your worries, anxieties and hang ups overcome you. Your whole demeanour will scream "don't come near me", and sure enough, everyone will stay away.

BREWING A POSITIVE VIBE

You can BREW positive energy by putting yourself in a good mood before you go out and socialise. For instance, you can listen to calming music, watch a funny outtake on YouTube or get on the phone with someone who makes you feel good about yourself. This way, you will remain upbeat.

Another way of brewing positive energy is to choose who you hang out with. If you're always around negative people, you will get soaked up in their energy and end up projecting it when you're around people you want to attract.

You probably know exactly who I am talking about. We all have them in our lives: the crabby office manager who always glares, the women next door who has nothing better to do than gossip, and the stressed out colleague who is constantly threatening a life change. Do yourself a favour and avoid rubbing elbows with these people.

A lot of self-help books add to the concept of a positive outlook. This is the main reason why the Chicken Soup Stories series has become so popular. People generally want to read inspirational stories because they recharge themselves and it gives them strength to cope with their own challenges.

Surround yourself with positive energy so that you can keep on having positive thoughts. At the same time, strive to be the "chicken soup for the spirit" to everyone you meet by giving out a comfortable vibe that attracts people anywhere.

WHAT TO DO WHEN PEOPLE PUT YOU DOWN

There are times when other people intrude into your personal space and deliberately try to alter your positive frame of mind. You will never know the reason, and my advice is to avoid investigating their motives. The truth is that more often than not, it has absolutely nothing to do with you, and your interpretation needs to be as such.

The fact is, you cannot change other people's perceptions of you. More importantly, you cannot change the way they think about themselves. With this said, it might seem difficult to control a situation where in another person shows his or her disdain, but I can tell you right now that it's one of the easiest things to do.

First of all, you can start by controlling the things you CAN control. The other person's agenda and the emotions linked to it are his or hers, and you cannot do anything to change these. However, your mental processes and emotions are YOURS, and you can control your own thoughts and interpretations as you please.

Therefore, if you want to deal with a negative person, you need to adjust your thinking. Instead of rebutting that person and getting into a heated argument, you can do the following:

Ask yourself if the insults can be interpreted as feedback that can help you grow.

Some petty insults and jibes can actually help you improve, dependant of course on who is handing out the report card. You can turn any negative situation around by interpreting the commentary as feedback. Even if the insult was meant to make you feel bad, you don't have to let it. Again, remember that it is your interpretation that elicits the positive or negative mindset, not the action itself.

Here's an example:

A condescending co-worker says "You're lazy; you always seem to be on a break!" If you adopt a positive mindset, you can reply in a neutral, light-hearted manner, like this: "I can always use more helpful advice. Thank you!" Your message should be clear. The key here is not to act pissed off or defensive. If they cannot elicit that reaction from you, they have no power over you.

This is essential when you are engaging with girls and trying to start up a conversation. The most important qualities to portray under these circumstances are calm, cool and collected.

How to Deal with Your Past Failures

Everyone has a sad story my friend, with meaningless failures and scars attached. It's not just you. If you're a little resentful about the hand you've been dealt or the way you have played it, it's ok… That is, as long as you use the past to propel yourself forward. For the most part, your past indiscretions have nothing to do with what you are about to embark on at this very minute. But you will need to find closure.

Before we get deeper into this chapter we call "Forgiving Yourself", think about this question: What is the difference between a stud and a geek?

When you think of the word "geek", what comes to mind? A geek is someone whose mind is always on video games, gadgets and books. He can't possibly know how to dress in a debonair manner and attract women. A stud on the other hand cannot possibly achieve academic honours because he only knows how to chase women and drink beer.

The common stereotypes like these make one unable to imagine a geeky guy who can attract women or a jock who can graduate Magna Cum Laude in Physics. These stereotypes affect the way you see other people and more importantly, yourself. They are incongruent with development, naïve and reinforce fears. There is too much grey in people to paint them with a single colour. And this includes you.

People use stereotypes for comfort and the act itself is driven purely out of fear. We tag people so freely in our everyday lives without realising that putting people in neat 'boxes', categorised according to our limited impressions of them, is one way of debilitating our minds with useless and unproductive notions.

Believing in stereotypes and dwelling on the past creates a victim like mentality. Worse, you will develop the kind of mindset that is the hardest to shake: you vs. them. Get it out of the system now!

This leads us to an important lesson ...

FORGIVING YOURSELF

This is probably one of the hardest mindsets to achieve, but in terms of self-esteem and personal development, it is the most essential. The fact is you are going to need to love yourself if you are expecting someone to return the favour. So, how do we go about letting go of the past?

Firstly, look at the events that have shaped you and decide if your interpretation is congruent with self-appreciation. If it is not, change it. The fact is we have all regretted certain life experiences and if we had to do it over again, chances are there would be some serious changes. But guess what, we can't and thus we are left with a single alternative, which is called coming to terms with it all.

Secondly, remember that your past interpretations of the events that have led to regret are not accurate. You have created this and I guarantee you, you have compounded the guilt by maximising your responsibility. Remember, I am talking about the true self, not what you portray to other people. Our mind remembers and heightens the drama of traumatic situations, and over time, it is only those heightened states, which are reminiscent. This distorted view accentuates guilt and responsibility, which creates a victim like state. It is critical to understand that you are judging yourself far more cruelly than anyone else would.

Thirdly, you are not alone. Every single person on this planet has an event, which has lead him or her to guilt and an onus of responsibility, which became debilitating. Do not look into the window of a friend, family member or complete stranger and imagine their world is any different. They have their stories. The essential element here is to understand that mistakes and indiscretions are human and communal. How you learn to deal with them is what separates you.

Finally, remember that the easiest way to eliminate guilt from your life is by taking actions and acknowledging responsibility. This in turn leads to growth, personal development and results in admiration for oneself. It is a state of harmony, attraction and inner peace with the end result being love. So if there are any regrets, feelings of inadequacy and roads you wished you would have travelled on, I suggest you take an action right now to find some form of resolution. Remember, the outcome is not what is going to make you grow; it's the action you take in trying to achieve the outcome.

ACTIONS

Negative to Positive Outcome

Write down a list of ten negative thoughts you have had over the last two days. Now write an alternative to each and every one with a positive outcome.

Disabling a negative response

I want you to do some more mirror work. Imagine you have approached a woman and she is rude to you. I want you to disempower the comments by finding a suitable response based on my advice.

Change through Action

Write down a list of all the events in your life that you wish you could change. Now, I want you to write an action next to every one of them relating to how you could address them. You will know what to do next.

Dating, Chapter 5:
Attraction

This chapter will teach you how to create latent attraction with women you meet. You will also learn how to project your worth by showing the traits that women are looking for in the men they want to start relationships with. If you've always wondered what makes women throw themselves at men they just met; and what traits make women fall in love and commit to, read this chapter carefully.

A friend of mine had given up dating after several failed attempts to get digits (a woman's phone number). They either they gave him fake ones or they just gave him a seriously hard time. The rejections were so bad that he used to cringe every time he was asked to hit the town. That is, until he finally realised the big difference between initial attraction and long-term attraction.

What traits attract women initially?

If you ask a few hundred women what they are attracted to, the following traits will come up more than once:

- A good sense of humour,
- Someone with a great personality, and
- Someone who's interesting.

Now, if you asked them what would make them consider a guy as a long-term interest, husband or boyfriend, the answers will vary some more.

The Dating Agenda of Men and Women

Women have a different agenda to men. Their intention is to find someone who is more often than not, a long-term prospect. Now, I am not saying that guys are not looking for the same level of commitment. However, we are much more at ease with the 'try before you buy' approach.

It's rare to find women who will want to genuinely end the connection after your first night together. There may be hidden agendas, which portray a different disposition, but this is normally for effect only and driven through fear.

Now, I am going to assume that you are interested in a relationship, tired of being alone and in some dire need of showing and receiving affection. What I am saying is this my friend. The number you are looking for should be one, and not one hundred, as the latter is not going to lead you anywhere fulfilling.

So, how exactly do you connect with a woman if you are aware of her long-term objectives? The answer is simple... You highlight the traits that women associate with the things they want from a man who they would consider to be a long-term prospect.

MAKE WOMEN WANT YOU

Let's say you don't want to think about the complexities of relationship or connecting with a girl on a deeper level. You just want to be able to attract her, get to know her intimately and open yourself up leisurely to the possibility of spending more time with her.

Let me just reinforce something on this note. One night stands and numerous sexual encounters with the opposite sex do not generate fulfilment. That said, there is nothing wrong with a one night stand as long as both of you are aware of the others intent.

Now, let's look at attraction by assuming that it is present whenever a man and a woman meet for the first time. This is the atypical form of attraction. Cold logic, societal programming and the many rules that prevent humans from just going for it whenever we're sensually provoked, control it.

It's called 'latent attraction'.

WHAT IS LATENT ATTRACTION?

Latent attraction is the kind of gravitational energy that is present in any interaction between men and women. I'm talking about the most fundamental and basic source of attraction here: she's a girl and you're a guy.

Latent Attraction in itself won't make a woman throw herself at a man, and it certainly won't make a man give up everything he has to make this connection. Something has to happen before the man and the woman connect on the emotional and physical level.

Think of latent attraction as the firecracker that sits in the dark in a storage room right before the New Year. When it's time to let the whole world learn of the beautiful and powerful secrets it holds, the owner will take it out, ignite it with the rest of the firecrackers… and it will be one of the symbols of festivity when the world celebrates the New Year. For now, though, it stays there in the dark… its bursting power cold and dormant.

Think of this kind of attraction as the potential "main event" that could take place while you are talking to women. There are certain things that have to be in place before it can be released from its dormant state. Some conditions need to be met…

Awareness of the other person's single status.
You're both single and you've noticed each other. There are no wedding bands in sight, and you ASSUME that the other person is in that particular place is looking to meet someone.

Proximity.
She's seated or standing nearby. If you want to meet her or talk to her, you can just walk over and introduce yourself.

Likable Trait.
Maybe she has blonde hair, and you happen to like blondes. On her part, she might be looking around for guys wearing glasses, because she likes that particular look. This trait could be anything, but it's the one thing that's going to make you take the first step in her direction to say hello.

So how do you go about generating the spark?

INTERACT

To release latent attraction, you need to take **action.**

Obviously you can approach a woman who's covertly checking you out, as there is already an obvious level of latent attraction. If, however, attraction isn't present yet, you can generate curiosity, which in turn will lead to interaction. If attraction builds from that, good! If not, move on.

The bottom line is that you need to be in her vicinity. If you know some-one in her circle, get in there and start making conversation. The important thing to remember is that the two of you need to interact. This is going to require a proactive approach on your part. Remember everything I told you about the approach and implement it.

'Men Watching' and Women

Before we discuss the subject of what's attractive to women, let me tell you something about how women 'Man Watch'. You thought us guys were different...err, wrong! Much like babe watching is a hobby for most guys, so bloke watching is for girls. There is a difference though. Whereas we are stimulated by their physical prowess, they are on the lookout for men who have visible traits of a potential partner; and this has nothing at all to do with looks. Men are more visual and thus the excitement of a slim girl in a bikini is obvious. Women are more about the story and seeing a guy play with his niece or nephew in the park will end up sparking a serious amount of stimulation.

Getting a Woman's Attention

It's pretty simple actually. To make her notice you, you have to stand out, become accessible and most importantly; you must embody traits that she finds attractive. A woman finds a man desirable because they embody a particular trait 'a key figure' in their life either portrayed or should have portrayed, during their development years.

Think of a father figure. If he was generous and attentive, she will be attracted to those qualities in a partner. If he lacked the aforementioned qualities, she will be driven anyway to compensate for the missing qualities.

ALPHA MALE CHARACTERISTICS

Men who get noticed as soon as they enter the room or a woman's line of sight look comfortable, confident and charismatic. The three C's embody the characteristics of an Alpha Male.

They portray a high social status and a level of control. Remember that in its most basic evolutionary portrait, attraction stems from the capacity to provide and protect. Alpha males exude these characteristics.

Here are some more traits of men who automatically attract women.

MASCULINE PRESENCE

You've seen men who don't look at all like the typical stereotype (bearded and unkempt) and look incredibly masculine. Research has shown that women are aroused by broad chins, high cheekbones and large eyes and recognise a good body as indicative of discipline and control.

Men who are masculine are often regarded as leaders. They are central in groups and seem to direct everything that happens within the group. They laugh easily and look incredibly relaxed as the central character.

Their communication is slower than the norm and normally in a low baritone. High pitched or erratic voices are associated with insecurity. Now agreed, there is not much you can do about the physical attributes. However, you can work on voice projection and tonality with numerous exercises.

RELAXED DEMEANOUR

The more relaxed you are, the more attention you attract. Tension in men usually results in a refusal to interact. Uncross your arms, unclasp your hands, breathe normally, and lean back. Looking like a tightly coiled spring will drive women away.

There's an easy way to instantly relax in any situation: control your breathing. When you breathe deeply, visualize the air going down into your diaphragm and expanding sideways.

Breathing properly will also help relax your facial muscles. Your number one goal should be creating inner comfort and relaxation. You want to exude control. The majority of guys are going to be high energy and this is something I want you to avoid. They will keep you central if you remain in this state.

In terms of eye movement, you are going to need to keep a neutral gaze. Do not react to the environment. Let it react around you. So if a pretty lady walks across your periphery, do not follow her by ogling. You will get tagged quickly. Remember, while you are looking at her, so are plenty of women looking at you.

Men who are not affected by beauty are regarded as comfortable and alpha type. Here's why: alpha males are used to talking to beautiful women, so they don't get excited when one appears in front of them.

THE POTENTIAL TO SUCCEED

Now I am not going to lie to you. Women fantasise about men who can provide them with all the luxuries in life. The same way you dream about acquiring wealth to buy all the things you potentially never had growing up. It's the power of hope and ambition, which in terms of attraction is a powerful cocktail.

The harsh reality is that not everyone is born with a silver spoon or a surname called Gates. Men know this, and women are acutely aware of this too. Women's magazines make a lot of money out of female fantasies of wealth. This is the same fascination that keeps the hype about Paris

Hilton alive. Women love hearing about the lifestyle of a rich heiresses, and girls whose lives have been transformed through wealth acquisition.

Women are attracted to the potential of men to succeed. Because of this dream of living life to the fullest, most women qualify men according to what they are capable of.

This means that even if you don't have the spending power of Donald Trump, if you personify the same qualities that are inherent in men who have made it in life, women will become attracted to you.

Women are attracted to men who are passionate about their purpose in life, and men who seem to control their own destiny.

The formula of success is simple: luck + hard work + passion. Among these traits, passion is the one that will attract women to you. Women subconsciously know that the lucky and hardworking people in the world will not acquire much wealth if they don't have the same passion that successful men have.

Luck could run out if it's all you have; hard work is difficult to sustain when your body and mind start to get tired; but having passion will make sure that you can create your own luck, and maintain a level of enthusiasm which will help you achieve your goals.

In other words, because women want to be with men who can provide for them, they will only get attracted to men who show signs of being successful... and the passion you show towards your work and your life in general, alerts women to your potential for success.

Passionate men have the drive to be the best in their field. They are constructive in their ambitions and rarely will they compromise in their path to success. They understand the concept of having fun, without having to negotiate priorities.

Bottom line: Women are attracted to men who can potentially provide for them.

CONFIDENCE

This trait is often synonymous with a high level of self-esteem and control. A man who displays confidence looks relaxed in any situation, which translates to being in control. This means you are able to absorb and deal with situations that some men would not.

If you are unfazed through obstacles that come your way, women will respect and admire your ability to handle the circumstances. Think about it. They are looking for someone to provide and protect. The trait of confidence is related to knowing what you can and cannot deal with. If circumstances are beyond your control, there is no need to worry.

The different levels of confidence in men are evident in body language and are incredibly easy to notice. Make no mistake of it; a man who embodies confidence in a social environment is the one who attracts women.

SEXUAL CONFIDENCE

One of the covert requirements in attraction is the portrayal of sexual prowess. She will never openly admit this, but there is an expectation for you to know what pleasuring a woman is about. For a woman, the requirement is simple: you must know how to turn her on, and how to make her climax.

The only way she can make this assumption is through the level of comfort you portray when interacting. Sexual innuendos and the confidence to have fun will elicit the belief that you are competent in the sack. Acting and not reacting is a quality you should be looking for.

BAD BOY VS. NICE GUY

Q. A woman I met in a club chose my mate. He doesn't shave, dresses like a biker and has had more jobs over the last year than anyone I know. No bitterness here, just genuine curiosity as to why she was more attracted to him.

A. The Bad Boy vs. Nice Guy debate has been around for so long now that there are several schools of thought around the topic.

My take on this is simple: nice girls love bad boys because they trigger an unfulfilled emotional response in them. What do I mean exactly? There are certain qualities in bad boys that make women feel like they are filling a void. Here are some examples:

Rebellious Attitude

The bad boy persona is irreverent and uncompromising. A typical bad boy spits at convention. He simply does what he wants regardless of the way society frowns at his actions. This attitude appeals to women because of what it represents... freedom from judgment.

Women are under more pressure in society than men. There are more things that women, particularly the 'nice' girls, aren't supposed to do in comparison with men. Even the women who strictly abide by societal rules know about the repressive nature of the unspoken rules imposed on themselves (e.g. don't have sex on a first date, don't be too forward, don't wear skimpy clothes ... etc.)

Meeting someone who embodies a woman's desire to be acknowledged without judgment is attractive. Thus, the answer is simple. They are attracted to these personality types because of their lack of judgment on behaviours.

Adventure

Simply put, it's more exciting to date bad boys because they represent freedom. And freedom is the climax of every story. Remember earlier, I mentioned that men are visual whereas women play a story in their head, which leads to attraction. An adventurous personality embodies the capacity to live life free of society's regulations. They represent the ability to do what they want, irrespective of how it is portrayed.

Let me give you an example: A surgeon has always dreamt of leaving her practice to travel the world. The problem is that she belongs to a family of surgeons, and the burden of responsibility and expectation are extreme.

She meets a maverick photographer who gets by selling nature photography to big ecology magazines. He used to be a lawyer. In her eyes, everything about this guy is 'strange', from the way he carries himself, to the food he eats. She falls for him like a ton of bricks. Her attraction stems from a deep-seated need to see the life she wants to live in the eyes of someone who's actually living it.

The attraction women feel towards bad guys has nothing to do whatsoever with career or appearance. It has to do with their care free and non-judgmental approach to life. Adopting these qualities is a great way to stimulate attraction. When you meet a woman encourage her to talk about dreams, desires and burning ambitions by telling her that she's not risking judgment.

Remember, women are acutely aware of the pressure to conform. Meeting someone who can maintain respect for her regardless of how she lets her inner rebel come out to play every once in a while is captivating.

ACTIONS

Bad Boy Assignment

You only have one assignment tonight. I want you to turn yourself into a bad boy and this is not going to be fictional. You have a story, one that is unique and full of adventure. You may not be aware of it, but it's true. Now I want you to write 3 pages, a cover letter so to speak, and I want you to develop this as if Stephen Spielberg had decided to do a movie based on the events of your life. Once you have written it down – I want you to pitch it to your mirror.

DATING, CHAPTER 6: RAPPORT BASICS

In this chapter you will learn how to start communicating with women by first building your approach confidence and your rapport skills. You will also learn how to be completely comfortable with approaching women you don't know.

Starting a conversation is the most important skill you will need to learn before you can start attracting women you want. Why is it such a huge hurdle? The main reason is that feeling of apprehension that comes when you don't know whether or not the other person will respond to you in a positive manner.

To start a conversation with a stranger, you must develop your approach confidence and your rapport skills.

BUILDING YOUR APPROACH CONFIDENCE

What is a cold approach? Simply put, it's "striking up a conversation with someone you don't know". Talking to a total stranger is discomforting, to say the least, but you have to learn how to do this if you want to meet women.

Most guys get freaked at the thought of starting a conversation with someone they've just exchanged glances with; so don't feel that you're all alone. The good news is that there are a couple of things to help you overcome this fear.

Approach Confidence Tip#1 – Improve Your Speaking Voice

You inadvertently reveal a lot about yourself through your voice. You have in all probability become so used to the sound of it; you have forgotten how others perceive you though your tone. However, apart from your body language, this is one of the initial impressions that will make or break your approach. Thus, common sense leads us to work on it.

Grab a voice recorder and listen to your own voice. Now, objectively… assess the way you speak by asking yourself the following questions:

- Do you sound confident or submissive?
- Do you sound aggressive?
- Do you sound assured?
- Do you sound appealing?

Your mood, your emotions and your background influence your voice. Moreover, if someone wanted to get to know you better, your voice will provide insight into your personality. Intense emotions are evident in the way you talk, and you need to be aware of how these emotions become heightened when you approach women. Understanding this will help you while developing your neutral speaking tone.

What is a neutral speaking tone? It's the tone you automatically revert to when you suddenly pick up the phone. It's the way you automatically respond to people when there are no negative emotions filtering through. It is your true voice. Obviously, it needs to be pleasant and attractive enough to make the appropriate impression.

To develop your own "neutral speaking tone", do this:

Smile and say hello a few times, varying the tone of your voice each time. Then, say a generic greeting out loud; again, varying the manner a few times. You just need this one line to practice daily in front of the mirror, when no one's around to hear you talking to yourself.

Use this tone daily by adjusting the words to fit any situation. When you ride the tube for example, use this tone to say 'excuse me' or 'thank you'.

When you have your standard greeting tone perfected, here is a way to improve your speaking voice when you're talking to women:

Lower the pitch of your voice consciously. Clear your throat and transform your high-pitched voice into a lower baritone. When you're approaching women you don't know, they will build attraction to you the first time you say hello, if your voice is deep enough. Females are naturally attracted to men who sound masculine, and subconsciously get turned off when a man's voice is too high.

Approach Confidence Tip#2: Don't Think of the Results

You will feel more anxious if you think about getting her number or getting her to say yes, BEFORE you even approach her. Thinking of the end result will only create internal pressure. You will need to reframe the objective. Your success is about making an approach and not the outcome.

Analogy: The Smart Phone Salesman

Consider how you would feel if you were selling a high-ticket item to someone. It could be a state-of-the-art Smart Phone that has not been released on the market yet. You have a potential buyer in front of you and you're making him warm up to the product by talking about the features. If your mindset is 'result-oriented', you will have a harder time selling. Why?

This is because in the back of your mind, you know you're only in the conversation to sell the item. Your listener will feel your tension and will interpret it another way. He might think you're nervous because the product is not as good as you say it is. Or, he might just ditch the idea of buying it from you because you're too objective orientated.

However, if you concentrate on the conversation about the new features and your mind isn't on the sale, your buyer will relax. You will end up selling the Smart Phone because he knows you're genuine and not a hard-seller. The other person feels relaxed around you and you don't sound contrived or fake.

In a conversation with a woman, you will need to loosen up and really have fun talking to her, whether or not you get her number in the end. I'll say it again; it's about the interaction itself and not what you get out of it.

DEVELOP YOUR RAPPORT SKILLS

Rapport develops when you and the woman you're talking to acknowledge a mutual interest. It creates a unique bond between the two of you by exploiting commonality. She feels there is something particular between the two of you, which she may not find with someone else.

By demonstrating rapport, you're primarily elevating your connection, which in turn develops her security. Think about it like this. She is looking for someone who is beyond the one night stand and will have met plenty guys with that insular intent. By elevating the connection to more than just a pick-up, you are heightening her attraction.

Rapport is something that develops while you're talking to a woman. The pre-requisite for rapport is to start making her feel comfortable around you by making eye contact and smiling.

Rapport Skill #1: Being Aware of Your Environment

After the initial pleasantries, you can use your environment and the situation you're both in to begin your conversation. This is called thinking in terms of the "context" of your conversation.

You can say, "This coffee is a classic… "if you meet her in a Starbucks or "I love abstract art" if she's looking at something particular at an art gallery when you approach. If you meet her inside a bookstore, you can recommend a new book or ask her for advice on selecting a new thriller. The point is you are using the commonality of environmental interest to generate a connection.

Rapport Skill #2 – Be Enthusiastic

Sitting inside your office for eight hours can make you a little mechanical, so you need to warm up before you go out and interact. Modern working environments encourage anti-social behaviour and we spend more time communicating through email, Facebook and other social networking sites than face to face. Ultimately you end up spending an incredible amount of time in your own head. What transpires is an aloof nature, which is incongruent with your real self.

You can become upbeat very quickly if you spend a few minutes listening a good tune. I recommend Sweet Caroline by Neil Diamond. You should also get into the habit of watching comedy shows on online streaming sites, or simply downloading outtakes, a personal favourite. Anything that will create a positive energy is what you should be after.

Rapport Skill #3 – The "Talk Show Host" Attitude

When you portray confidence, you embody self-assurance and charisma. Now, does this image of an ultra self-assured guy remind you of something? A talk show host!

Here's a mini-assignment for you: watch a talk show. It doesn't matter if it's Oprah or Jonathan Ross, just pick one and watch how the host does his or her thing. You will notice that they control a small part of the conversation, and hand over a chunk to whomever they are interviewing. They are the stimulant for conversation and perfectionists in generating comfort.

As soon as you start watching, you will realise that a talk show isn't a monologue, it's a healthy exchange of ideas, and it FLOWS smoothly because the host knows how to steer the direction of the conversation.

You are going to need to apply this to dating. Let's suppose you're the talk show host and the girl you're going to approach is your guest. As soon as you start talking, your main objective should be to get her to relax. If you are successful, she will open up. The rationale behind this reaction on her part is simple: she feels close to you because your demeanour is positive and non-threatening... which brings us to the main point of this tip:

Be Non-threatening, But Be in Control

When a woman is relaxed, she will potentially ramble. When this happens, you will need to be able to steer the conversation in the direction you want.

To illustrate what this point, here's an example of a conversation that becomes unmanageable:

You meet a woman in the coffee shop and she's sitting alone. You strike up a conversation with her and make her relax by adopting a friendly tone. Soon, she's sharing her sob story with you (e.g. she just broke up with her boyfriend), and you feel uneasy. You try to stop the flow but she keeps going. You feel cornered.

In this scenario, you just turned into her friend, and she probably won't think you're hitting on her. You become safe (too safe) and she ends up pouring out her heart. This isn't a bad thing per se, but if you want her to think of you in terms of attraction, you need to alter the course of the conversation by subtly changing it.

Say something like "excuse me, I think my coffee is ready" and stand up. You can even go to the bathroom for a few minutes. When you come back, change the topic by sharing your own story. This should be similar to what she just shared, but with a definite ending.

In the example above, the girl shared a sad story of being dumped. You can share a similar one, but devote only one or two statements to that story before you change the topic completely.

You can say "Hey that story reminds me of the time I got dumped. Do you know what I did to get over feeling miserable? I went to Thailand on a backpacking holiday. Ever been there?"

The first part of the statement is meant to make her feel that you listened to what she said, the middle part is for closing the topic, and the last part leads her away from the topic which has created anxiety.

The key element to remember here is subtlety. If you make this obvious she will think that you are unsympathetic. The point is not to come across as disinterested; it is to gear the conversation into a more positive area, which makes developing rapport easier.

PRACTICE YOUR RAPPORT SKILLS

The only way you can practice your rapport skills is to expose yourself to as many people as you can, and I don't just mean women.

1. Approach Strangers Regardless of Gender

Wherever there are people, there's a chance to interact. Here's what I want you to do for the next three days:

- Don't wear your watch and start asking people for the time.
- Ask the waitress what her favourite dishes are when eating out
- In the coffee shop, ask the attendant which coffee flavour he or she recommends and why.

Add tasks for the rest of the week according to the places you go to. So if you are in a museum, ask someone for an opinion on a particular portrait. If you are in a book store, ask for some advice on choosing a new read.

You just need to practice getting comfortable talking to people and eliciting positive energy. By doing this, you will get used to people reacting to you, and you can adjust your speaking tone according to the situation. For now, don't discriminate. Practice building rapport on anyone you meet or anyone in your immediate vicinity.

I suggest doing this for a week until it becomes a habit to greet and say something nice or neutral to strangers regularly.

2. Talk to Women You Want to Date

When you've gotten used to talking to strangers, it's time to upgrade your rapport skills by approaching women you want to date. Go somewhere familiar, like a bar, cafe or a restaurant you've visited in the past. Look around and see if a woman is nearby. If you spot her, decide if she's your type or not. If she is, approach her.

Do this several times during the week in different locations. Your agenda doesn't include getting anyone's number. You just need to get used to approaching women you feel attracted to. Just dish out your greeting, exchange smiles and leave. If she opens up some more, have a short conversation with her. Of course, it goes without saying that you shouldn't say no if she hands over her number, but remember that this isn't your main objective.

Approaching beautiful women who know nothing about you is a little daunting if you don't put things into perspective. Remember, she is still just another girl with the same insecurities and ambitions as anyone else. You should not be entertaining any extra pressure because of the way she looks.

Remember, you don't need to do anything initially except start a conversation or ask a question. For now, do not worry about flirting, increasing sexual attraction or getting her number. You are learning how to build rapport.

3. Expose Yourself to a Large Number of Women in a Single Place

Ok, so you've become comfortable with talking to people in general and you have committed to starting up conversations. Here's the next thing on the agenda: go to places that women frequent like gyms, bars, clubs etc. Now I want you to make it your objective to meet at least 5 different girls in the vicinity.

GROUP SITUATION

The objective is to get the girl alone with you, but if she's a part of a crowd, don't worry.

You can talk to her by first involving her group in the conversation. Check if one of the members of her group is someone you've already talked to that night, approach that person first and get introduced to the group.

You'll create an opportunity to talk to the girl alone as soon as you get comfortable with her friends. Remember, she came with them, so they're going to be looking out for her. If they see you as a threat, there's a big chance that they will block your approach before you even try.

IDENTIFY THE 'MOTHER HEN'

Mother hen is a term I use to describe the woman inside the circle you are trying to access, who will make or break your approach. She's the Alpha female in the group, and keeps tabs on what her friends do, whom they talk to and essentially whom they go home with. Think about her in terms of an older sister. If you can befriend or charm this woman and get her to endorse your efforts, you'll have no problem getting close to the girl you actually like.

USE A WINGMAN

A wingman is your personal support system when you're out there approaching women. They highlight your capacity for being social. It's much easier to approach women with a friend, than on your own. It portrays a less desperate demeanour and creates a sense of ease in terms of whom you approach. The important aspect here is to regard yourselves as equals and not to let the outcome dictate your behaviour.

A simple illustration: Picture yourself in a club with a friend. You see this girl dancing and you want to meet her. If you're feeling anxious, your friend can approach her first (before other guys move in). He can either let you cut in while he's dancing with her, or he can introduce you.

FREQUENTLY ASKED QUESTIONS ABOUT APPROACHING WOMEN

Q. She's seated near the bar and she looks like she's waiting for her friends, how long should I wait before I approach her?

A. If you see a girl who's your type, go to her immediately. Don't wait. If you hesitate for even a minute, you might talk yourself out of it, or worse you might lose your momentum.

In a bar situation, a beautiful woman will only be alone for a few minutes before someone else takes notice of her and strikes up a conversation. In your case, you might wait too long and never get a chance to any one on one time because her friends have already arrived or she has already been approached.

Seize the moment and own it completely. Remember, the guys who get to meet women are the ones who actually approach, not the ones who sit by watching other men connect with the women they saw first.

Q. I attended a conference and starting chatting up a girl. I talked to her for about 30 minutes. Everything was fine initially, but then she started to act restless until she eventually excused herself. Did I bore her?

A. Keep the initial approach to 10 minutes. Always have somewhere else to be. If you're sure you will talk to her later on (during conference breaks and when the conference ends), you can afford to leave her after your initial approach.

Women find it discomforting when a man hangs around her for a long time hoping that something will happen. It embodies desperation, and that is the one quality you are going to have to avoid if you are looking to stimulate attraction.

Women, in general, do not like telling someone to go away, especially when the guy seems nice and friendly. If you opened well and she gives off a friendly vibe, graciously exit and tell her you'll talk to her again later.

Q. I've been asked how I'm doing in the past and I have always answered "fine, thank you". Is there more stimulating response?

A. There is. It's "better now, thanks." This is best said with a cheeky smile. You can use this as a starting point for a conversation if the situation is ideal (neither of you have to hurry off).

It's probably best to use this line when you're talking to a girl you're attracted to otherwise you may give off the wrong signal, but you can try this on anyone and still get good results.

Q. I went out last night and saw two girls in a club. I was more attracted to the girl in a red dress, but this other girl in a white blouse was giving me the 'look'. I was undecided on whom to approach and ended up bottling the whole approach. What should I have done?

A: I would approach the girl who seems more interested. If you end up successfully striking up a conversation with her, and she enjoys your company... you will have a much better chance engaging someone else you're interested in.

The reason for this is simple: women are always observing other women. If the girl in red saw you talking to the girl in white, she will get curious about you. She will also notice that you're fun to be around and socially adept, which will, in turn, drive her your way eventually.

Food for thought:

Just look at how the cosmetics companies feed off female endorsements. They can easily sell a high-end item if they have a celebrity endorsing it to other women... The female instinct of "I must have that too!" will kick in and the item will be in their bathroom cabinets in hours. This female characteristic is evident in the dating scene too.

Finally, think about the mindset of a girl before you approach. If she is on her own, she could be antisocial for whatever reason. The approach is obviously riskier. If you have spotted someone with friends, it's evident that she is in a more social mood, making the approach more attractive.

ACTIONS

Record Your Voice

I want you to record your voice tonight and listen to what you sound like. Play around with your tonality and pitch as discussed earlier in the chapter.

Talk Show Host

Watch an episode of 'Friday Night with Jonathan Ross'. Pay particular attention to how he manages to build rapport with his guests. A particularly interesting episode was an interview with 'Lady Gaga'. She was difficult to build rapport with and he managed it brilliantly. Take notes on how he does this.

Talk to Strangers

I want you to start striking up conversations with strangers. I don't care where you are or who it is, just make this demand on yourself and start interacting with people you do not know.

DATING, CHAPTER 7:
CONVERSATION TOPICS

Your first conversation with a woman is the "getting to know" stage. During this phase, you introduce yourself to a total stranger who might or might not be someone you end up dating for the next few years. In this chapter, you will learn how to demonstrate your high social value using conversation. You will also learn which red flag topics to avoid when talking to a girl for the first time.

PIQUE HER CURIOSITY

A woman normally assumes she has a higher status in comparison with men who constantly try to get her attention. Beautiful women have been conditioned to think this way because they have spent their adult lives accepting offers of drinks and gifts from men. Understand the mindset though; women will think there is someone better if you try too hard to please them.

This is an important lesson you will have to learn when dating for the first time. The guy who buys all the drinks, tries the hardest and seems the sweetest, has the lowest value.

For you to show up on her attraction radar, you need to highlight your uniqueness from the herd that have grazed before her. If you can do this, she will in all probability do all your work for you.

How to pique a woman's curiosity in three steps:

1. Talk about yourself in a unique way
2. Make your story memorable
3. Notice things about her that won't ordinarily be apparent to most guys.

BETTER THAN 20-QUESTIONS

When you first meet a woman, she'll want to know more about you. In particular, she will want to know what you do for a living, where you went to school, your hobbies, if you're intelligent or sporty etc.

So how do you creatively present the different aspects of your personality to a woman? Here are some of the most effective methods:

1. Play the 'For a Million Pounds' Game

This game is great for breaking the ice and getting her into a sporting mood. It's really simple. Ask her the following questions:

Q:' For £1000, would you sleep with your boss?'
A: 'Are you crazy, no way'

Q: 'Ok, would you do it for £10 000?
A: 'No, I definitely wouldn't.

Q: 'What about for £100 000?
A: '£100 000?

The rule here is that you have to get her to agree to do something she would normally never do, with the incentive of cold hard cash. You can play around with this as much as you like...and more often than not, it ends up in a pretty hilarious place.

2. "What's the story behind...?"

If she's wearing something flamboyant, ask her to tell you something about that item. It could be a piece of jewellery, her bag, her clip, or her shoes. If she says there's nothing special about anything she's wearing, say something like this…

"I know for a fact that women take an hour or so get ready. Those earrings should have won you an award tonight…they're exquisite"

Give yourself permission to be flippant and child-like when talking to a woman for the first time. This behaviour translates as 'fun' to her and that's what you need for her to anticipate a good evening.

It goes without saying that you should also wear something that will get her asking questions. For instance, a pin that represents your passion for animals or a tee shirt with a bold statement or weird a design will generate curiosity. It also separates you from the crowd. It's known as peacocking in the game.

BE INTERESTED IN WHAT'S HAPPENING IN YOUR WORLD

Running out of things to say? Talk about the things on television right now, or the upcoming shows you're looking forward to. If she doesn't watch television, talk about the industry in which she works or your own personal opinions on current events.

Remember to keep it all positive. Do not bash anything, be it a general idea or political ideology; even if it's something that people would normally form a negative opinion about.

THE MOST OBVIOUS TOPICS

Sometimes people look for topics of conversation without considering the most obvious ones.

- Your job or your industry
- The city or town where you grew up
- Your hobbies…
- Past experiences
- Sources of inspiration
- Favourite vacations
- Dream vacations
- Best summer experiences
- Uplifting news or events
- Dreams and aspirations
- 'What if' scenarios

The trick to talking about these things is to keep all exchanges positive. You can debate about issues, but you should not berate her point of view or approach a topic negatively.

YOUR STORIES

"You"-centred stories are your best dating props. Just look at how the stand up comedians tell theirs. It's something you can use to promote your personality.

Tell a Story in Response to Her Questions

When you get her curious about you, she will undoubtedly ask many questions about your background and your experiences. This is the time to tell your story in a captivating and humorous manner.

Here's an example:

Let's say a good friend of mine told me about a colleague of his, Parker Jr. who always found it embarrassing to tell women what his real name was, which led him to always introduce himself as "Park". He would make up several renditions around that name. When they went out for work drinks, a woman called him out for giving out a fake name saying no parent would ever name their child 'Park', so he told her his classic 'name story':

"My parents couldn't decide on a name so they looked out the hospital window together and named me after the first thing they saw... a park."

He went home with her that night. The fact is no one ever took him seriously, but the mischievous nature of his response was captivating enough to generate some serious attraction.

Sort through your life experiences and think of the adventurous or embarrassing situations you've been in. Select the ones that are funny and incorporate some level of self-depreciation.

Never be negative or bitter when you're describing something that happened in your past. If you have to describe a negative situation, make it seem like you've learned a lot from the experience and create a positive spin off it. You are aiming to generate comfort and ease in terms of your rapport, and creating anything other than this will make her feel like she has to tread lightly, which in turn will make her anxious.

Women can sense tension better than men because of a gender-specific intuition, so make sure you're able to laugh at yourself when revealing your past. This will help develop your persona into a sensitive and sexy one. Women in general love men who are able to laugh at themselves, as it denotes very little baggage. It comes down to being comfortable and in control, which results in attraction.

FIRST-TIME CONVERSATION QUESTIONS

Q. Is cocky behaviour funny? I've heard that women find it attractive when men act arrogant, but I'm not sure?

A. Many people have marvelled at the concept of using arrogant behaviour to attract women. Arrogant men turn women off. But cocky and mischievous men are attractive. It all comes down to how serious they are in terms of the role they play. Don't forget. Arrogance stems from a low self-esteem. It is compensatory behaviour and does not create an environment associated with attraction.

Let me introduce the concept of being 'pleasantly cocky'.

Turning yourself from a man who is soft spoken about his achievements into someone who's outwardly proud of his achievements can get you in trouble if you don't infuse an amount of self-deprecation in your personality.

Self-deprecation in itself is a negative, but it's rather attractive and humorous when you have the self-esteem to pull it off. Men who are pleasantly cocky can pull off a mock-humble approach to dishing out personal jokes at their own expense.

With that said, it's perfectly fine to be overly confident if you grasp the concept of 'respectful interaction' before you start acting cocky. If you want to pull this off, you will need to keep two things in mind:

Firstly, you need to make a woman feel comfortable around you before you start being cocky. So build the communication first before trying to elevate your status.

Secondly, always respect her opinion by letting her drive the conversation when she wants to. Ask questions and value her opinions.

Q. I will never be a jerk because I've been raised to be chivalrous at all times. How can I prevent getting pushed around by women I try to engage with?

A. There's a huge difference between being chivalrous and being a pushover. Let me explain…

When you have made a woman feel valued, you need to show her that you're not a part of the multitude of men who tolerate women who think old-fashioned chivalry and servitude are synonymous. Being too respectful can sometimes do more harm than good. If you find yourself in these waters, become pleasantly cocky to her just to remind her that you're attentive out of choice.

ACTIONS

Women's' Magazines

Get a copy of any women's' magazine and read it from front to back to find out what's hot and what's not in the female world.

Talk to Strangers...Do it this time!

I know you have not done the previous chapters actions, so I am going to give it to you again. Get out there and start striking up conversations with strangers.

DATING, CHAPTER 8:
EMOTIONAL CONNECTION

This chapter will teach you how to establish an emotional connection with a woman, and how to use the concept of "like attracts like" to deepen any interaction.

LIKE ATTRACTS LIKE

You will start emotionally connecting with a woman if you relate to her in terms of commonality as well as showing character traits that she values. For instance, you talked to a woman and she used language that was similar to yours. At first you won't be able to explain why you're drawn to the way she expresses herself, but you will be aware that there is an affinity.

The way she talks reminds you of a place you love.
There is a sense of comfort in what we know. Meeting someone who grew up in the same city, with the same accent and familiar colloquialisms is attractive.

She uses similar words.
You get instantly attracted to people who use the same words you use daily. For instance, if you work in the same industry, you are bound to speak in a similar manner.

These examples show you how instant emotional connection can be triggered by similarities. People will always act friendlier around others they consider to be kindred.

How do we apply this to dating?

You need to make her realize that you're SIMILAR in certain respects. She will find it easier to relate and develop rapport with you. Remember, people gravitate toward familiarity because it makes us feel safe.

MIRRORING BEHAVIOUR

To deepen the feeling of familiarity, you can learn to mirror her behaviour. Smile when she does, and use the same gestures. You can even mirror her posture. Sometimes, these actions are automatic when you're completely comfortable with someone. You will find yourself enjoying the same song or laughing at the same jokes.

Next, use the same vocabulary she does.

For instance, she's describing her job and you deduced that she's an actress. You should say 'rehearsals' instead of 'acting practice', because the former is more applicable to her mindset. The same rule applies when you're talking to a lawyer, a doctor, a policeman or an entrepreneur. You don't say 'office' when you're talking to a doctor; you say 'clinic'.

Note the places she has been and the activities she partakes in. If she says she goes to the gym, talk about your experiences in the gym. If she mentions her love for travelling, you can tell her about the places you've been.

KEEPING IT REAL

I know it's tempting to say grand things about yourself to a woman for attention purposes, but my advice is to refrain from lying about your similarities if you want your connection to survive over the long term. If you lied about one thing, she will most likely find out. That is just the nature of lying. And this is obviously not an attractive quality as it is fear driven.

GETTING HER TO SAY YES

When you've made an emotional connection with a woman, getting her number and setting up the date should be your next objective.

Use Scarcity as a Tool

Now that you know how to make a woman see you as an attractive proposition, how to establish rapport with her and how to talk to her on a level that she finds familiar and comforting, it's time to make her feel alarmed at the thought of never talking to you again. You've created a need in her; she wants to talk to you some more because she values your company.

- Leave Early. When she is in this frame of mind, you can cut the interaction short. Trust your gut and observe her reaction to your teasing. It is a bit of push and pull, but it will get the result you are looking for.
- If she asks 'do you come here often?' she could be looking for a way to stay in touch with you. Tell her you go there weekly, but not for a period of time because you're trying out a new bar next week. You can use this as an opening to invite her to go with you.

Appeal to Her Social Needs

If you want to make a woman say yes, you must appeal to her need to be "in", be popular or be in an envious position. Before or after you talk to her, make sure she sees you talking to other people, even if they're just your friends or friends of friends.

The more well connected and desirable you appear to be, the more her resistance will erode. You can approach her afterwards and tell her that you have something planned for the weekend, and would she like to join. If you have raised your social status enough in her eyes, she will be thinking "what will I miss out on if I don't do this?" and her innate need to have what others have 'endorsed' will do your work for you.

ACTIONS

Google "Mirroring"

I want you to research mirroring in terms of dating and the effects it has. Use Google to search for this.

Google "Peackocking"

I want you to find out what separating yourself from the herd actual entails. Research the term "Peacocking". Use Google to find out more about this.

Socialise

If you are still waiting to find the right moment to get out there and socialise, then wait no more. It's now! Get out there and make yourself proud.

DATING, FINAL WORDS

Congratulations, you've completed this section on dating and you're on your way to being a pro-active go-getter that women find themselves attracted to. I want to re-emphasise a few points here. Firstly, being social with women does not equate to copious amounts of alcohol to numb those internal fears. From a women's' perspective, one of the most attractive qualities a man can possess is committing to being vulnerable and open to the consequences of approaching without the aid of being drunk. Talking to a woman you've just met when you're pissed costs you nothing in terms of overcoming your fear, and believe me, she will be well aware of this. Let me align this with a true story.

A guy I knew had been friends with a girl who he had fallen head over heels in love with for over a year. The day she was supposed to be moving in with her boyfriend, they went for a pub lunch. She had a glass of white wine and he ordered a large bottle of sparkling mineral water. She could see he was agitated and asked him what was wrong. After umming and aaahing and stumbling over his words for a minute or two it came out.

"I think I'm in love with you."
She responded with "What?"
"I think I'm in love with you."

The rest of the meal was awkward, and she reiterated how grateful she was that he had opened up to her. After around thirty minutes of small talk and two vegetarian burgers later they hugged and said their goodbyes. The following day, he was sitting at his desk when she walked up to him looking like death. She had been awake all night crying. The consequences of his actions, his openness to being vulnerable and talking from his heart resulted in her not moving in with her boyfriend and the two of them becoming a couple a day later.

Secondly, I want to dispel the myth that approaching women is an exclusive exercise for extrovert personalities. As stated previously, there are books like "The Game" which are based on introvert anti-social behavioural type personalities becoming players who would get your mothers telephone number if they wanted to. I don't care what your Myers-Briggs Personality Test says about you, it remains inconsequential in terms of your success in the dating game. The same obstacles face every personality type. Introverts will have resources at their disposal that many extroverts will envy, and vice versa. The dating game is a level playing field; don't use your personality type as an excuse to avoid taking action.

Before you move onto Section 4, Nutrition, here are some final recommendations:

Bedtime Reading

Read this section before you go to bed so that your brain can assimilate everything while you sleep. Section 3 isn't meant to pressure you, and I know you will be able to enhance your social life at your own pace if you take on board my advice. Treat it as your cheat sheet to attracting girls, as well as your personal development guide to help you achieve more.

Take Action Immediately.

Let me remind you that the success of Section 3 is based on your actions and not your interpretations. Simply reading this material won't get you the dates you want. You will need to get out there and live it!

The best way to go through life is with direction in one hand and passion in the other. With these two attributes, you can always create your own possibilities. You are the master and commander of your own vessel and it's time to start steering it where you choose. So let go of your insecurities and live your life to the fullest. Remember, everything you ever wanted is on the other side of fear.

NUTRITION

NUTRITION

Let's all sound a resounding yawn for the fact that far too many diets are aimed at females! This was one of the main reasons why I decided that it was time to set out the benefits of the optimum diet for men in Section 4. After twelve months of research I managed to gather the best information out there, filter it and create an optimum nutritional blueprint for you. The food you put into your body effects just about everything you can think of. Thoughts, motivations and desired energy levels are directly proportional to what you eat. In addressing the truth about your intake you will embark on a journey of realisation and excellence that I am sure you would not have envisaged before.

I've made every effort to address the modern concepts and attitudes towards food as well as identifying the fundamental nutrients that need to be included in your daily consumption. So many 'faddy' diets are proven to pose serious health implications to the body and the aim of Section 4 is to provide you with a long-term alternative. It is my complete intention to introduce you to a suggested nutritional guide that is known to offer you a far better lifestyle and greater chances of increasing your life expectancy.

FEMINISM IS DEAD - TIME FOR MEN TO TAKE A STAND AGAIN!

As I typed the title above, it almost seemed to me that the fairer sex have taken over most chapters of lifestyle nowadays. This is abundantly clear when it comes to talking about human nutrition and the associated health implications.

The majority of diets feature reviews from women all over the world who have tried and tested various regimes, but rarely include feedback from men. Let's face it guys, the women's vehement challenge to shrug off a male orientated society has now come out on the other side and they are definitely leaving us in the dark when it comes to health and well-being.

So, with this in mind, let's place all of the feminine diet programmes to one side and get down to the business of addressing the Optimum Male Diet. We require a more substantive regime and one that is going to provide all of the essential nutrients to keep you healthier for longer.

THE PURPOSE OF THE OPTIMUM MALE DIET

I am a living and breathing testament to the OMD (Optimum Male Diet) and as such, I am going to translate my findings and experiences for you. There were a number of nutritional related health problems that I was aware of when I began my journey in search of the OMD and as such, I will be referencing the chronic illnesses that can potentially arise out of the consumption of certain foods. It will hopefully motivate you to address the serious implications of bad nutrition. My aim was to conceive a diet, which would provide confidence, weight loss and longevity in terms of life expectancy.

I fervently believe that the OMD hits the nail right on the head. A large number of programmes that I came across were dangerous to pursue in the long-term. They restricted certain essential nutrients to the body, which lead to inconclusive evidence in terms of health and well-being. So rest assured, this section is genuine in all respects. You will enjoy a healthier lifestyle if you follow some of my advice and there is nothing inconclusive about that!

Governments of certain western nations are not taking the basic steps towards ensuring the health of their citizens. Consider the amount of diets and the damage they have caused by not purporting the full extent of the facts.

So... before we go any further, let's get a couple of points ironed out:

1. This Optimum Male Diet is based on scientifically proven research. It identifies a lifestyle that will be of significant benefit to you in the long-term.
2. This section on Nutrition will be presented in a no-nonsense and factually based style.

It is my full intention to present you with a multi-faceted diet that will achieve the following objectives:

1. To inform you of the proven benefits of pursuing the OMD.
2. To give you an overview of the nutrients that are essential to the health and wellbeing of every individual.
3. To introduce you to some hard-hitting facts that will enable you to make a more informed decision as to the type of lifestyle you will look to pursue in the future.
4. To help you to put some of the information and findings into practice.

In Nutrition, Chapter 1 we will start to evaluate the way in which your present diet makes you feel. This may well reveal how certain types of foods can have a significant impact on your energy levels and general state of mind. We will go much further than this, in that we will also show how certain common food sources are known to be associated with serious health problems. These include the UK's biggest cause of death - coronary heart disease and certain types of cancers.

In Nutrition, Chapters 2 through to 4, we will look at the three macronutrients in the diet separately. We will focus our attention on carbohydrates, protein and then fats. This will involve dispelling the many myths that surround these essential nutrients.

All three of the macronutrients are vitally important to your diet, and you will be able to identify the very best sources to obtain optimal nourishment. Macronutrients are more complex than you would first believe, so we'll identify the best types and eliminate the harmful ones.

In Nutrition, Chapter 5, I will give you all the facts on micronutrients. These are the vitamins and minerals, which are imperative to your diet, but are required in much smaller quantities (hence the micro bit). The aim of this chapter is to help you to pinpoint the types of foods with suitable levels of these nutrients.

The chapter will then move on to the consideration of dairy products in your diet. Expect some truthful revelations here, which may very well go against the grain of what the media has been telling you ever since you were a child. Place all of what this industry has ever told you to the back of your mind and learn how dairy products are known to be associated with severe medical problems.

In Nutrition, Chapter 6 we will discover what it takes for your favourite meat dish to be furnished to you. We will also cover what you are really consuming every time you scoff down a burger.

In Nutrition, Chapter 7 we will look at sugar and address all its negative side effects. If you are looking to lose weight, pay particular attention here, as it is a sure fire way to get you dropping those unwanted pounds.

In Nutrition, Chapter 8 we are going to get you kicking all the bad habits and look at what you need to give up if you are going to get on the straight and narrow.

In Nutrition, Chapter 9 we will look at how all of the information you have accumulated can be culminated and consolidated into a healthier and more informed you.

In Nutrition, Chapter 10 will continue along the same lines and look at your Optimum Male Diet for the future.

In Nutrition, Chapter 11, I'll give you some excellent recipe ideas and suggestions that you can choose to include in your weekly menu. Towards the end of this chapter, you're encouraged to investigate other suggestions, so that you can compile your own menu for the coming weeks of your new diet.

In Nutrition, Chapter 12 you're almost ready to begin implementing the Optimum Male Diet for the rest of your life.

KEEP AN OPEN MIND

Before you venture further into the OMD, I want you to keep the following points firmly in the back of your mind:

1. Our understanding of human nutrition has advanced at a considerable rate over the last twenty to thirty years. With this in mind, this chapter on nutrition is in line with the most up-to-date research and scientific opinions.
2. You may feel that the OMD is a little radical at times. This is only because there are so many industries (e.g. the dairy industry) that seem to have gags over the mouths' of experts who could make a difference. Your ability to keep an open mind is essential.
3. Read the information carefully as you go along. Remember that the Actions have been included in each chapter to ensure you are grasping the most important concepts.

Before we move onto Nutrition, Chapter 1, let's test your current understanding of nutrition by taking a simple quiz: (there are points allocated for each question in brackets):

Nutrition Quiz

Slightly Easier Questions

1. Name the three types on macronutrients (3)
2. Other than saturated fat, name another type of fatty acid chain (1)
3. What is the average calorie intake for a male of between 19 and 50 years of age? (1 point for being within 51-299 calories here, or 2 points for being within 50 calories)
4. Milk, butter, cheese etc are all types of which products? (1)
5. Are complex carbohydrates or simple carbohydrates proven to be more beneficial to our health? (1)

Harder Questions

6. Amino acids make up what type of macronutrient? (2)
7. If a fatty acid chain contains three carbon double bonds along its length, what type of fat will it be? (2)
8. Which of the following food items would contain the most saturated fat: Steak; peanuts or bananas? (1)
9. What is the leading cause of death in the UK? (1)
10. Which of the following food items contains the best source of protein: eggs; Soya flour or jam doughnut? (1)

Answers

1. Carbohydrates, protein and fat.
2. Monounsaturated or polyunsaturated.
3. 2,550 kcals.
4. Dairy products.
5. Complex carbohydrates.
6. Protein.

7. Polyunsaturated.
8. Steak.
9. Coronary heart disease.
10. Soya flour (not eggs, which is a common misapprehension).

If you achieved a score of more than 10 in this quiz, pat yourself on the back as your knowledge would be well above the national average. A score of around 6 would be the average and if you managed 12+, you've definitely studied nutrition before or were paying attention in nutritional classes.

NUTRITION, CHAPTER 1: TIME FOR A CHANGE?

Far too many men become apathetic to lethargy. Their ambitions and overall ability to communicate and socialise have diminished through the consequences of following an unhealthy diet. This chapter is designed to not only identify the negative impacts of a bad diet, but also to provide you with the opportunity to take stock of your present eating habits.

Are you sick and tired of always feeling sick and tired? Well there's a perfectly simple explanation for why you're probably feeling this way - namely your diet! If you become accustomed to eating all the wrong types of foods, your body gets used to this and will essentially crave more of the bad stuff, which results in exhaustion and fluctuating blood sugar levels. Alternatively, if you introduce your body to a healthier option, you will enjoy the benefits of having more than enough energy.

There are a number of fundamental adverse side effects to eating the wrong types of foods. We're all aware that if you eat too many foods that are high in sugar and saturated fats, you're likely to put excess weight on, but the impact on an individual's health and psyche go much further than this.

A LACK OF ESSENTIAL 'BUILDING BLOCKS' FOR YOUR BODY

Nutrients are imperative for the overall maintenance and upkeep of every human being. For your body to renew it requires more and more cells to be formed and unless it is being provided with the necessary 'building blocks' (ingredients) to enable this to happen, you are going to suffer.

This is the most fundamental reason why nutrition experts advise us all to eat at least 5 different types of fruits and vegetables every day. They provide us with the building materials we require to remain healthy and refreshed, which result in the body being as efficient as possible.

Protein forms an essential part of our diet and you are likely to be surprised at the number of ingredients that contain sufficiently high levels of this macronutrient, as an alternative to meat derived products. It is made up of a number of amino acids, which are the basic components of life on this planet and when we deny our body sufficient quantities of these raw materials, we're inviting a whole heap of trouble. We will touch on the 'Truth About Proteins' in more detail in Chapter 4.

FEELING LETHARGIC ALL OF THE TIME

If your general diet is poor in nutritional content, you are going to feel sluggish and constantly tired. The 'empty calories' that are in most junk food products affect your overall state of mind. It has been scientifically proven that these food types contribute towards stress, anxiety and depression. This is mainly due to the fact that your blood sugar level can be altered so detrimentally as a result of these foods. In short, the body punishes us in its own way, by failing to provide us with sufficient drive and energy. Fibre (especially soluble fibre, like those in legumes, grains, nuts, and seeds) provides fuel for the friendly intestinal bacteria and supports healthy digestion and healthy fat metabolism. Whole grains are one of the best sources for the full spectrum of the key vitamins for energy generation, especially the B-vitamins.

KNOCKING YOUR CONFIDENCE

Eating the wrong types of food can have a direct knock-on effect on your confidence and self-esteem. On top of the weight gain comes inconsistent sleeping patterns, erratic emotions and addictions, which will leave you short on feeling good about yourself. If you are not getting enough Omega 3 & 6 (walnuts and flaxseed), vitamins B1 and B3 (Brown rice), vitamins B6 (Whole Grain Oats), Vitamin C and Folic Acid (Cabbage) and selenium (Molasses and Nuts), you are asking for a whole heap of depression.

THAT BLOATED FEELING

The body struggles to cope with junk food. In fact, often, some of these food items may not be shifted through the gastrointestinal system at all and will instead remain within our intestines, fermenting and producing the excess gas that is commonly known as flatulence. This leads to an uncomfortable feeling of bloatedness.

What's more, as these food items run through our intestines, they are not broken down which results diarrhoea. This is because bodily enzymes break down nutrients in foods as they pass through the gastrointestinal system, so if the food is poor in nutrient content, it is not going to be of any use to these enzymes. If constipation is a problem, gradually increase the amount of fibre-rich foods you eat such as fruit, vegetables, wholegrain cereals, bread, whole-wheat pasta, brown rice and beans.

YOUR OVERALL HEALTH

Not only will your body react in the ways that we've already looked at above, but you will also run the risk of going on to develop serious diseases and medical conditions in the future.

These illnesses include certain types of cancer, diabetes, raised blood pressure and levels of cholesterol and the UK's biggest killer - coronary heart disease. If you want to reduce the risk of heart disease you will need to balance your diet with less saturated fat from red meats, more fresh fruits and vegetables, less sugar and more fibre.

YOUR WEIGHT

Fast food and junk food are far too cheap, readily available and it is unfortunate that so many people are unable to resist the temptation of over-eating. This has led to a crisis in terms of obesity levels, which in turn has had a massive impact on the National Health Service and the billions of pounds required for research. You, the taxpayer, foot this bill. Foods that are high in fat and sugar work on our brains like opiates – painkillers – and the more we eat, the more we want. This consequence is also increased by the "empty calorie" effect of junk food. It fills us up for a short period of time, but then, like any addict, we begin to feel tired, depressed, and hungry all over again, and we keep coming back for more of the same. Let me assure you of one thing. You will not lose weight if you don't give up junk food.

DECREASED SOCIAL SKILLS

It all ties in with the areas above (e.g. lethargy and confidence), in that you are likely to feel as though you cannot be bothered to socialise with your friends or make any effort with women. This decrease in the ability to socialise stretches across the spectrum of your entire life. It will impact on your relationship with your partner, potential partner, family and friends and it may even hold you back in your ambition to progress within your career. A healthy mind is proportional to what you decide to put in your body.

ETHICAL AND MORALISTIC COMPROMISE

Carnivores have an uncanny ability of switching off their conscience when it comes to eating meat and men are probably the guiltier sex. In Chapter 6 I will heighten your level of knowledge and understanding towards the involvement of getting your favourite meats onto your plate, which will enable you to make a more informed decision on the type of diet you choose to follow in the future. I will let you think about this for starters: farming animals for food causes forty percent more green house gas emissions than cars.

EVEN YOUR LOVE LIFE IS AFFECTED

This is where all of the above factors culminate together to leave you lacking in confidence, overweight and de-energised with no self-esteem. No doubt you can see where this is all leading now? That's right - a definite inability to communicate with the opposite sex and attract the right partner. Ninety percent of dieters regain the weight they lose in less than a year. Adapting a diet plan and sticking with it is one thing, but having to maintain the weight loss by following the same plan for life is quite another. If you can't make it for life, you will end up feeling disparaged and inconsequential in terms of the choices you make. The effects on those near and dear will be prevalent and you will continue to be a victim of your cravings. I don't need to stipulate where this will lead but I can assure you one thing. It won't be a healthy love life.

NOW IT REALLY IS TIME FOR A CHANGE!

It's got to be time for you to say - no more! You can either go through the rest of your life living in a relentless haze or you can take the very first step to a more positive future, one that includes more energy, confidence and attraction!

Take your time to work through the remaining chapters of Nutrition, where you will be introduced to the fundamentals of the optimum diet in a stage-by-stage format. I will concentrate on presenting you with the relevant facts and then leaving you to make an informed decision at the end of it.

WORKING TOWARDS THE OPTIMUM DIET

We're going to work through this section on Nutrition together and familiarise ourselves with the imperative areas of knowledge which will provide you with the building blocks to sustain this diet. This will involve evaluating human nutrition in sufficient depth, so that you have a clear understanding of exactly what you are choosing to put into your body. Moreover, you will be taught exactly why the OMD will be of significant benefit to you in the short and long term.

Crucially, this section on Nutrition is designed to introduce a practical and optimal diet that is proven to provide you with far more energy, positivity and a healthier lifestyle. The knock on effects will be vast and you will start to entertain the reality of becoming healthy, attractive and booming with confidence.

DIET DIARY

For at least one week, please maintain a diet diary of all of the food that you eat. Don't change your eating habits at this stage, as it is imperative you record the exact consequences of the different types of foods you are consuming. My anticipated conclusions will be that you will realise there is a direct link between what you eat and how you feel. Record a score between 1 to 10 for how you have felt in terms of your health and overall state of mind.

MEASURING YOUR LEVELS OF CONFIDENCE

At this stage, I want you to ascertain your confidence levels. Record how confident you feel in the following situations and we will come back to this assessment later.

- Your confidence level at work. (dealing with colleagues and senior stakeholders separately)
- Your level of confidence walking down a busy street.
- Your ability to socialise with others.
- Your general feeling of confidence within yourself. (e.g. your self-esteem).

NUTRITION, CHAPTER 2:
THE TRUTH ABOUT CARBS

Carbohydrates have been under the spotlight ever since The Atkins Diet hit our shelves. Some nutrition experts were in favour of their consumption while others regarded them as contenders for all forms of weight gain. It is therefore essential to get over these misinterpretations and finally conclude what carbs actually do for us. The truth is that men need a larger intake of carbohydrates than women and they will thus play an important role in our diet. But not all carbs are necessary. So we will also distinguish between the ones that are essential for you and those you can disregard.

Carbohydrates are vital for our body but the way they have been portrayed has led us to believe that they are bad for us. Eating a low carb diet only helps with temporary weight loss and can lead to some serious health problems. They are also not the real culprits behind weight gain. It is the proteins and fats that you take along with them that are the real cause for your putting on those extra pounds.

Let me introduce you to some of the true facts about carbohydrates:

- Carbohydrates make up one of the three essential macronutrients, the other two being proteins and fats, which are vital for a healthy body.
- Carbohydrates are the greatest source of energy production and are vital for various functions of the body. They provide energy to the muscles, nervous system and specifically the brain, which relies completely on carbohydrates to pump in the glucose, which is essential for its functioning.
- During the process of digestion the carbohydrates are broken up

into glucose molecules, before they are allowed to get into the bloodstream, with the help of insulin. These glucose molecules travel to the cells and work as fuel to help aid the functions of various organs.

- The most important source of carbohydrates are foods derived from plants such as vegetables, fruits, cereals, wholegrain and beans; while other sources include dairy products, sugar, molasses, corn syrup and honey.

To understand carbohydrates better we need to absorb some more detail about the kinds of carbohydrates available, where they are obtained from and what effects they have on the body. Carbohydrates are categorised into three different types – Simple carbohydrates, complex carbohydrates and fibre. They can be distinguished into these three categories depending on their molecular structure.

Simple carbohydrates (monosaccharides) break into glucose very quickly. These carbs generally consist of one or two units of sugar contained in a single molecule. Some simple carbs; such as honey, molasses, syrup, jam and soft drinks to name a few, are not the best types of carbs to include in your diet because they can cause an increase in your glucose and insulin levels. These then trigger off hunger pangs leading to overeating, resulting in fat accumulation. Simple carbs can be available through natural food sources too and it should be noted that not all simple carbs are bad for you.

There are several simple carbs, which provide other useful nutrients, such as fruits and certain vegetables. These provide a healthy source of essential vitamins, minerals, fibre and water.

Complex carbohydrates (polysaccharides) take more time to digest and hence break into glucose gradually, influencing only a slight increase in insulin levels. They also help to keep the stomach full so that an unnecessary craving for food does not occur, thereby allowing low accumulation of fat. Complex carbs also known as starch, commonly consist of thousands of complex sugar molecules conjoined together. Some of the vegetables and leguminous foods such as lentils, beans, soybeans, peas and whole grains are a great source of minerals, vitamins, fibre as well as protein, on top of the carbohydrates they supply.

Fibre (polysaccharide) is the third and final form of carbohydrate. These are hard to break into smaller molecules and hence cannot be absorbed by the body. Although fibre does not play any role in the production of energy, it helps in digestion, bowel movement, reduces heart problems, maintains sugar levels and is equally essential for you.

We have just seen the significance of carbohydrates in our diet, how they are available to us and which ones are the best for consumption. If your diet lacks enough carbohydrates, the body will begin to look for other energy sources. An example could be from your muscles. What are the consequences?

How A Low Carb Consumption Can Be Disruptive

When your body fails to get the required carbohydrates, it begins using the energy available from proteins. This in turn deactivates the initial functions of proteins, which include creating new cells and tissues, antibodies, hormones, enzymes and regulating the flow of fluids.

If the body lacks carbohydrates it makes it difficult for fats to burn normally. Carbohydrates in combination with fats break down to produce energy. But without the presence of carbohydrates, fats are unable to break down normally. This results in a substance called ketones being produced that embeds itself in the urine and blood causing ketosis, an anomalous state that brings in a loss of appetite.

- You feel extremely lethargic, listless and do not feel up to any physical exercise.
- The lack of fibre can cause constipation.
- A continued low carb or no carb diet can lead to severe health conditions such as cancers, kidney stones, and accumulation of uric acid crystals in the blood causing gout.
- A high protein diet, especially one that you get through meat, can lead to heart problems and a lack of calcium causing osteoporosis.

I think by now I've been successful in driving home the fact that carbohydrates are important for us and need to be included in our daily dietary intake. Let's now take a look through your daily carbohydrate requirements and the sources from where they can be derived.

DAILY CARBOHYDRATE REQUIREMENTS AND THE AVAILABLE SOURCES:

Like all macronutrients, carbohydrates need to be taken in the right amounts in your daily diet. 55 to 60 percent of the calories should come from carbohydrates alone. The daily intake of carbohydrates for the average active male is around 2,550 calories. The recommended amount of 130g of carbohydrates can produce the required quantity of glucose that the brain needs each day. It is also advised that you must not take more than 25 percent of carbohydrates that are derived from simple carbs.

Not all men have the same calorie requirements. The amount of exercise you subject your body to should be considered as the deciding factor in terms of calorie intake. For example; an athlete would probably need to take in anywhere between 1,400 to 2,800 calories from carbohydrates alone, which is much more than the average man would consume. Why would an athlete require so much more in carbohydrates?

- Boost their calorific requirements.
- Improve the storage of glycogen. (energy stored in the muscles that have to be replenished after a stressful workout)
- Enable muscle revival after strenuous physical exercises.
- Offer a good source of energy for endurance.
- Maintain glucose levels in between meals.

So if you are into strenuous exercise, you must make sure that your diet contains an adequate measure of carbohydrates.

You need to consume carbs in the right amount and from the right sources. As I discussed earlier; simple carbs such as sugars should be taken in very low quantities because they only temporarily satisfy your hunger and in fact trigger off cravings for more. They also cause the insulin levels to shoot up and remain there for several hours, thereby exposing your body to an excessive fat accumulation. Simple carbs that you should include in your diet are fructose, available through fruits. These are better options as compared to jams, chocolates, sweets etc.

Complex carbohydrates are considered far better, as they digest slowly and provide energy for a longer period of time. Potatoes, rice, oats, pasta, most vegetables and some fruits make up complex carbohydrates and must be included in your diet. Wholegrains are also regarded as a highly nutritious source of carbohydrates, for example, brown rice, millet, sorghum and the most recent wonder grain - quinoa. They will keep you full for longer and prevent further food cravings.

Carbohydrates can also be responsible for mood swings. When you fail to take carbohydrates, your brain ceases to organise the production of serotonin. Serotonin is a substance produced in the brain that stimulates the mood and also reduces hunger pangs. Without it, even a large portion of food, minus the carbs, will make you feel as if you are still starving. Men have a greater amount of serotonin than women and can control those hunger urges with more ease.

You can experience different moods with various food intakes. For instance, if you consume a protein rich diet, you are more likely to be short-tempered or agitated. Foods containing a lot of fats will bring about lethargy. Thus a proper intake of carbohydrates will produce the right amount of serotonin, which in turn will regulate the amount of food you consume by registering with your brain, that your stomach is full. You will neither overeat nor be in a bad mood. Well, not as a result of your diet anyway.

How Can You Tell When You Are Eating A Carbohydrate Enriched Diet?

Most foods that you buy at your local supermarket have the nutrient contents mentioned on the reverse of the package. See which foods provide you the prescribed amounts of nutrients and include that in your shopping basket. Make sure the carbs in the basket do not add up from all the junk foods. Select different varieties of fruits and vegetables, legumes, cereals, starches and beans. Work out how many calories these foods will give you in a day and also how many calories your body type needs.

Remember, as men we require more carbohydrates than women. This is because of our more muscular build, which in turn requires more energy reserves.

ACTIONS

Some Must Haves In Your Diet

How do you decide what to include or exclude with your daily meals to ensure that you are taking in the right amount of carbs? Chalk out all the foods that are carbohydrate rich and then divide them into the three categories. You know by now that your diet must contain more complex carbohydrates and fibre and a small amount of simple carbohydrates. Let's work out a simple meal plan for a day:

- About two to four servings of fruits
- Between three to five servings of vegetables
- Six to eleven servings of food such as brown rice, wholegrain breads, cereals, pasta etc, which come under complex carbohydrates
- One to two servings of fibre such as, beans, peas, legumes

You could include very small portions of white rice, fried vegetables, refined flour products and fruit juice. What you must exclude are foods that contain sugary carbohydrates such as doughnuts, cakes, pastries, fizzy drinks, chips, sweets, sugar, jam, honey and all those foodstuffs that only taste sweet.

Stop Snacking On The Wrong Types Of Foods

If you are a constant snacker, think twice before you open the kitchen cupboard to fish out a bar of chocolate, slice of cake or a bag of crisps. Remember it's not your body that needs these constant sugary snacks; it's your brain that has stopped producing serotonin and is urging you to indulge yourself. Be practical, think clearly, work out a diet chart of what you have been eating until today and see where you have been going wrong. Give your body what it requires and see what it gives you in return; a perfectly healthy body and a happier, more cheerful you.

In the previous chapter we mentioned using a diet diary. It might be a very good idea to record all of your findings from the two suggested activities above. If you don't record how the different types of foods affect you, you are not going to be able to spot trends and you will definitely forget how you felt one week later. So use the diet diary to honestly acknowledge the way in which you're affected by the foods you eat. This way you can start to recognise the extreme effects on your mind and body. Something you were unaware of up until now.

GOOD CARBOHYDRATES FOR YOUR SHOPPING LIST

Make sure you include the following carbohydrates in your shopping list.

CARBOHYDRATE SHOPPING (TICK OFF)

- Bran
- Wheatgerm
- Barley
- Maize
- Buckwheat
- Cornmeal
- Oatmeal
- Brown Pasta
- Macaroni
- Spaghetti
- Brown rice
- Potatoes
- Root Vegetables
- Wholemeal Breads
- Granary Bread
- Brown Bread

- Pita Bread
- Bagel
- Wholegrain Cereals
- High Fibre Cereals
- Porridge Oats
- All Bran
- Weetabix
- Shredded Wheat
- Ryvita Crispbread
- Muesli
- Cassava
- Corn
- Yam
- Oatcakes
- Peas
- Beans
- Lentils

Nutrition, Chapter 3:
The Truth About Proteins

In Chapter 3, I provide you with a very gentle introduction to the importance of protein and how this macronutrient is used for the essential maintenance of the body. We're going to take the extent of this knowledge much further and discuss the different types of food items where protein can be obtained.

Cell Production And General Body Maintenance

Crucially, every single living organism on this planet, from plant species to animal, is made up of proteins, which perform different roles. In short, our body would not survive if it were not for this essential nutrient. That is why it is so important for you to ensure that you consume a sufficient supply of protein in your diet.

When food enters our gastrointestinal tract, clever little enzymes work hard to break it down and remove the essential proteins inside. Different enzymes work for different types of macronutrients needed in the body. So while one type deals with proteins, separate enzymes break down carbohydrates and fats. This is one of the main reasons why you have heard 'eating one type of food at a time' is best. Once the enzymes have broken down the food and removed the amino acids, they are distributed to areas of the body where there is a need for them.

When you refrain from consuming enough protein in your diet, your body is not provided with essential building materials to keep you fit and healthy. However, having said that, you must make sure that you do not consume too much. As a guide, the following figures provide the estimated average requirement per day (in grams) for different adults:

Men (19-50 years of age)= 44g
Men (50 years plus)= 42g

Women (19-50 years of age)=36g
Women (50 years plus)=37g.

Whilst the human body can store fats and excess carbohydrates, it is unable to store excess protein. So aim to get your balance just right.

PROTEIN IS NOT JUST FOUND IN MEAT

There are advocates who believe that the only reliable source of protein is through meat and fish. While there is plenty of protein in these types of food, it's fiction to believe that your sources must consist of animal derived food items.

There are more efficient protein-rich sources of foods, which do not require you to eat copious amounts of saturated fats at the same time. Animal derived sources of protein are notoriously high in fat content. If this is your primary source of protein, you are asking for trouble. Saturated fat is found to increase cholesterol production by the body. It also decreases insulin sensitivity, which causes the body to store food more often as fat.

Saturated fats and trans-fatty acids lead to a plaque residue in the arteries around the heart. Over time, this can lead to coronary heart disease and premature death. Coronary heart disease is the most common cause of death in the UK and it is suspected that large amounts of meats, prevalent in our diet, are to blame.

There are plenty of alternatives to meat derived products that can ensure that you are not risking the possibility of consuming too much fat at the same time and risking your health.

HIGH-PROTEIN ALTERNATIVES

Protein can be just as prevalent in plant-derived foods as their animal counterparts. In fact, there are certain types of plant foods that contain significantly higher protein levels. The best way of assessing the level of protein, within a particular food item, is to analyse the overall mass that is devoted to the Protein.

Let's take a look at this mass for the most popular types of meat and fish products:

- Lean bacon= 20%
- Lean beef= 20%
- Cod= 17%
- Herring= 17%
- Eggs= 12%
- Milk= 3%
- Butter= less than 1%

Both cod and herring score a rather mediocre 17% each. Eggs tend to be the biggest shocker, as it is assumed they are one of our best sources of protein. However, their overall protein content is a mere 12%. Take a look at the list of plant-derived foods below:

- Low fat Soya flour= 45%
- Peanuts= 24%
- Wholemeal bread= 9%
- White bread= 8%
- Rice= 7%
- Peas= 6%
- Potatoes= 2%

Even apples and bananas contain about 1% protein and are therefore a reliable source. Potatoes are always associated with starchy carbohydrates (as we discussed earlier), but still have a 2% protein mass.

It's the food items that are at the top of the list that are the most eye-catching. Look at low fat Soya flour as an example; where nearly half of its overall mass is devoted to protein. No animal-derived food source gets close to this.

THE ULTIMATE SOURCES OF PROTEIN

It has long been recognised that Soya and wholemeal bread are fantastic sources of protein. In the UK we spend around £1.2 billion on pre-sliced, pre-packaged bread each year and if bread protein is combined with certain other plant foods, it will produce a complete protein source that your body requires. As long as your diet is varied and contains vegetables, beans, grains, nuts, and seeds, you will be getting enough protein.

Yes, even vegetables have a moderate level of it. This is yet another reason why you should include 5 portions of fruit and vegetables in your diet every day. Make sure you vary these portions too. It might be a good idea to eat two pieces of fruit and leave the other three portions for a selection of different vegetables.

As a staple, consider substituting the potato with rice. With there being a 5% difference in the protein content between the two, this would obviously increase your intake.

ACTIONS

In this chapter we have discussed the importance of protein to the body. There are literally thousands of uses for protein with cell renewal being the most important. Plant-derived food sources really can offer the highest levels of protein content. Also, these types of foods tend to be far healthier and less fatty. I want you to start on the following exercises and to try and make them habits.

Reading Product Nutrition Labels

Do this at home or when you are on your next shop. What I want you to be looking at specifically here is the amount of saturated fat you find with products that are high in protein (animal-derived). Then compare these with plant-derived high protein foods.

You will notice that plant-derived food items will tend to be higher in other types of fat content such as monounsaturated and polyunsaturated fats. These types of fats are actually essential to our body and they should never be confused with the potentially damaging saturated fats. We will look at these differences later.

WORKING OUT YOUR DAILY INTAKE OF PROTEIN IN YOUR DIET DIARY

I would like you to work out how much protein you are consuming every day. Simply consult the nutrition labels on products and there should be a protein content for each 100g. Use this to roughly work out how many grams of protein you are consuming. Write this in your food diary.

The average amount of protein that each adult between the ages of 19 to 50 should consume is 44g. Compare this figure with what you have calculated and adjust your intake accordingly.

Good Protein Rich Foods for your Shopping List

Make sure you include the following protein rich foods in your shopping list.

Protein Shopping (Tick Off)

- Tofu
- Alfalfa Seeds
- Artichokes
- Asparagus
- Avocados
- Baked Beans
- Kidney Beans
- Cowpeas
- Soybeans
- Beet Greens
- Beets
- Broccoli
- Cabbage
- Carrots
- Cauliflower
- Corn
- Lentils
- Mushrooms
- Onions
- Peas
- Spinach
- Buckwheat
- Cornmeal

- Quinoa
- Peanut Butter
- Almonds
- Brazil Nuts
- Cashew Nuts
- Peanuts
- Pine Nuts
- Hazelnuts

NUTRITION, CHAPTER 4: THE TRUTH ABOUT FATS

This chapter will reveal that it is vital for men to consume a certain amount of fat each day. Moreover, we will be looking at the different variants of fats to highlight how some dietary choices can be affecting your long-term health levels and possibly reducing your life expectancy.

PUTTING FAT INTO CONTEXT

The simple fact of the matter is that not all fats are the same. While some types of fats can actually be of significant benefit to your body, others should only be viewed with caution. All individuals require a certain amount of fat to be included in their diet but problems arise when we consume too much of this macronutrient. This will be true even for the better types of fats, as fat is the one type of macronutrient that the body is able to store. This translates into excess weight.

SATURATED FATS AND TRANS-FATTY ACIDS

These types of fats are the ones you need to be careful of. In truth, your body would survive if you eliminated them completely from the diet. The fat you would require to stay alive would be obtained through monounsaturated and polyunsaturated fats. The creation of trans fat occurs when liquid oils solidify by partial hydrogenation, a process that stretches food shelf life and changes "safe" unsaturated fat into dangerous fat. Trans fats are concentrated in margarine, doughnuts, crackers, cookies, chips, cakes, pies, some breads and foods fried in hydrogenated fat.

Saturated fat and trans-fatty acids are a real problem for the body. They provide little, if any, actual nutritional benefit to our gastrointestinal system. This system struggles to move all of this food through its entire length (literally tens of feet long) and often it will be unsuccessful in eradicating all of the material from the body. In turn, this leaves behind a build-up within the intestines, which is thought to be a leading cause of stomach and other gastrointestinal cancers.

As this material festers inside of us, it ferments and gives off gas, which we then experience as excess bloating and flatulence. On a chemical level (which is something we are going to consider at a basic level with all fats), saturated fats consist of a more basic structure than the monounsaturated and polyunsaturated fats. This means that the material that does make it through the gastrointestinal system will tend to do so more quickly than other types of fats, with the resulting faeces likely to be of a diarrhoeic nature.

I cannot emphasize enough how bad these types of fats are for you. Heart disease, clogged arteries, and high cholesterol are the main health risks, but some studies indicate trans fats as triggers for diabetes and various forms of cancer as well.

THE GOOD FATS

Monounsaturated and polyunsaturated fats are what you should be aiming for in your diet. These fats will actually help lower your cholesterol and in turn put you at a lower risk for heart disease.

The chemical make-up of these types of fats means that they are of far more use to the body. They contain longer and more complicated shaped chains of fatty acids, which means they take longer to be digested through the gastrointestinal system. The enzymes that are used to breakdown fats in the body are more likely to make use of the fatty acids from monounsaturated and polyunsaturated fats, compared with the saturates we have just been looking at.

The Best Types Of Foods That Contain Monounsaturated And Polyunsaturated Fat

Let's start with the worst types of foods first. These are the ones that are known to be high in saturated fats and are nearly always derived from animals. Butter, certain types of hard margarine, palm oil and animal fat (e.g. lard) should be avoided. Butter could not be any worse for your health as it contains numerous different types of saturated fats. If you use it on a regular basis - stop now! It really is just like smearing a massive heart attack all over your toast!

As a general rule of thumb, the harder and more solid the type of fat, the worse it is for you. Look out for brands of margarine that are labelled "trans-fat-free." If you can't find one, choose a liquid or semi-soft margarine over the stick variety.

Olive oil and sunflower oil are an excellent substitute for animal and vegetable oils. They are high in essential monounsaturated fats and other antioxidative substances. Olive oil is also very well tolerated by the stomach. In fact, olive oil's protective function has a beneficial effect on ulcers and gastritis. It also activates the secretion of bile and pancreatic hormones much more naturally than prescribed drugs. Consequently, it lowers the incidence of gallstone formation.

There are many plant (e.g. vegetables) foods that are known to be high in polyunsaturated fats. Nuts and seeds are high in this regard and you should aim to consume as many omega 3 and omega 6's as possible. Both of these fatty acid chains are essential in our diet and play a crucial role in brain function and development. They are also necessary for stimulating skin and hair growth, maintaining bone health and regulating metabolism.

A More Informed You= A Healthier You

Okay, so we all know that the things that are worst for us often tend to taste the best, but you can actively re-educate your palette? Your palette has become accustomed to junk food, which is high in saturated fats and trans-fatty acids. But remember the very first time you had a beer? Not tasty. My point is simple. You can create healthy habits, which will bring as much pleasure to your palette as the negative alternatives.

Here are the average daily amounts of saturated fats that are considered to be acceptable for men and women respectively in the UK:

Men= 30g
Women= 20g

When you sit down and start to do the maths, you will see that it is very easy to exceed this 30g level if you have a real penchant for junk food and fatty treats. Maintaining a healthy balance of fat intake is going to be crucial for you if you want to shed weight and remain healthy.

Actions

Measuring Your Daily Intake Of Saturated Fat

Let's take a closer look at the average amount of saturated fat you are consuming each day. To do this; look at the nutrition labels on the products that you consume. These will always tell you how much saturated fat there is in every 100g of applicable product. Work out how much you are consuming each day. If your figure is over the 30g limit - red lights, sirens and plenty of alarm bells should be sounding.

The Solid Fat Theory

I want you to examine fatty products. Look at the products, which contain high levels of saturated fats and you will notice that they tend to be in a more solid form at room temperature. This is especially true for different types of margarines. Conversely, softer spreads tend to have higher levels of the best types of fats. Research this next time you are grocery shopping.

LIST OF FOODS THAT CONTAIN MONOUNSATURATED AND POLYUNSATURATED FATS FOR YOUR SHOPPING LIST

Make sure you include the following Monounsaturated and Polyunsaturated fat rich foods in your shopping list.

Good Fats Shopping (Tick Off)

- Olive Oil
- Peanut Oil
- Canola Oil
- Avocados
- Nuts
- Seeds
- Safflower Oil
- Sunflower Oil
- Soy Oil
- Flaxseeds
- Flax Oil
- Walnuts

NUTRITION, CHAPTER 5:
THE TRUTH ABOUT MICRONUTRIENTS
AND DAIRY

To complete your basic understanding of all of the different types of nutrients we are going to delve into the fundamental details of micronutrients. This will be split into vitamins and minerals. We will take a closer look at how insufficient quantities of these micronutrients can lead to serious illnesses. We will then focus on the impact dairy products have in our lives and on our health. At this stage it is a good idea to start to contemplate exactly what we have in common with four legged ruminants that eat grass in a field.

People are more likely to neglect the intake of adequate amounts of micronutrients, than they would with the macronutrients. Their education of protein, fats and carbohydrates tends to extend a little further than vitamins and minerals. But it is important to understand that our bodies need them in small amounts, to support the chemical reactions our cells need to survive. They affect digestion, the nervous system, thinking and various other body processes.

VITAMINS

Vitamins are either fat-soluble or water-soluble. In the first instance, the body is able to maintain and store the vitamins. It is not, however, able to store water soluble vitamins and thus you need to ensure that you consume regular and sufficient supplies.

WATER SOLUBLE VITAMINS

The best known micronutrient of them all is vitamin C. It is one of the easiest vitamins to lose in our body. The best source of vitamin C comes from blackcurrants and oranges, but you will find this vitamin present in many other types of fruit, vegetables and even potatoes. It is used for the development of tendons, cartilage, bones and in the skin. It is also essential in assisting the body with the absorption of iron for red blood cell creation.

You've probably all heard of the stories of sailors developing scurvy on long ship voyages hundreds of years ago, which was caused by the lack of access to fresh fruits and vegetables containing Vitamin C.

The other major water-soluble vitamins are referred to as vitamin B complex. These vitamins are easily lost in the body and you will need to take regular supplies. A lack of vitamin B can cause dermatitis, severe headaches, aching muscles as well as a number of neurological problems. Vitamin H (Biotin) is also included and if you are looking to prevent baldness, it is essential your body gets' enough of this.

FAT SOLUBLE VITAMINS

Vitamins A, E and K are all types of fat-soluble vitamins, which need to be included in your diet. Unlike the water-soluble vitamins, these can be stored in the body but it is essential that you get the balance just right. Vitamin A can be toxic if it is consumed in excess. There are stories of arctic explorers who have been killed by eating polar bear liver in large quantities (where vitamin A is abundant), as they were unaware of its dangers.

Only very small quantities of vitamins are required on a daily basis and it is not that difficult to obtain sufficient levels. Breakfast cereals, fortified non-dairy margarines, plant oils, nuts, seeds and certain green leafy vegetables all provide excellent sources of these fat soluble vitamins.

ESSENTIAL MINERALS

When we looked at the importance of protein to the body, we saw how this macronutrient was essential in providing the raw materials for the renewal and upkeep of the body. Well, protein only really provides part of these raw materials and building blocks. Many other ingredients are also required for cells to function and other vital processes to occur. Even communication between cells requires a sufficient intake of certain micronutrients. Omitting one miniscule micronutrient from your diet can have dire results.

Let's take a look at the types of minerals that are imperative for our health:

CALCIUM

It is the major component of bones and teeth and is essential for growth. Calcium is also in demand by certain enzymes in the body and provides the necessary ingredients for the process of blood clotting to transpire. If you were to weigh the amount of micronutrients that are present within the body, you're likely to find that calcium has the most, with around 1000g being present within the average adult individual.

It is a myth to think that calcium can only be obtained from dairy products. Yes, there is a lot of calcium in milk, cheese etc, but dark greens, legumes, dried fruits, nuts and seeds, soy, and fortified cereals and juices are all excellent sources of calcium. These plant-based sources are thought by many to be superior to dairy, because they are also excellent sources of antioxidants, fibre, folic acid, complex carbohydrates, iron and other important vitamins and minerals which you won't find in milk products. Also, the high protein content in dairy products makes our urine acidic, prompting the body to draw calcium, an alkaline mineral, from the bones.

MAGNESIUM

Magnesium is present inside cells and like calcium; it is required by enzymes for bone growth and development. A lack of magnesium can cause fatigue, muscle spasms, confusion and an irregular heartbeat. Again, you do not need to turn your attention to dairy products for your supply of this mineral, as sufficient amounts can be obtained from bread, cereals, potatoes and other vegetables.

PHOSPHORUS

Approximately 85% of the body's phosphorus is found in bone and it is essential for the creation of DNA in our bodies. If you do not get a sufficient supply of phosphorus, it is likely to impact on the cells' ability to duplicate in the body. Phosphorus also helps to maintain normal acid-base balance (pH) by acting as one of the body's most important buffers. Bread, cereals and nuts provide a source of phosphorus. Inadequate phosphorus intake can result in a loss of appetite, anaemia, muscle weakness, bone pain, rickets (in children), osteomalacia (in adults), increased susceptibility to infection, numbness and tingling extremities as well as difficulty in walking.

POTASSIUM

This micronutrient is essential for the conduction of nerve impulses. A deficiency of potassium can trigger muscle weakness, nausea, vomiting and diarrhoea. You will find that potassium is quite widely available through vegetables, fruit and fruit juice drinks. Bananas also contain high levels of this mineral.

IRON

Interestingly, females require a higher amount of iron than men. This is because women use up reserves of iron in their menstrual cycles and it is much more common for females to suffer from anaemia (lack of iron), than it is for men. This mineral is imperative for the creation of haemoglobin in red blood cells. Non-dairy suggestions for sources of this mineral include: bread, flour, potatoes and vegetables.

ZINC

Zinc is an essential item required by our immune system to stay healthy and function properly. It is used in combating problems on the skin, like boils or acne. Zinc is also used for muscle growth. This Micronutrient can be obtained from bread, cereal products, peanuts and pulses.

The list above provides you with some of the examples of the most commonly known and vital micronutrients that we need to include in our diet. There are many others and these range from copper right through to molybdenum. Ultimately, the necessary processes that occur within the body cannot be maintained if we do not eat right.

THE TRUTH ABOUT DAIRY

If there is one thing that is guaranteed to get my back up, it's the dairy industry. The mindset that has been bestowed upon us from an early age, about milk being so good for us, is completely false. What's more, it seems that they have Government backing due to the financial repercussions that would be involved if the industry were to collapse.

With genetic manipulation and intensive production technologies, it is common for modern dairy cows to produce 100 pounds of milk a day, 10 times more than they would produce in nature. To keep milk production as high as possible, farmers artificially inseminate cows every year. Growth hormones and unnatural milking schedules cause dairy cows' udders to become painful and so heavy that they sometimes drag on the ground, resulting in frequent infections and overuse of antibiotics. Cows, like all mammals, make milk to feed their own babies and not humans.

It also takes a great deal of grain and other foodstuffs cycled through cows to produce a small amount of milk. Not only is milk a waste of energy and water, but the production of milk is also a disastrous source of water pollution. A dairy cow produces 120 pounds of waste every day, with no toilets, sewers, or treatment plants. You can only begin to imagine the disastrous effects.

Children lose their taste for a mother's milk for good reason. Milk is designed specifically by a mammal mother's body to nourish her babies until they can eat solid food. At this time, it is no longer required for survival. Humans are the only animals in nature who continue "nursing" (albeit with a switch from human to cow's milk) after this period.

Scientific evidence most certainly exists to prove that animal milk is not good for us and it goes without saying that these liquids have never been intended for human consumption. Dairy foods are linked to all sorts of problems, including obesity, heart disease and cancer. They are also likely to be contaminated with antibiotics, hormones and other chemicals such as dioxin, one of the most toxic substances in the world.

Our gastrointestinal systems find milk and dairy products to be totally alien. They struggle to digest these ingredients and this is one of the reasons why dairy products are a leading contributing factor towards bloating and Irritable Bowel Syndrome (IBS).

ELIMINATING DAIRY PRODUCTS FROM YOUR DIET

First and foremost you need to get the notion out of your head that dairy products are a wonderful addition to your diet. They contain no fibre or complex carbohydrates and are laden with saturated fat and cholesterol. Thus, we need to identify other food sources that can provide us with the nutrients that dairy does, without the negative side effects.

Such alternatives really do exist. Soya milk is an ideal alternative to cow's milk. It contains vegetable proteins, which results in less calcium loss through the kidneys. It also has no lactose. 70% of the world's population is lactose intolerant. Soy protein is also beneficial in reducing cholesterol and it is proven to do far less damage to our gastrointestinal system. In a nutshell, it contains more essential nutrients than dairy.

When we took a look at the minerals above, you noticed that all of the essential nutrients required by the body can be obtained through non-meat and non-dairy alternatives. Moreover, these sources are much healthier options for us as their overall fat content is miniscule. This is especially true for the worrying saturated fat content. Cereals, vegetables, fruits and their juices, pulses, nuts, starchy carbohydrates (such as potatoes for example), contain exactly what our bodies need in terms of vitamins and minerals. See the complete vitamin and mineral list below.

ACTIONS

We've covered quite a lot of ground in this chapter and there's definitely been quite an appreciable amount of information for you to digest. So, let's consolidate all of this knowledge and start putting it into a little light practice. As there are two main elements here, let's tackle an activity from each.

Finding Out Your Daily Requirements Of Micronutrients

Fortunately supermarkets are tending to bow to pressure and provide detailed information on most of their products with regards to your recommended daily intake of micronutrients. Take a look at your breakfast cereal box and find the names of all the vitamins and minerals as well as the recommended daily amount beside each one. Most of these amounts are written in thousandths and even millionths of a gram. The product will usually state how much of the vitamin or mineral is being consumed within every portion (for breakfast cereals this is usually per 30g portion). Write down all the essential vitamins and minerals you require, with our cheat sheet, and which meals will provide you with the necessary intake.

Monitoring The Effects Of Dairy On Your Health

I want you to monitor the way you feel after you've consumed dairy products. Pay particular attention to the feeling of excess bloating. You can write this down in your diet diary. Remember, the best way to find out if something is good for you or not, is to listen to your body. Some of the effects of lactose intolerance can include abdominal pain, bloating, flatulence, diarrhoea, vomiting, nausea and severe weight loss.

VITAMIN AND MINERAL CHEAT SHEET

Nutrient	Info	Fruit Source	Vegetable Source	Nut Source
Vitamin A	Helps cell reproduction	Tomatoes, Watermelon, Peaches, Oranges, Blackberries	Sweet potato, Kale Carrots, Spinach, Avocado, Broccoli Peas, Asparagus Squash - summer Green Pepper	Pistachios Chestnuts Pumpkin Seeds Pecans, Pine Nuts/Pignolias Sunflower Seeds Almonds Filberts/Hazel nuts
Vitamin B1 (Thiamine)	Important for the production of energy	Watermelon	Peas, Avocados	
Vitamin B5	Important for metabolism of food	Oranges, bananas	Avocado, Sweet potato Potatoes, Corn, Lima Beans, Squash, Artichoke, Mushrooms Broccoli, Cauliflower Carrots	
Vitamin B6	Important for the creation of antibodies	Bananas, Watermelon	Avocado, Peas Potatoes, Carrots	
Vitamin B9	Important in producing red blood cells and components of the nervous system	Kiwi Blackberries Tomatoes Orange, Strawberry Bananas	Lima Beans, Asparagus Avocado, Peas Artichoke, Spinach Broccoli,	Peanuts Sunflower Seeds Chestnuts Walnuts Pine

		Cantaloupe	Squash Corn, Sweet potato Kale, Potatoes Carrots, Onions Green Pepper	Nuts/Pignolias Filberts/Hazel nuts Pistachios Almonds Cashews Brazil Nuts Pecans Macadamias Pumpkin Seeds
Vitamin C	Important Antioxidant	Kiwi Strawberry Orange Blackberries Cantaloupe Watermelon Tomatoes Lime, Peach Bananas, Apples Lemon, Grapes	Artichoke, Asparagus Avocado, Broccoli Carrots, Cauliflower Corn, Cucumber Green Pepper	
Vitamin D	Promotes absorption of calcium and magnesium		Mushrooms	
Vitamin E	Important antioxidant	Blackberries Bananas Apples Kiwi		Almonds Sunflower Seeds Pine Nuts/Pignolias Peanuts Brazil Nuts
Vitamin K	Critical for blood clotting	Spinach, broccoli, kale	Pine Nuts, Cashews, Chestnuts, Hazelnuts	

Calcium	Eases Insomnia and helps regulate the passage of nutrients through cell walls.	Oranges, Blackberries, Kiwi, Tomatoes, lime, strawberry, lemon, grapes, apples, bananas, peach	Artichoke, peas, squash, broccoli, lima beans, spinach, carrots, avocado, asparagus	Almonds, Brazil nuts, peanuts, walnuts, chestnuts, macadamias, peanuts, sunflower seeds, pumpkin seeds, cashews
Copper	Involved in absorption, storage and metabolism of iron and the formation of red blood cells.	Kiwi, apples, bananas, blackberries, grapes, lemon, lime, orange, peach, strawberry, tomatoes	Artichoke, avocado, broccoli, carrots, cauliflower, corn, cucumber, green peppers, kale, lima beans, mushrooms, onions, peas, potatoes, spinach, squash, sweet potato	Most nuts have traces of copper in them
Iodine	Helps regulate energy production and body weight.	Fruits grown in iodine rich soils contain iodine.	Vegetables grown in iodine rich soils contain iodine.	Nuts grown in iodine rich soils contain iodine.
Iron	Iron deficiency affects the immune system and can cause weakness and fatigue.	Blackberries, kiwi, strawberry, tomatoes, bananas, grapes	Lima beans, peas, avocado, kale, spinach, broccoli, squash, potatoes, corn, carrots, mushrooms	Most nuts have traces of iron in them.

Magnesium	Needed for cell generation, relaxing nerves and muscles, clotting blood and in energy production.	Kiwi, bananas, tomatoes, blackberries, strawberry, orange	Avocado, artichoke, peas, squash, potatoes, corn, spinach, kale, broccoli, sweet potato	Brazil nuts, cashews, almonds, pumpkin seeds, pine, peanuts, walnuts, macadamias, sunflower seeds, pecans, pistachios, chestnuts, hazelnuts
Phosphorus	Necessary for the formation of bones, teeth and nerve cells.	Kiwi, tomatoes, blackberries, bananas, strawberry, orange, peach, lime	Lima beans, peas, artichoke, avocado, corn, potatoes, asparagus, broccoli, mushrooms, sweet potato	Sunflower seeds, Brazil nuts, cashews, pine, pistachios, almonds, peanuts, walnuts, chestnuts, pecans, pumpkin seeds
Potassium	Essential for growth and maintenance of the body.	Bananas, tomatoes, blackberries, strawberry, orange, peach, grapes, apples, lemon, lime	Avocado, lima beans, potatoes, peas, squash, sweet potato, broccoli, corn, carrots, spinach, asparagus, green pepper, mushrooms, onions, cauliflower, cucumber	Chestnuts, sunflower seeds, pumpkin seeds, almonds, Brazil nuts, peanuts, cashews, pine, walnuts, pecans, macadamias, hazelnuts

Selenium	Functions as an antioxidant.	Bananas, kiwi, strawberry, blackberries tomatoes, orange, peach, apples, grapes	Lima beans, peas, mushrooms, kale, corn, sweet potato, potatoes, squash, onions, spinach	Brazil nuts, sunflower seeds, cashews, peanuts, walnuts, almonds, chestnuts, pecans
Sodium	Regulates blood pressure	In most fresh fruits.	In most fresh vegetables.	Peanuts, pumpkin seeds, cashews, chestnuts, almonds
Zinc	Important in protein and carbohydrate metabolism as well as growth and vision.	Blackberries, kiwi	Peas, lima beans, squash, potatoes, corn, sweet potato	Pumpkin seeds, pine nuts, cashews, sunflower seeds, pecans, almonds, walnuts

NUTRITION, CHAPTER 6:
MEAT YOUR DEMONS

I am sure you feel that eating meat is the best way to meet your daily requirement of protein. It is true that meat can provide you with a rich source of protein, but are you aware of the dangers it can pose to your health and the environmental effects of farming these animals?

We have always blamed carbohydrates for causing obesity. It is in fact high protein diets and fats that are responsible, with excessive meat in our diet topping the list. Have you ever seen an obese vegetarian? Not only that, but as I mentioned in the previous chapter, the foods that we eat have a direct effect on our moods. Excessive meat consumption is responsible for fits of anger, irritability, crabbiness and bad temper. On top of these unsociable mood swings, there are a number of other health hazards.

ILL EFFECTS OF EATING MEAT

- You are exposed to a series of health problems that include constipation, gout, piles, indigestion, varicose veins, arthritis and appendicitis, heart problems, high blood pressure, colon cancer, diabetes, anaemia, obesity and prostate cancer.
- Meats are high in saturated fats, which increase the blood cholesterol levels, especially LDL Cholesterol, which is a cause of strokes and heart disease.
- It is accountable for the manufacturing of free radicals, which are the most harmful components that can be housed within the body.
- Red meats are accepted as being a contributory factor towards a lower life expectancy.

- Most of the animal breeders and farmers use various medications to keep their animals fit for consumption. Tranquilisers are often used before slaughtering the animal.

You are causing harm to yourself, animals and the environment. Let's take a look at some of the global predicaments that are triggered as a result of meat consumption.

THE MEAT ON YOUR PLATE COULD HAVE FED SEVERAL HUNGRY MOUTHS

Animals reared for their meat are fed with more than 400 million tons of grain each year. Famine-struck nations have more than 500 million people facing food deprivation and the reality of literally starving to death. A United Nations report in 2006 accounted the meat industry to problems with land degradation, climate change, air pollution, water shortage and pollution. An area of rain forest the size of seven football fields is destroyed every minute to make room for grazing cattle. It is grossly inefficient as these animals eat vast quantities of grain while only contributing minor amounts of meat, dairy and eggs in return. About 20 percent of the world's population could be fed with the grain and soybeans fed to U.S. cattle alone.

Giving up meat will not prevent your body from getting the right amount of protein. There are a number of powerful plant proteins like lentils, canned legumes, soybeans, nuts, pumpkin seeds, wholegrain cereals, grainy bread and grains like quinoa. You will also be avoiding saturated fats and lowering blood pressure as well as constipation.

Meat was never destined to become a part of our dietary intake. This is because our body does not have the provision for fully digesting it.

WHY MEAT IS NOT FULLY DIGESTIBLE?

Meat takes long to break down into smaller molecules and never gets fully digested. It requires an excessive oxidation process, which is the burning of oxygen to aid the breaking down of food particles. Oxidation is believed to produce free radicals, which are considered to be a major cause of health problems in our body. Since the digestive process of meat is slow, heavy oxidation takes place and can result in a large accrual of free radicals.

A large amount of toxic waste is left behind after the meat has been digested. These rotten toxins, known as purines, are forced to move down the intestines and release unhealthy bacteria and toxins that create free radicals, until they are slowly expelled from the body. These can lead to foul breath, diarrhoea and other gastrointestinal diseases.

By eating meat we are not only risking our health, but also causing damage to the environment by exhausting its natural resources.

HARMING OUR ENVIRONMENT!

The increasing demand for meat has caused hundreds and thousands of acres of cultivable land to be transformed into farms for cattle. This has led to a large decrease in the cultivation of grains, especially in the European countries and the United States. It is estimated that seventy per cent of land is used for cattle rearing food consumption. This extensive land use has reached a stage where natural reserves, such as the rainforests, are also slowly being cleared away.

Livestock accounts for more than 18 per cent of all greenhouse gases. There is also a massive amount of animal waste that is polluting the earth's water resources. These animals produce 130 times the human excreta every second, which flows into streams and rivers and leads to severe water pollution.

You are also kidding yourself of the pain and suffering these animals have to endure, in the process of getting them reared for consumption. If you think one person does not make a difference understand this. The average person can be responsible for consuming more than 2,000 livestock in a lifetime.

HOW INHUMANE CAN WE GET?

Animals reared for consumption are kept in highly constrictive areas where there is no room for movement. Chickens are de-beaked with hot blades, so they do not peck each other. Pigs' tails are chopped off and their teeth clipped with pliers whilst male cows and pigs are castrated without any pain relief.

THE HORRIFYING TRUTH ABOUT ABATTOIRS

Sheep have had their throats slit before they are stunned, while some regain consciousness during the slaughter. Likewise, cattle are often still conscious through this process. Young calves face castration and de-horning, while most factory farms practice branding. Pigs share the same fate, as they are not fully stunned before they are butchered. There are instances where chickens, ducks etc are thrown into scalding tanks before the blood has drained out of them. In truth, they are confined to tiny filthy warehouses and induced with powerful drugs to enhance their growth. The resulting consequences are their organs and hearts cannot keep up and they end up becoming crippled or enduring heart attacks.

There are a lot of alternatives, which are far more healthy and nutritious than meat. Plants can provide your body's entire requirement for all the essential micro and macronutrients. Studies have actually revealed that people who live on meat-free diets have a longer lifespan than meat eaters.

BETTER ALTERNATIVES THAN MEAT

You can eat whole grains, cereals, beans and nuts, lentils and a whole range of fruits and vegetables. Soy is also a very good alternative to meat and is rich in protein, vitamin B and iron. Also try using tofu, which is derived from soy. There are several other foods available in the market that give you the flavours of meat but are actually derived from plant sources. Quorn products are an excellent example. You will never miss meat in your meals again.

ACTIONS

In this chapter we have uncovered some of the shocking truths about meat consumption. We have seen what it takes to get this meat to your plate and the devastating effects this process is having on our environment.

Put Your Ignorance Completely To One Side

I want you to research meat production and the process of slaughtering animals. There are an abundance of articles on the Internet. It is all about being well informed and making pro-active decisions based on the facts. This is a pretty crucial exercise in terms of your development, so please don't ignore it. I also want you to research meat substitutes that are currently available on the market. Look for brands like Quorn and Linda McCartney.

NUTRITION, CHAPTER 7:
SWEETS ARE NOT SWEET

Sugar has become part of our staple diet and can be found pretty much everywhere. The bottom line is simple. If you are consuming too much of this, you will get more wrinkles, immobility in your joints, dry and brittle nails as well as a number of more serious health related disorders.

WHY SUGAR MAKES YOU FAT

Sugar comes from the juice extract found in cane plants. It is refined which results in all of its vitamins and minerals being destroyed leaving it with absolutely no nutritional value. It has been linked to mental and emotional disorders and an imbalance of neurotransmitters in the brain.

There are essentially two ways that sugar causes fat storage. When you fill your body with more fuel than it needs, it exceeds its storage capacity. This results in excess sugar being converted into fat, returned to the bloodstream and then stored as fat in the stomach, butt and chest. Excess insulin is the second problem. High levels of this hormone are released when consuming too much sugar and this results in the body's fat burning process shutting down so the ingested sugar can be used for energy. The long and short of it is this. If you eat too much sugar, you are going to get fat.

What else?

The raised insulin levels, caused by sugar, depress the immune system, which results in an inability to fight diseases. On top of this, as refined sugar contains no vitamins and minerals the body ends up drawing on its reserves. When these reserves are depleted your body struggles to metabolize cholesterol and fatty acid. In summary, sugar has the following effects:

- Suppresses the immune system
- Upsets the body's mineral balance
- Causes anxiety and depression
- Causes drowsiness
- Elevates harmful cholesterol
- Can cause hypoglycaemia
- Can cause kidney damage
- Promotes tooth decay
- Speeds up the ageing process
- Increased the amount of fat in the liver
- Causes hypertension

HEALTHY ALTERNATIVES TO SUGAR

Good substitutes for refined sugar are maple syrup, brown rice syrup and molasses. Do not substitute sugar with sweeteners containing aspartame, as they are carcinogenic.

ACTIONS

Research Healthy Sugar Alternatives

I want you to do a little research on the Internet. Try finding some other healthy alternatives to sugar and look into some of the long-term side effects that are associated with this substance.

NUTRITION, CHAPTER 8:
STOP IT NOW!

If you are going to concern yourself with nutrition and begin implementing the OMD, there are a few other vices you will need to throw out the window.

STOP SMOKING

I am not going to go into detail about the harmful effects of smoking. If you are not aware of them, quite simply, you have been in a coma for the last 20 years and nothing I can say here is going to open your mind. Just keep this statistic in the top of your head. Smoking decreases your life expectancy by ten years.

STOP GETTING DRUNK

Alcohol raises the level of hydrochloric acid in your stomach and causes havoc with your digestive system. Excess alcohol consumption also results in increased blood-sugar levels, which results in binge eating. If you want to look good, shed fat and become nutritious, you are going to stop getting drunk. There is nothing wrong with the occasional drink, but if you can't control it, give it up.

STOP SODA

Soda has high levels of phosphorous, which increase calcium loss in the body. There are also vast levels of sugar in canned drinks, resulting in you putting on fat. Diet sodas contain aspartame; so don't drink this as an alternative. Research has shown that the combination of this substance with carbohydrates leads to decreased serotonin production. Bottom line – you will drink yourself into a depression. You need to be consuming eight glasses of water per day.

STOP COFFEE

Caffeine can cause headaches, fatigue, anxiety and depression. It basically raises stress hormone levels as well as increasing blood pressure. It is also highly acidic, along with all those decaf options you were thinking of. Acidic foods result in your body producing fat cells. Decaffeinated green tea is absolutely amazing for your body as it contains numerous antioxidants.

ACTIONS

Draw up a list of all your current food and drink habits that you think could potentially be harmful to you. Now, I want you to do some more research on the Internet. Find out if they provide your body with any nutrients and if not, what alternatives are available. Example: Research Fat Free products sold in supermarkets.

NUTRITION, CHAPTER 9:
MORE INFORMED MEN = HEALTHIER MEN

I have highlighted the importance of a fully functioning body in terms of life expectancy and general well being. Changing to the OMD means getting all of these issues into perspective and taking a serious look at the way you live your life. It involves keeping abreast of the facts about nutrition, diet and lifestyle choices.

WHY IT IS CRUCIAL TO GATHER ALL THE FACTS ABOUT HEALTHY OPTIONS

Our bodies are communicating with us all the time. If you have pains in your stomach and you are in and out of the bathroom every half an hour, your body is giving you a distinct message. It is holding up a big red flag and asking you to sort it out. And nine times out of ten this problem has been caused by what you have chosen to put in your mouth.

We have become far too dependent on fast food and products containing synthetic additives and sugar. There is little or no nutritional value in these kinds of meals. Our bodies are in truth being starved and a large part of the problem is being ill informed.

KEEPING OUR BODIES HEALTHY

Okay, let us sum up all the nutritional facts that are important for keeping our bodies healthy. Firstly we need to cut down or eradicate all the foods in our diet that contain saturated fats and trans-fatty acids. These are two of the biggest contributors to developing serious illnesses and diseases. The recommended daily amount of saturated fat a man requires is no more than 30 grams. We need to be wary of foods such as butter, cheese, sugary snacks, crisps, crackers and all meat derived products. Remember that the foods with high levels of saturated fats are usually thicker and come in a more solid form.

Similarly we should increase the amount of polyunsaturated and monounsaturated fats that we have in our diet. Again, we need to control the balance of these micronutrients as even healthy food consumed in excess can have detrimental effects. Use olive oil or sunflower oil for cooking and consuming products such as avocadoes, mixed nuts and seeds. Shop for food products with these nutrients as well as those containing omega 3 and omega 6.

Protein is present in a variety of foods and there are far better sources than meat and the "bad" fat that comes along with it. Some of the foods you currently eat may not be as protein enriched as you are led to believe, particularly eggs and milk. By substituting meat derived products for foodstuffs such as wholemeal bread, rice, potatoes, oatmeal, Soya and bananas, you can give your body all of the protein it needs.

Dairy products can wreak absolute havoc with our digestive systems and can contribute to health problems such as IBS (Irritable Bowel Syndrome). Cutting dairy products from your diet is essential and there are a number of healthier alternatives like Soya.

Vitamins are essential for long term health. Water soluble vitamins, which include Vitamin C, are easy to come by in plant based food. Oranges, mangos and green leafy vegetables are great sources of this micronutrient. Fat soluble vitamins include Vitamin D, Vitamin K and Vitamin E. We only need a small portion of these, as they can be stored in the body.

Finally, we have minerals such as Zinc, Iron, Magnesium, Potassium and Calcium. These contribute to strengthening our bones, teeth, cell regeneration and many other benefits. Fruits and vegetables have a high concentration of these minerals.

BENEFITS OF THE OPTIMUM MALE DIET

One of the purposes of a nutritional lifestyle is the prevention of chronic illnesses and diseases. We are led to believe that merely eating a balanced diet, with moderate fruit and vegetables, is enough to sustain a healthy body. There is much evidence to suggest that this is not the case and that meat is infact counterproductive. It is directly linked to certain cancers and coronary heart disease as a result of the high content of saturated fat. They are also associated with blocked arteries, which can result in other health issues such as impotency and chronic back pain.

Following the Optimum Male Diet will lead to greater health, more energy and confidence as well as some serious weight loss. You will lower your blood pressure, decrease the risk of heart disease, avoid more toxic chemicals and ultimately live longer. You will also be doing the planet a huge favour by preserving natural resources, cutting down on pollution and reducing famine.

ACTIONS

In this chapter we have taken the time to re-evaluate the fundamental aspects of nutrition. This meant going over the main points in connection with the macro and micronutrients and of the types of foods where these can be obtained.

Do Some Deep Thinking

Grab a pen and paper and write down everything you know about leading a healthier lifestyle and why it is important to you. This is essential, as it will draw on your own personal references, which will help you maintain the diet.

Gather More Information

Now that you have all the important facts relating to why The Optimum Male Diet is a healthy option, do some of your own research. There is an abundance of information on the Internet relating to healthier lifestyles. You will also see that facts I have presented to you are completely true.

Nutrition, Chapter 10: Turning Your Life Around With The Optimum Male Diet

There are a number of reasons why you follow the Optimum Male Diet. Personal and social responsibly are prevalent as well as the numerous health benefits that are associated with it. This chapter represents a new chapter in your own life.

Better At Preventing Illness

Changing to the OMD brings nothing but good news on the health front. The amount of men suffering from serious illnesses such as cancer, diabetes and obesity in the UK is on the rise, and it does not look like the trend is going to buck anytime soon. Medical research has established for years that there is a link between the food we eat and these conditions.

The single biggest killer of men in the UK is the heart attack. By eating foods that are lower in cholesterol such as oatmeal, walnuts and plant derived foods with omega 3, you can keep this at an appropriate level. This can be achieved in as little as two weeks and will contribute to boosting your immune system and protecting you from developing other potentially killer diseases.

Cancer is the other significant illness that can be prevented by changing your diet. The most common types that affect men are prostate cancer, lung cancer and bowel cancer. Research has found that once meat and dairy products have been eliminated from a person's diet, they are less susceptible to developing these cancers. When these foodstuffs are eradicated, a person's body will create more and more white blood cells, which are used to fight cancerous cells and prevent them forming. Vegetables such as carrots, cabbage, cauliflower and broccoli are known to have cancer-busting properties. A fruit such as the tomato, which contains a phyto-nutrient called lycopene, has been hailed as one of the best weapons against prostate cancer.

For heart disease and cancer alone, eliminating the meat and dairy elements of your diet can reduce the risk of developing them by as much as 57%. That's an incredible figure. Other illnesses and diseases that can be prevented by include hypertension, diabetes, obesity and osteoarthritis. Even conditions like gallstones or kidney stones are greatly reduced.

A lot of illnesses can be directly linked to each other. For instance, it is thought that those who have blocked arteries because they have a poor diet could have pain located in their back due to the blockage. Lack of blood flow to nerves in the spine causes the pain and can make the discs of the spine deteriorate. So blocked arteries can cause more than just a heart attack.

THAT WEIGHT THING

Obesity is a big problem in the Western world and the bottom line is simple. If you eat the wrong foods and do not exercise enough, you are going to get fat. With all of the information contained in this section, you will be able to work out what your daily intake of nutrients, fats and protein should be. This, in turn, will ensure that you do not overeat and your portion sizes will be balanced. The right nutrients, vitamins, minerals and proteins will be delivered to your body and it will be able to function as nature intended. Eliminating all of the trans-fatty acids and saturated fats that cause you body to deteriorate will shed those unwanted pounds at an incredible rate.

BETTER FOR YOUR MIND

As well as the physical benefits of eating a diet full of nutrients, proteins and good fats, there are mental benefits too. If the brain does not have the right "brain food", problems occur in terms of emotional and mental well being.

When you have a diet that is full of sugar and saturated fats, your levels of confidence will decrease dramatically. Combined with a lack of fibre in the diet, which can result in aggression, you could potentially have an overall feeling of complete negativity. Simply put, eating foods such as nuts, legumes, oatmeal, beans, soy and spinach will lift your mood and help you start to enjoy your life again.

BETTER FOR YOUR APPEARANCE

For starters, do you have a history of baldness or hair loss in your family? Research has indicated that this could be down to the amount of red meat that past generations consumed. Red meat is full of fat, which turns testosterone into a powerful hormone known as DHT. This hormone attacks the hair follicles and basically kills them off. If you were to cut out the meat from your diet, hair loss and baldness could be slowed down to a natural pace. Switching your diet can also help with things such as excess sweating, body odour and halitosis.

If you suffer from acne or dry skin then the intake of a variety of fruit and vegetables can help. Vitamins A & E, Zinc, Selenium and Essential Fatty Acids (known as EFAs) all contribute to your skin being healthy. The best out of the lot is a Vitamin B Complex nutrient known as biotin. This is a fundamental nutrient, which is essential for good nail, skin and hair growth.

ENVIRONMENTAL AND SOCIAL CONCERNS

The amount of land to farm animals that are destined for our plate comprises 70% of farmed land. The land that is being used to grow food for the livestock could be being used to feed thousands of starving people around the world. On top if this, waste products from animals contain ammonia, which lead to acid rain and deforestation.

There is a lot of ignorance in the UK on how animals are slaughtered and it may be a bit more gruesome than you think. Understand that animals do not have a painless death when they are farmed for our consumption.

IT'S NOT AS HARD AS YOU THINK

Even if you're not concerned with land to animal ratios and you'll never encounter a lycopene in your life, the bottom line remains the same. It is ultimately you that is affected by what you put into your body. If you have carrots and potatoes alongside the meat on your plate, then all it takes is one last push to substitute the meat product with a healthier alternative.

ACTIONS

Do Some Forward Thinking

Make a list of all of those aspects of your life that you are looking to change; from losing weight to seeing your grandchildren grow up. Now think about how your current lifestyle is affecting your objectives. With the information you have about the OMD, implement ways in which you could achieve these objectives by making changes today.

Nutrition, Chapter 11: Optimum Male Diet Menu Suggestions

I have provided you with the fundamental information about why the Optimum Male Diet is the right lifestyle choice for you - all that is left is to find out how to make some healthy and attractive meals. Below are some great recipes to get you started on your new and improved lifestyle. These particular recipes are designed to be quick and easy to prepare, taste exquisite and help ease you into this new diet. There is a selection from each of the "three courses", namely starter, main dish and dessert. As you progress and grow more confident, you can advance to cooking more complicated and time consuming dishes with even more exotic ingredients. You will also find an abundance of recipes online, so do some research. I have also listed these recipes with "sugar alternative", *if required,* just in case you have not done any of that research. Google healthy options on the internet, there will be an abundance for you to enjoy.

Carrot and Coriander Soup

Ingredients you will need:

25g margarine (Non Dairy)
500g carrots (sliced)
1 medium potato (chopped)
1 small onion (finely chopped)
1 celery stick (chopped)1 garlic clove (finely chopped)
900ml water
1 tsp. ground coriander
Pinch of sugar alternative (*If required*)
Salt and pepper
2 tbsp. coriander (roughly one man-sized handful!)

Method:

Melt the vegetarian and non-dairy margarine in a pan, add the carrots, potato, onion, celery and garlic and cook gently for 10 minutes.

Add the ground coriander, sugar and water and season to taste. Bring to the boil. Cover and simmer for 1 hour or until the carrots are tender. Cool slightly.

Add the fresh coriander (including the stalks), reserving a few leaves for decoration. Whiz in a food processor until smooth. Add a little more water to loosen, if required, decorate the soup with coriander leaves and serve.

DELICIOUS & NUTRITIOUS NUT ROAST – THE OPTIMUM MALE DIET ALTERNATIVE TO MEATLOAF!

Ingredients you will need:

200g mixed nuts (chopped)
1 stick of celery (chopped)
1 green pepper (chopped)
1 onion (chopped)
1 medium carrot (grated)
50g mushrooms (sliced)
25g wholemeal flour
50g breadcrumbs
125ml vegetable stock
1 tbsp. vegetable oil
1 tbsp. mixed herbs

Note: These quantities will serve 2-3 people.

Method:

Preheat the oven to 190°C/375 °F/Gas mark 5.

Heat the vegetable oil in a pan and add the chopped onions, frying for several minutes. Then add the celery, mushrooms and pepper, frying for 2 minutes. Add the grated carrot and fry for a further minute. Remove the pan from the heat; add the wholemeal flour and stir. Finally, add the vegetable stock, mixed nuts, breadcrumbs, mixed herbs and season with a dash of salt and pepper. Grease the inside of a loaf tin adequately. Pour the mixture into the loaf tin and press down with a spoon. Bake in the oven for approximately 35 minutes.

VEGETABLE CURRY IN A HURRY

Ingredients you will need:

3 medium sized potatoes (chunks)
Half a cauliflower (cleaned and cut into florets)
1 carrot (peeled and sliced)
1 small tin or 300ml of processed peas
1 large onion (chopped)
2 bay leaves
1 tbsp. curry powder
2 tbsp. tomato purée
1 aubergine or green pepper, chopped (optional but tasty)
3 fl. oz of olive oil or sunflower oil

Method:

Heat the oil in a sturdy pan and fry the onion for several minutes. Add the carrot, potato chunks and cauliflower florets. Fry for a further 10 minutes. Next, add the pepper or aubergine (optional). Add the curry powder and a pinch of salt. Allow to cook for 5 to 10 minutes. Sprinkle in the processed peas, and then add the bay leaves and the tomato purée. Cover over with water, bring to the boil and then simmer for approximately 30 minutes. For a further smattering of protein, serve on a bed of rice.

APRICOT AND APPLE CRUMBLE

Ingredients:

3 apples, sliced thinly
2 oz dried apricots, cut into quarters
1 tbsp sugar alternative (*If required*)
4 tbsp water
For the topping you will need:
3 oz of vegetarian and non-dairy margarine
6 oz flour

Method:

Put the apples and apricots into an ovenproof dish. Sprinkle with your sugar alternative and water. Make the crumble by rubbing the margarine into the flour and then mixing in the sugar alternative. Pile the crumble on top of the apple and apricot mixture. Bake in a moderately hot oven for 45 minutes to an hour. Serve hot with vegan ice cream.

BANANA PARCELS

Ingredients you will need:

Bananas
Puff pastry
Soya milk
Sugar Alternative (*If Required*)

Method:

Peel one banana per person. Wrap each banana in puff pastry. Brush the pastry with Soya milk and dust with your sugar alternative. Cook in a hot oven till golden brown.

WALNUT AND MUSHROOM PÂTÉ

Ingredients you will need:

60 ml water
100g firm tofu (mashed)
Half a medium onion (sliced)
2 crushed garlic cloves
50g walnuts (chopped)
Salt and pepper to taste

Method:

Heat some water in a pan and add the garlic, mushrooms and onion. Simmer for 5 minutes until the mixture is soft. Place the mixture and tofu into a blender and mix until smooth. Add the walnuts and season with salt and pepper. Blend for approximately 5 minutes. Transfer to serving plate.

Note: The pâté needs to be chilled in the fridge for at least 2 hours before serving.

HEALTHY GRAVY

Ingredients you will need:

Vegetable stock
Vegan Worcestershire sauce
Balsamic vinegar
Cornflower or thickening granules

Method:

To make vegetable gravy tastier I always make it using water from boiled vegetables if I have any. Carrot water is especially nice as it has a nice sweet flavour. You need to strain off the vegetables and then boil the water down so that it reduces. Then you will have a more concentrated flavour.

If you don't have any vegetable stock made up you can make your own. Finely chop or grate 1 large onion, 1 carrot and a stick of celery. Put into a pan of boiling water cover vegetables with water then add the same amount of water again. Boil until the vegetables are really soft and the gravy has reduced down considerably. Then strain the veggies. The left over vegetables can be blended and made into soup and the stock is ready to be made into gravy.

You can of course use a stock cube to make the gravy, or to intensify the flavour of yours, but they are very salty and sometimes the flavour can be too intense for a delicate dish.

Put your stock into a saucepan and add a dash of vegetarian Worcester-shire sauce, and a dash of balsamic vinegar and some salt if required. Then add slowly some thickening granules or some cornflower until the gravy is of the desired thickness. Make sure you stir it quickly so it can mix well. If you have lumps in it, strain it through a tea strainer before serving.

STARTING TO COOK WITH THESE RECIPES

The recipes provided are all very basic and quick to prepare, making it easier for you to adapt to your new diet. If you build up a library of 10 or 12 simple recipes like these, you can easily alternate them until you become more confident with more intricate dishes.

It is likely that it will take a while for your body to adjust to this new range of food that is being introduced. It can take anything up to a month to stop craving the sugar and saturated fats that you were used to consuming.

ACTIONS

Search for More Recipes

Take a look on the Internet for more recipes that contain only fruit, vegetables, tofu, Soya, pulses, beans and rice. You will be amazed at how many you find and how tasty they all look. Use the information you have found in the previous chapters to check the fibre, protein and fat content of these food products in the recipes. Now search for a typical meat based recipe. You will find a stark comparison between the two.

Invite Friends To Dinner

Why not invite a few family members and friends over to try out your dishes? It will help you practice making each dish and will impress them no end.

Nutrition, Chapter 12:
Working Towards A Healthier
And Happier Future

This section has explored the food we eat and why it is so crucial to our overall health and wellbeing. We have discovered the importance of the right kind of fats, protein and nutrients. In this chapter, I would like to emphasise how important the OMD is in contributing to your overall health and happiness of your extended life.

More Health Please

The proteins, nutrients, good fats, vitamins and minerals that are found in plant-based foods increase your body's immune system. They help to ward off potentially fatal diseases.

It is a common case that as many as three out of four men, by the age of 23, already have blocked arteries. These life-sustaining channels can become clogged up as a result of the build up of cholesterol, which forms a slimy plaque on the artery walls. Once this plaque hardens it can cover as much as 90% of the artery wall. The blood flow is restricted and there is a greater risk of suffering from a heart attack. The blocking of the arteries can also lead to diseases such as Coronary Artery Disease and Cardiomyopathy. Saturated fats and trans-fatty acids contribute to this. The OMD will greatly reduce the risk of having a heart attack, due to the fact that it eliminates saturated fats from your diet.

The other biggest killer in the UK is cancer. Men are 16% more likely to develop cancer than women. And to scare you even further, 40% more men die from cancer than women. There are several factors that contribute to this figure, one of which is the fact that women are much more aware of the foods they eat.

The two most common forms of cancer affecting men are prostate and bowel cancer. Prostate cancer tends to affect men in their 50's. For every 100 confirmed cancer diagnosis', 24 are prostate related. Research has indicated that dairy products are a fundamental contributing factor in this disease.

There are 20,400 men diagnosed with Bowel Cancer every year. 90% of the time it is treatable with early diagnosis. Increasing your daily intake of foods that are high in fibre will significantly lower the risk of developing Bowel cancer. Eating meat will increase the chance of the cancer forming.

The lowest cancer rates occur in Third World Countries, where plant based foods are predominantly consumed. In nations where meat and dairy are in abundance, cancer is prolific. This includes countries such as France, the UK, the Netherlands and the United States of America.

OTHER HEALTH BENEFITS TO CONSIDER

As well as the reducing the development of serious illnesses, the OMD will help you lose weight and increase your level of self-esteem. As your confidence grows, so your moods will improve with your energy levels becoming more consistent.

WHY IS THE KEY

Sit down and ask yourself the reasons for turning your back on your current nutritional lifestyle. Take time out to pinpoint your exact motivations. This is important in maintaining your goals and achieving longevity.

WAYS TO ENSURE YOU FULFIL YOUR TARGET

Talk to other people who have been through or intend to go through the same process. You can even find someone who is willing to take the plunge with you. Having a nutritional buddy to motivate you will be a great asset.

Keep it interesting. This is one way to ensure longevity. There are 101 things that you can do with a potato. You can make potato soup, potato roast, potato wedges etc. When giving up meat and dairy, make sure you find suitable alternatives that have the same texture and taste. Corn based products and Soya are fantastic substitutes.

ACTIONS

Write things down

I want you to start a journal. Write down all the things you are feeling before you implement your diet. This could be a myriad of feelings from anxiety or apprehension to excitement and anticipation. Ensure you put pen to paper regularly as it will give you a boost in terms of monitoring your achievements.

FINAL WORDS

Here's To You and a Far Healthier Life

You are about to embark on a far better and longer-lasting life. One that is not thwarted with serious health problems. I can only speak from my personal experiences when I talk about impact it had on my life. By implementing its core concepts, I lost weight, gained confidence and began to feel healthier. It certainly did take some getting used to and I would be lying if I said I had initially found it easy. As with all worthwhile things in life, it required dedication, conviction and the capacity to learn. But the benefits were numerous and I started to feel the difference after a week. There are certain choices you make in life, and if this is one of them, you have begun an exciting and liberating journey. Now let's move onto the final section on grooming.

GROOMING

GROOMING

"Good habits, once established are just as hard to break as bad habits" - Robert Puller

Before we go further, let's have a short discussion on habits. I am intentionally going to state the obvious here because when it comes to Grooming, it's this simple. A habit is an automatic action that you embodied at some point in your life. Positive or negative actions became reinforced leading to continual habits being formed, resulting in your personal definition. Indulge me while I point out the obvious with some elementary examples:

- A person who repeatedly smokes is called a 'smoker'; a person who habitually drinks is called a 'drinker'; and a person who consistently never gets things done is called a 'procrastinator'.
- In a similar manner, someone who is great in the sack is a great lover, someone who always looks good regardless of the location or event is stylish and someone who can generally charm women at any time is...yes, you guessed it...a charmer!

Needless to say, the formation of good habits become your most potent tool in terms of developing self-esteem and positive perceptions of the self.

The truth in regards to the formation of habits is that bad ones are just as easily disposed of with good ones. The moment this active decision takes place, you subconsciously realign yourself with becoming better than before.

It is no longer enough to say 'It's a girl thing' when it comes to Grooming! If you are feeding off your mates' behaviour and sweating it out in an old T-shirt, you are going to need to adopt a new set of habits. If your overall appearance has consistently turned people off and resulted in some dishevelled self-esteem, then it's time to make some changes.

This section is here help you transform your bad grooming habits into good ones by giving you a blueprint of some basic, yet essential tips in looking and feeling your best in terms of grooming!

Let's quickly go through what we are going to be covering.

In Grooming, Chapter 1, Your Skin, we are going to look at some essential tips in keeping your skin looking fresh and younger. We will also identify certain skin types as well as identifying some of the more harmful substances that can result in premature ageing.

In Grooming, Chapter 2, Teeth and Mouth, we are going to look at some alternatives for keeping your teeth white and sparking. There will also be a bit of advice on keeping your breath mint fresh and the importance of flossing.

In Grooming, Chapter 3, Hair, we will discuss which styles are most suited to your shape of face. We will also include some colouring options.

In Grooming, Chapter 4, Body Hair, we will dedicate our attention to facial hair and preferences that women find sexy. Finally, we will look at dealing with that hair in all the wrong places.

In Grooming, Chapter 5, General Body Hygiene, we will look at some useful product ideas as well as dealing with the concept of tanning and always smelling fresh. This will include post gym grooming.

GROOMING, CHAPTER 1:
YOUR SKIN

According to University of Toledo psychology professor, Dr. Frank Bernieri, first impressions are formed within 30 seconds and often make the crucial difference on a first date. Because your skin is the first thing that women notice about you, your success starts with having clear skin. Smoothing out wrinkles, getting rid of acne and avoiding products that can damage your skin will go a long way to being your presentable best.

A few changes in your skin care routine will have women in awe of your attentive commitment to health, hygiene and cleanliness. Moreover, clean, unblemished skin will give you a tremendous sense of personal confidence. So, what does it take to have that smooth, soft and healthy skin that women find attractive? Let's list some of the best ways to care for your skin:

EXFOLIATE AND MOISTURISE

You can start exfoliating by washing your skin with a cleanser and then exfoliating with a washcloth. After this, apply a good moisturising lotion. By doing this daily, you are blotting away the excess oil that makes the skin look shiny and unhealthy. To maintain firmness and elasticity, you should also use toners.

HERE ARE THE ESSENTIAL ITEMS THAT SHOULD BE IN YOUR BATHROOM CABINET:

Moisturiser

Moisturisers should be applied both in the evening and in the morning. Make sure your moisturiser is oil free as this means it will not clog your pores. Also look out for one that includes UVA and UVB protection. Apply a thin layer all over your face and neck and make sure it has completely blended into your skin. If your face feels tight after you wash, identify the 'tight' spots and pay extra attention to them when massaging in your moisturiser.

Eye Cream

You should apply eye cream every morning and every evening. This helps to reduce the puffiness or bags under your eyes. Remember not to apply too much cream. Place the cream on your index finger and gently pat around the area where the puffiness occurs.

Facial Scrub

You only have to use a face scrub a couple of times each week. Do not use it every day. It wipes off all the dead skin and keeps you looking fresh. Don't forget to focus on the oily areas of your face like your forehead and nose. Face scrubs with fine granules are a lot better for your skin because they clean your skin more effectively, particularly in problem areas (between your nose and your cheek). A good scrub will remove dead skin cells too.

Not all skin care products are created equal, so here's simple list of things to remember when buying them:

- Always use alcohol-free moisturisers on your face after shaving.
- Make sure the brands you choose for general skin cleansing are free of chemicals and preservatives. Those that don't induce an allergic reaction on your face could affect the other areas of your body differently (such as your torso or your back), so make sure your brands are hypoallergenic.

- Don't forget that toners with alphahydroxy and glycolic reduce pore size. Always look for skin friendly toners that contain substances like aloe and omegas.

So from cleansers for your face to the right moisturiser for oily skins or dry ones, there is always going to be a product that will work best for you. Check the labels of exfoliating products in the pharmacy and look for those that address your specific skin care needs.

What if there are no products in your pharmacy that are "for men".

Research has shown that many skin care products that make products just for men, have the same ingredients as women's products. Clever manufacturers just put a more masculine label on these products to attract the male market, but the ingredients are essentially the same. Considering this, don't be afraid to try a product that claims it's made for women or comes in a flowery box! It may end up being the one that works best for your skin.

CARING FOR YOUR FACE

The face is the mirror of our soul and this should be cared for appropriately. It's always a healthy looking face that grabs a woman's attention. Maintaining a healthy diet, having regular sleep, cutting out stress and doing regular exercise will go a monumental way to keeping your face looking fresh. Also, products such as good cleansers, moisturisers and sunscreens are essential to keeping your face in the best possible shape.

Here is a list of face care must-do's

- Frequent washing - You need to clean you face at least twice a day with a face wash.

- A separate facial soap – In general, you shouldn't use deodorant soap on your face, as they have harsh ingredients. This means you should buy separate soaps for your body and face. If possible, clean your face before you bath or shower so you don't have to wash your face when you're bathing.

- Exfoliate - Facial exfoliating is also essential in removing damaged skin cells. It is best to exfoliate before shaving as it makes the process much more comfortable and prevents razor burns.

- Treat cracked lips early - Lip balm is also advisable as it prevents your lips and the general area around your lips from getting chapped and cracked.

- Apply toner and moisturiser to the most visible areas on your face like your forehead and cheeks - Do not leave the house without putting these on, as they will safeguard the skin from any sort of dehydration. They will normally also have a UV protector included, which is essential for obvious reasons.

- Apply eye cream – Removing the saggy bags around your eyes is essential, but be careful when applying them as they can cause irritation to the eyes. It is best to apply eye cream at night before you sleep.

A crucial step to caring for your facial skin is getting to know your skin type. It's very important that you know which skin products apply to you specifically. There are a few basic skin types, and you have to figure out which one you have:

1. DRY - tends to be flaky in certain areas and it feels dry and tight

2. NORMAL - not flaky, not shiny or oily, in the middle, feels comfortable

3. COMBINATION - oily forehead and/or nose, normal to dry cheeks

4. OILY - shiny and oily all over, tends to break out and feel greasy, especially on your forehead and nose.

In general, men have combination or oily skin, but yours might be oilier or dryer than most so when you go shopping for a skin care product, make sure you remain attentive to your type.

But what if you aren't sure about your skin type? The best solution to finding one that works for you is through trial and error. Dab a small amount of the product (there are 'tester' samples available in stores) on the inside of your wrist or elbow and let it stay there for a few minutes or a few hours. If no allergic reaction occurs, buy the product.

Night-Time Skin Care

Evening is the ideal time for men to clean their faces because unlike women, it isn't usual to see men rushing to the bathroom during the day to cleanse their faces or apply toners. It's also important to clean your skin at the end of a long day because even if you can't see the dirt and grime that's on your face when you get home, it's there.

If you cringe at the thought of sleeping with all that creamy goop on your skin, just think about this: your pores NEED to be cleaned or else your skin will become irritated and dehydrated, which can cause pimples, blemishes and blackheads.

Pollutants in the air mixed with the oils on your skin, equate to clogged and dirty pores. These toxins get expelled from your skin during the night and you can simply wash them off (together with the moisturisers and toners) in the morning.

Note that the guidelines for facial care I described apply to those who don't have particular skin issues that require special care. Special treatment is needed for men with the following skin conditions:

SPECIAL SKIN ISSUE #1: ACNE AND PIMPLES

If you want to keep your skin looking firm and fresh you will need to avoid foods that cause inflammation of pores, redness and swelling. Consuming large quantities of sugar or fats tend to cause these conditions, so cut back on the chocolates and fatty foods.

As a rule, acne treatment should not be DIY. Consult a professional to find out which skin products to use. In the meantime, use purified water (lukewarm) to cleanse your face. Refrain from using facial scrubs with granules to avoid further irritation.

SPECIAL SKIN ISSUE #2: FLAKING SKIN AND BURNS

If you shave, you naturally exfoliate the dead skin cells, which in turn will result in softer smoother skin. The only negative is that frequent shaving can result in rough skin developing along the cheek and jaw lines. Razor burns or sunburn may also cause flaking skin.

Solution:
Moisturise skin after shaving. If your aftershave does not have moisturising elements, use a separate moisturiser or toner after you shave. After this, you need to apply sunscreen with an SPF (Sun Protection Factor) of

15 or higher. Pay attention to your ears, the back of your neck as well as any balding areas on the scalp. If you do get burnt during the day, apply crushed aloe vera or a lotion with aloe extract to the burns. A bath with cooked oatmeal will also help to reduce the burning sensation.

SPECIAL SKIN ISSUE #3: LARGE SKIN PORES

Men's facial skin generally has larger pores compared to women's, which results in the accumulation of more dirt and the production of more oil in the pores.

Men with larger-than-usual pores must clean their face whenever they can. Besides cleansing during the morning and during the evening with a very mild cleanser, you should also keep a pack of smooth facial tissues or finely textured oilpaper ready to mop up the oil during the day. If you are conscious of doing this publicly, find a private spot like the office bathroom.

FACTORS THAT AFFECT SKIN HEALTH

Ageing

Premature ageing can be caused by excess sugar in your diet, lack of exercise, work-related stress, emotional instability or a hormonal imbalance (testosterone production decreases as you age). Testosterone is the chemical in men's skin that makes it thicker. These factors may also cause age-spots, particularly the sugar content in the food you eat (age spots appear due to the sugar in the system binding with collagen and causing a chemical reaction called glycosylation).

Anything that reduces stress is beneficial to your skin. Most of the time, natural ageing slows down or hastens up depending on how you handle stress. **Relax and take it easy every once in a while.**

I am sure you have seen some people your own age who look a lot more youthful than yourself. Their secret usually isn't related to cosmetic surgery, but rather, exercise and a good diet, which results in less sagging and wrinkling of their skin.

Free Radicals

Free radicals are unpaired electrons that attack healthy cells in our body. These may be caused by exposure to too much solar radiation and pollution. Damage to healthy cells is through a reaction called oxidation and thus leads to skin damage as well as premature ageing.

If you have too many free radicals in your system, you will have more wrinkles, an unhealthy skin tone and your skin will lack firmness. Thus, if you work outdoors, you need to be more aware of the effects of these free radicals. Consumption of highly fatty foods, alcohol, caffeine, stress and low blood supply can be the internal reasons for oxidation.

Since these free radicals are oxidants in cells, the best way to control them is by drinking supplements and foodstuff rich in antioxidants. Some examples of these include fruits (particularly berries), ascorbic acid tablets and vegetables.

Smoking

When you inhale smoke from a cigarette the carbon monoxide is absorbed by the haemoglobin in your blood. Carbon monoxide is a highly toxic gas, which is also found in the smoke from car exhausts. The blood absorbs carbon monoxide 200 times faster than oxygen, which results in a lot of oxygen being displaced.

If you smoke, your skin is starved of oxygen and thus you are slowly poisoned by the carbon monoxide. Added to all the harmful chemicals such as ammonia and hydrogen cyanide, the results are devastating. Your skin loses its healthy glow and takes on a yellowish – grey pigmentation. The more you smoke the worse the effects become. Smoking also causes premature ageing in another way. It uses up the vitamin c in the body, which cannot be manufactured. One of its functions is the preservation of collagen in the skin, the substance that gives you a youthful appearance. Premature wrinkles around the eyes and mouth occur when the collagen breaks down. The bottom line is you cannot have a healthy skin if you smoke.

Coffee

Caffeine intake tends to increase the levels of various stress hormones produced in the body, which speed up the ageing process. Switching from coffee to tea is a good way to reduce the chances of corisol hormones getting too high.

Like most drugs, caffeine from coffee, tea or other sources can be useful to give that extra 'lift' when we need it. The body can, however, become tolerant to it with more being required to give the desired effect. Caffeine used in a proper way, as an occasional stimulant, can be helpful, but when taken regularly, it is definitely harmful.

Dehydration

Your skin consists of 90% water. Water results in your skin being clearer, younger and smoother. It moisturises the skin from the inside out and results in a glowing effect. The cells in your skin dry out or die if they do not get sufficient water, which in turn, causes a number of skin rashes.

Drinking water keeps the skin cells active and also flushes unwanted toxins from your body. Moreover, frequent water consumption can lessen the formation of pimples when they are premature. Warm water can get rid of black heads and makes large skin pores smaller.

Other than drinking water, you should consume foods with high water content (such as aubergines), as these can help make your skin glow.

Alcohol Consumption

Every time you have a drink blood vessels become dilated and remain permanently so until your skin loses its tone. Excessive drinking will lead to the development of telangiectasias or chronic dilation of the capillaries and a permanent flush on the face will appear. Alcohol also worsens acne rosacea, a skin disorder that is characterized by redness, flushing, pimply bumps and telangiectasias. Remember that alcohol depletes the body of vitamin A, which is an important anti-oxidant.

YOUR ROUTINE

Cleanse Your Face Twice a Day

Do this every morning and every evening. Rinse your facecloth in some warm water. Wipe your face and neck, which will eradicate the first layer of dirt. Now place the cleanser in the palm of your hand and rub back and forth until lather forms. Apply the lather to your face and neck in a circular motion for approximately one minute. Finally rinse off the cleanser with your facecloth. It is advisable to do this twice.

OVERNIGHT TREATMENTS

Find an overnight mask that deals with your particular skin type. For combination and oily skins, clay works a treat by absorbing the toxins and balancing the oil. Clean your face and neck with your cleanser. Then apply your mask. After applying it wait for the recommended duration until removing it. Do this by taking a warm damp cloth and wipe it off. Don't forget to apply your moisturiser after finishing.

PROFESSIONAL CARE

Taking some time out at least once every month for a professional facial treatment will make you more aware of your skin needs. Get a facial once or twice every month. This is a great way to treat yourself and keep your skin looking and feeling completely refreshed.

Steam treatments and facials are also a great way to rejuvenate the skin by removing the dead skin cells and will leave you with a very satisfying feeling when done. Proper facial treatment is also a great way to deal with pigmentation caused by the sun and helps remove dark circles from around the eyes.

FRESH AIR, DIET AND EXERCISE

Exercise increases oxygen supply to tissues, which results in young and healthy skin. The capillaries function better and thus decrease premature ageing. Your diet must include fruits and vegetables, which supply the skin with essential vitamins and minerals.

GROOMING, CHAPTER 2:
TEETH AND MOUTH

Oral hygiene is not optional and you are going to need to pay more attention to your teeth if you want to look good. A bright and white smile is essential for fitting the profile of someone who pays attention to their grooming.

Here are two reasons why your pearly whites and minty fresh breath can get you more phone numbers than lines and lines of memorized glib:

- Women are attentive to your mouth and teeth – It will never be acknowledged but they will be looking at your mouth and wondering what intimacy would be like. Bearing that in mind, imagine the difference a set of pearly whites will make.
- A big and frequent smile is infectious. It exudes control, comfort and confidence. The average person smiles up to 50 times a day. Get your teeth white and get up to a hundred.

Now that you have your motivation for getting that brilliant smile you've always wanted, it's time to learn what you can do to whiten up your teeth and freshen up your breath.

TEETH BLEACHING

The most common procedure in getting your teeth looking clean and super white is with bleaching. Cosmetic bleaching is the fastest way to get the coffee, tea and cigarette stains out. Most dentistry's will have this procedure available.

Bleaching can be done in two ways. One is far more expensive and takes between an hour and two to complete while the other is a lot less expensive but is spread over a number of weeks.

- In the first instance, laser treatment is used to bleach your teeth. It can be an expensive way to get your teeth done (the price varies from dentist to dentist) but if you have the money, why not?
- In the second type of treatment the dentist will use a mould for your mouth. This will be filled with a bleach type solution. You take this home with you. You will need to wear it up to an hour every day for a few weeks. The cost can range between £150 and £400. This is a slightly more cumbersome way of achieving the result but may be the only option if you are financially constrained.

Bleaching though is a temporary solution and the results last for 3 years at best. If you have sensitive gums you will need to be careful.

On the other hand, we have on our shelves today products like whitening toothpaste. You may wish to try them out. The best brands according to the British Dental Journal are Macleans Whitening, Aquafresh, Rapid White and Super White. A fair warning: remember that toothpaste comes with chemicals, fluorides and dyes, which can be quite harmful to your teeth.

As an alternative to toothpaste, there are tooth soaps on the market that clean your teeth without these harmful substances. These are a fantastic alternative to the more well know branded pastes.

If you don't want to get your teeth bleached I suggest making sure they are constantly brushed after meals. Since we see our teeth every day as we brush them we fail to see just how discoloured they have become in time. Brush your teeth after meals and make sure you have a mouthwash to keep your breath fresh. Mints are also handy. Coffee and meal breath are two of the biggest turn offs.

FLOSSING

Brushing alone cannot remove plaque that is located in places that a toothbrush cannot reach — particularly in between teeth. In addition to removing plaque, flossing also helps to:

- Remove debris that becomes embedded in between teeth
- Polish tooth surfaces
- Control bad breath

Flossing should take place at least once a day for two to three minutes each time to be most effective.

Regardless of what type of dental floss you end up using, the oral health benefits remain the same -- regular consistent flossing is your best weapon against plaque – maybe even more important than your toothbrush.

MINTY FRESH BREATH

Good oral care consists of effectively brushing your teeth several times a day, flossing and cleaning the surface of your tongue. All of these will help reduce plaque build-up, loosen particles of food from the teeth and gums, and avoid their fermentation in your mouth. They will also eliminate the foul odour that's created during the process of food fermentation. A good mouthwash can also go a long way to preventing bad breath.

Foul breath can also be caused by your dietary habits. Your choice of food has a direct affect on the presence of bad breath in your mouth. Certain foods tend to produce volatile sulphur compounds, which are the culprits behind bad breath, such as garlic or onions. Here are some more examples of bad breath-causing foods, divided into four main categories:

- Drying Agents like alcohol (some mouthwashes contain alcohol which enhance the problem of bad breath)
- Dense Protein Foods (nuts)
- Sugars (even those found in breath mints which mask breath and worsen sulphur production)
- Acids like coffee or citrus juices

After eating, be sure to gargle a few times with pure water to dislodge any food particles still stuck around your gum line or in your teeth. If you cannot brush or floss immediately, you can drink water before and after you gargle just to clear your throat of food debris.

One effective way of getting rid of bad breath is scrubbing your tongue with your toothbrush after meals or before you go to sleep.

GROOMING, CHAPTER 3:
HAIR

Well groomed body, facial and head hair increases confidence and makes you far more presentable to the opposite sex. It is a well-known fact that women have strong opinions in regards to male hair.

Also, did you know that women are particularly attentive to hair fragrance? The scent of a man's hair is a huge turn on (or turn off, if it smells bad). Bearing this in mind, let's take a look at a few pointers for body hair and mane maintenance.

YOUR MANE

A good haircut can make or break you.

Speak to your stylist before and enquire on the most suitable style and shape for your particular hair type. Be educated and responsible with this. If you have thin hair, asking for a George Clooney cut is pointless and will leave you regretting the cut.

Before we discuss hairstyles but let's get one thing clear: if you have a preference for you current style, you don't need to reinvent the wheel but you will need to trim it regularly.

A good hair trim (or regular shaving for bald-by-choice men) will do wonders if your hairstyle is your 'trademark'. You must also wash and condition regularly; otherwise, your style will not be maintained.

What I'm saying is that although a great new style might do you good, if you find yourself missing your old hairstyle, you might be too self-conscious about the new style to really relax and enjoy it. So, read with the intention of getting a new cut only if you really need one.

HAIRSTYLE TYPES

Your hairstyle must match the shape of your face.

The general rule is that the oval face shape is the most appealing to women, so tell your hairstylist to create a style that will make your face more oval in shape. If your face is long, you need to create the illusion of shortening, while wide faces need to create the illusion of lengthening.

If you have an oval shaped-face, congratulations, as most hairstyles will look pretty good on you. Here are some more tips if you're having a hard time deciding what hairstyle suits you best.

- If you have a round face you need to focus on balance. Keep the sides lean and make sure you have a bit of styling on the top. Round faces look good with square hairstyles.
- If you have a square face keep the sides leaner and short and wear the top longer. Make sure the hair around the ear area is kept clean.
- If you have an oblong face, create a style which is longer on the sides and shorter on top. Disguise the front hairline with some layers. Go check out the Thehairstyler.com and try a few different styles to see what looks good.

Short Hairstyles

- Suitable for men with a dynamic characteristic
- Suitable for all face shapes except a square one
- Short haircuts look nice when applied to straight hair with a soft or medium texture

Short hair can make you look a lot younger and exude masculinity, strength and sexiness. Short hair works for most faces barring the square shaped face. If you can pull off a short haircut with a bit of stubble, the girls will be knocking down your door. Oblong faces look fantastic with short hair too.

Medium Hairstyles

- This type of style exudes maturity
- Suitable for all face shapes
- Textured choppy style looks good

These are more common and classic cuts. They do require more maintenance but allow more freedom in choosing a particular look than short hairstyles. Layered and choppy looks are common with this length and look great. Medium hairstyles require partings from one side of the hair and combing across to the other. If you have an oblong face, medium length hairstyles are probably the most suitable.

Long Hairstyles

- Exudes youth and exuberance
- Suitable for oval and spherical shaped faces

These hairstyles look good on oval faces. I do not recommend growing your hair beyond your jaw line. If you have a long face, avoid this type of hairstyle, as it will just elongate your face.

Out of Bed Look

This look has become increasingly popular over the last few years and as long as you have had a good stylist to look after your cut, it can exude sex appeal. This unkempt look comes across as carefree, but don't be fooled, it can require more maintenance than a conventional cut.

If you decide to go for this kind of cut be sure to find out what type of product will work best with the texture of your hair. You will also need to keep this style maintained which means getting it trimmed every 6 weeks.

WHAT ELSE CAN YOU DO WITH A HAIRCUT?

If you're short...

You can add height (a few centimetres) by choosing a hairstyle with a lot of volume on top. Stay away from flat shapes with little volume, as this will accentuate your lack of height. Use conditioners that don't flatten your hair.

If you feel you're too tall...

Keep your style shorter and flatter on the top. Use hair conditioners for that sleek look. Puffy hairstyles are a major no go as they add height and accentuate your tall figure.

If you have a big nose...

A fuller style helps draw attention away from your nose. Make sure the cut is more voluminous in the front than the back. Also, stay away from a centre parting as it draws attention to the centre of your face.

If you have big ears...

Don't go for a short on the sides. Make the length fuller but not too full as if the hair covers the ears completely, it looks like little Frisbees' are hanging off your head. Just remember to keep a balance.

If you're losing your hair...

Men who are losing their hair are better advised to go in for really short cuts. If you already have lost half your hair and half the crown of your head is showing, it's best to think about a crew cut.

HAIR COLOUR

Stop letting your hair go all pepper and grey, unless you have chosen this look yourself and have full control over the mature colour. Get down to a salon and let them find the right colour for you. Better yet, describe to them what kind of look you're aiming for (youngish, more mature, summer sun-friendly etc.), and let them work their magic.

I can't emphasise this enough: beginners should get professional advice

If you are new to hair colouring it is advisable to take a cautious approach. Consult experts if you are looking for a procedure that requires double process techniques (bleaching and toning). There are a variety of DIY kits but be warned, there are numerous horrific stories of colouring gone wrong. Good brands to look out for include Clairol and Herbal Essences.

If you're doing it yourself however, the following tips might come in handy:

- Be wary of wild colours. Make sure you don't choose colours that are too far apart from your natural one.
- Check out your clothes and find out if most of the items you own will clash in terms of the colour tone.
- Do a patch test. It may be a wise idea to do a patch test on your arm, as hair dyes are toxic and contain some very harsh

chemicals. If your product is available in a sachet, get that first before you buy the whole bottle. Put a dab of the product on your arm (on the sensitive skin around the inside of your elbow). Leave it overnight and observe for any allergic reactions. If you're using the whole bottle, a few hours will do (the product heats up with time so it's not wise to keep a whole bottle of potentially volatile chemicals lying around).

- Get a tub of petroleum jelly and apply it on your neck and forehead, just below the hairline. A good tip when applying colour to your hair is rubbing some Vaseline around the hairline. This will prevent any staining of the skin. To remove the Vaseline after colouring, just rub some cream cleanser on some cotton wool and remove it gently.

- Don't shampoo too soon after you colour. The best hair colourants already have conditioners in them so you don't need to wash with your regular shampoo right after colouring. This is to prevent fading. Also, remember that you are going to have to use conditioner and shampoo that is made for treated hair to prevent fading.

Temporary Colouring

What if you only need to go blonde for a day or one night? Temporary hair colouring is done by applying a thin layer of a colourant on your hair. The effect of the colour is not harmful to your hair so this is the best choice for those changing their hair colour for a special event or occasion. There are a few products that are made specifically for temporary colouring needs so you have to check if you have these at the pharmacy. If you don't find one, you can use normal colourants.

Another way of temporarily colouring hair is to reduce the "colour incubation" time to half. For instance, the instructions say you have to let the colourant stay on for an hour before you wash. You can let it set for just a few minutes. The colour won't be as vivid, but if your natural hair is light enough, you will still get the desired effect.

There are some down falls when it comes to temporary colours. If you have dark hair, the temporary colour will probably have no effect at all. Temporary colours work best on blonde or light-coloured hair. The most vivid are temporary colourants of the red and blue spectra.

Semi-Permanent Colouring

The semi-permanent colourants contain oxidizers and therefore are more permanent than the temporary ones. Although the semi-permanent colours won't stay forever, they will last you a good ten to twenty washes.

During this duration of time, the colour will fade slowly back to your natural colour. Fortunately with this type of hair colour, your roots will not show and the change will be almost unnoticeable. Semi-permanent hair colour gives the natural colour with added shine and brightness. Semi-permanent hair colouring is great for those looking to try a new colour without having the risk of permanency.

Permanent Colouring

Although permanent hair colours will give you the look that you want without it washing out, it can cause unwanted damage to the hair. Permanent hair colour contains strong oxidizers that cause the colour to last. Permanent hair colours are used for colouring grey hair or simply just for lightening.

HAIR ISSUES

1. Grey Hair

Early greying of hair can be a huge confidence buster for a lot of men, unless you can pull it off like Richard Gere. Grey hair can be caused by stress, particular genes or even environmental pollution. There are a number of herbal and cosmetic products that offer instant results for greying hair, but it's important to research the different types so you can buy the right kind for your hair type.

Temporary colour is good for treating grey hair up to 50% and usually lasts for six to twelve shampoo rinses. They should be free from ammonia and peroxide, which will result in them not lightening the hair.

Semi-permanent colour is stronger and used to cover approximately 75% of the grey area. This will last for approximately twenty shampoos.

Permanent colour offers the longest and most comprehensive effects in terms of concealing grey hair. The process requires the expertise of a hairdresser to go through the combinations required for mixing chemicals for colouring and the subsequent touch–ups. Permanent hair dye products require bleaching - a complex method used because of the longer colouring process.

2. Dandruff

There are many shampoos out there that claim to deal with dandruff, and you may have to try them out before you stick with a brand that suits you. Usually, infrequent washing causes dandruff. A dirty scalp will be a conducive place for a micro-organism called pityrosporum-ovle to breed. Dandruff may also be caused by fungus or even extreme sunburn to the scalp. Dandruff shampoos will help moisturise the scalp and destroy any micro-organisms.

If your dandruff is the result of dry skin, select a dandruff shampoo that is used to treat dry scalp. It will help moisturise and wash away lifeless skin cells. If you have flakes and your scalp is oily, you may have seborrhoea dermatitis. These flakes are thick and crusted instead of light and flaky. Over the counter products are available as treatments, which include selenium that helps with this condition.

3. Lice

An itchy scalp will alert you to the presence of lice on your head. If this is the case, refrain from lending out your comb to housemates or family members to avoid contamination. The best thing to do is to buy an anti-lice shampoo and follow the instructions to the letter. You will need to change your bed sheets, your pillow covers and your towel. If you can, air out your room and clean your cabinets to get rid of any residual lice eggs.

Grooming, Chapter 4:
Body Hair

Numerous surveys state women find too much body hair unattractive. Not a revelation, is it? They much prefer the smooth and sexy image of a sleek look. For hygiene purposes, it is essential to minimize body hair. It is an accepted fact that the new age look involves a fitter, cleaner body; so shaving is very much in vogue.

Here are some shaving tips you can use if you decide to get rid of the body hair once and for all.

- Always shave in the shower or after a bath. The steam prevents skin irritation and you will have a much smoother shave.
- If you are a first timer, get started with a beard-trimming tool to save time and avoid frustration. Shaving takes time and it could take a long time if you do it manually.
- Trim your hair with clippers or scissors before you shave.
- After trimming, have a long bath. Bathing in lukewarm water will allow the hair to soften, and hence become easier to shave.
- Use a gel after patting your skin dry and shave slowly. Do not rush the job. Remember that you can nick yourself if you try to do it too fast.

Facial Hair and a Women's Preference

In a survey by aftershave manufacturer Lynx, the following information was revealed: beards, moustaches and goatees are a huge turn-off for women, particularly when left unkempt and dirty. Here are some statistics:

- 92% of women preferred their men clean shaven
- 95% of the women complained about the discomfort of facial stubble
- Seven out of 10 women regarded moustaches as "out of date"
- Two thirds were opposed to the idea of goatees, and a whopping
- 86% said they found beards totally unattractive.

SHAVING YOUR FACIAL HAIR

If you are going for the clean-cut look, shaving at least once every two days is essential. The appeal of the clean-cut look has something to do with the fact that it makes you look well groomed. Here are some tips for shaving your facial hair:

- Always shave in the shower or after you have had a bath so your skin is clean and smooth when you shave. The steam from the shower also prevents skin irritation and softens the hair on your face.
- For a much smoother shave, make sure you have the best shaving gear and do not use old razors as they can cut the skin and leave it irritated.
- Massage the gel gently into your skin with circular movements so that the skin can soften further. Never scrimp on shaving gel and razor quality because the quality ones will help nourish your skin instead of causing abrasions and infections.
- Start shaving from the side burns down, as they are flat surfaces and the easiest to start on.
- Make sure you rinse the razor with each swipe of the blade.
- Leave the more difficult parts, like the chin and lip, until last. Allow for the gel to work longer, which will make them easier to shave.

- Do not use old-fashioned aftershaves, as they tend to irritate the skin.
- Look for aftershave gels, which are soothing and have effective moisturisers.
- Finally, avoid putting on cologne that contains alcohol after you shave, as this will dry the skin out.

A note on electric razors: these gadgets are certainly much easier to use than manual-powered razors but beware, over time they can stretch the skin and leave you with a sagging appearance. If you do use one, make sure your blades are always kept clean and that you always place a cold facecloth over your face after the shave.

DEALING WITH STUBBLE

Stubble is hard to deal with because it does not grow out fast. Moreover, if your skin is really dry in the places you've shaved, it can itch like hell. Remember, well kept stubble can be sexy, but will it make the girl you're with itch as well? If you insist on keeping it, deal with it in the following manner.

- Grow your entire whiskers for two or three days. Make sure your shaver is on the lowest available setting and even out the growth on your cheeks, upper lip and chin.
- Position your trimmer guard attachment between 1.5mm to 2.5mm (depending on the length of your beard); then hold the trimmer in a horizontal position. Take care to face the cutting unit either upwards or downwards, (whatever your preference is) and shave languidly, taking care not to trim off too much lest you end up with an uneven look.
- Next, use the foil shaver to remove unattractive hair on the lower neck; if these are too long and starting to curl, then you can also target that stubble by aiming for a balance, which is the subtle difference between looking stylish and looking unkempt.

YOUR BEARD

There are men who let their beard grow long and they still look cool. Why? It's because they groom it well. However, the main problem with having a beard you can groom and shape to your liking is growth. You will need to have good hair growth on the chin, upper neck, around your cheeks and the upper lip to groom a full beard properly. That means dealing with the temptation of shaving the hair off every single day and keeping the hair smooth and well trimmed for it to grow out properly.

Here are a few tips on beard grooming:

- Longer length allows for more versatile sculpting for your face, especially if you are going to try a home-trim job. When using a beard trimmer, comb the hairs on the beard-line (upper neck) and cheek-line (a little below cheekbones), which makes judging the trimming easier as well as manoeuvring the unit's head.
- Remove hair on the upper cheeks, sides and the lower two thirds of the neck by setting the unit's measure to the not-too-close trim number.
- Consider sharp side-whiskers for a debonair look and dab on some mousse, which will help set the hair.
- Always remember to shampoo and condition your beard, as this will keep it looking clean and aid you with the styling.
- If you suffer from itching it can be a good idea to rub some organic olive oil into the skin and beard. Be careful not to use too much.
- Remember to always check your beard after eating and drinking.

Beard Styles to avoid:

- The chinstrap, which wraps around the chin area
- The inverted horseshoe, think Hulk Hogan.

If you are going to go the beard route, you are looking to make the right impression by appearing suave. Think of a manly and rugged appeal.

- Make sure the style is symmetrical.
- When using your beard trimmer, always remember to first comb your hair in the direction of the hair growth to gain maximum hair length.
- If you want to shorten your beard hair length to a medium length, remember to first place the trimmer guard attachment on the apparatus, and the front of the cutting unit should be facing away from you.
- You can begin trimming from right beneath your chin and work the trimmer around your jaw-line toward the ear and upper beard area in an upward motion.
- Grooming your beard is simple when you learn how to follow the natural contours of your face.

MOUSTACHE AND GOATEE

In this day and age it is advisable to ignore the moustache and the goatee. However, if you want to go this route then make sure it is thick and manly.

- Grow your hair for 3 – 4 weeks so that you have a decent length for shaping it. Use a good quality trimming kit, which will offer some variety when trimming. For example a wide setting could be used to make your moustache straighter.
- Try placing a finger on your upper lip so the hair is separated from the skin and trim in an upward direction. When you reach the length you like, change the motion of the trimmer unit to downward so the hair is uniformly shaped.
- Remember to apply only light pressure so you don't end up with an uneven moustache. For a basic, fuller goatee, grow the stubble

out and don't forget to use a good quality electric shaving system to clear away any hair on the cheeks and neck.

- After using the trimmer head to trim the 'borders' of the goatee around your chin and moustache area, use the smaller trimmer head for creating a thinner and cleaner goatee.

BACK AND CHEST HAIR

Hair growth is longer, faster and thicker on the back and chest. To trim or remove these completely, use an electric trimmer. Remember, you can choose to let it grow it you're not self-conscious about it, but if it becomes an issue, get rid of it.

Another option for dealing with back and chest hair is to remove it completely by waxing. Chest hair can be a turn on for women, as long as it is well kept. Unfortunately back hair is no go, so do something about it.

For a quick and easy way of eliminating back hair, get a friend to help out with an extendable shaver and some shave gel. Remember to apply a soothing moisturiser afterwards so the stubble on your shoulder is not off-putting. The other alternative is using a waxing kit with ready to use wax-strips, which are great for men with soft to medium hair growth. If you have coarse hair, it's better to use hair removal creams if you don't have sensitive skin.

ARMPIT HAIR

The armpit area is where the sweat is produced, and so maintenance of your armpit hair is crucial if you want to avoid body odour. Keep your armpit hair tidy by trimming every once in a while. If you don't feel comfortable shaving it off, make sure it's short enough to never interfere with washing.

INGROWN HAIRS

Have you ever felt pain a few days after shaving because the hair follicles seem to have been trapped under the skin? This painful occurrence can be unsightly because the protruding inflamed skin resembles acne, pimples or rashes. Some may even think of these as razor bumps.

If you don't want redness, swelling and scarring because of a trapped follicle, you can use skin care products that contain salicylic acid. It is basically a dermatological-grade ingredient that helps in exfoliation. It also helps moisturise the skin. Also, if you use specialised products on your ingrown hair, your skin can recover faster.

You can opt to replace your current shaving solution with something that does not encourage acne. Look out for products that are designed for sensitive skin and are very good in preventing razor bumps.

EAR & NOSE HAIR

Nose and ear hair require trimming because they turn women off, plain and simple. Even if the rest of your body isn't that hairy, you might still have very long nose and ear hair. Adult nasal hair grows at a rate of approximately 0.35mm per day, approximately 1 cm per month. If you don't trim regularly, you won't be able to control which direction it grows.

There are a number of useful products that help with this type of hair removal. Nose and ear hair trimmers are mechanical devices with rotary or oscillating blades, which are specifically designed to trim nose and ear hair without nicking or cutting the nasal membrane or sensitive areas of the ear. A nose/ear hair trimmer is a safe, painless and effective method of quickly trimming nose/ear hair. When performed properly, trimming your nose/ear hair is no more painful than getting a regular haircut.

You can also trim these hairs with small safety scissors. Remember, you don't have to go deep, as you only want to remove the hair that is sticking out. If you have hairs appearing on the outside of the nose it is best to use strips or tweezers for the long hairs. Ear and nose hairs are a complete no go, so make sure you do something about them.

PUBIC HAIR

Big bushy pubic hair is very unattractive. Besides your sex life, one major reason why you should trim and maintain your pubic hair is its vulnerability to infection. Women like this area well kept, it means they have a respect for their body and are conscious of it. You must at least trim the hair on your pubic region if you are looking for more appeal.

There are several ways to deal with pubic hair: waxing, shaving, electrotherapy or simple trims every week or month. This is one area you don't want to nick with a sharp razor so make sure you know what you're doing. Here are some tips to help you out.

- You can 'trim the bush' by investing in an inexpensive shaving tool with a trimmer option or else get fast results by using scissors (to shorten the hair first) and then applying the trimmer to get closer to the root, for an even trim.
- The downside in using a trimmer for shaving pubic hair is that hair grows back fast and requires regular maintenance jobs to keep it from looking scraggly. Another alternative is to shave it all off with a razor, which is equally affordable and a technique men are typically familiar with and so are guaranteed good results.
- When shaving off pubic hair, make sure it's done in the shower, preferably using hot water and gel to lather and soften the coarse hair to get a closer, smooth and appealing look to the scrotum

area. You do need to watch out for razor burns, ingrown hair problems and keeping the area smooth.

- Finally, you can also consider hair removal creams that also moisturise the sensitive groin area after removing the hair painlessly.
- Professional waxing will get rid of the hair for nearly a month and is the smoothest way to remove pubic hair and discourage re-growth.

EYEBROWS

Eyebrows need to be trimmed regularly to "open up" your eyes. Use safety scissors for the strands of hair sticking out. You can check which ones these are by using your index finger and pushing against the line of the hair. You can also use a fine-toothed comb to gauge the length of each hair strand and to find out which one needs to get trimmed first.

Comb the hairs in the opposite direction to which they fall. Right eyebrow hairs will fall right and left eyebrow hairs will fall left. Mono brows are a turnoff unless you are a cast member on Star Trek. Use tweezers to pluck out this unnecessary hair. You can also use a trimmer to get rid of the hair but the effect will not last long, unlike when you pluck. Trim or pluck after a shower so your eyebrows are wet and the individual strands are visible.

NECK HAIR

Neck hair will make you look sloppy so you need to get rid of it as soon as possible. Fortunately, this is one hair problem that's easy to solve. An electric razor will do an excellent job. Again, make sure you have a mirror so that you can monitor the whole thing or ask your mate to lend you a hand.

GROOMING, CHAPTER 5: GENERAL BODY HYGIENE

Most guys associate general body hygiene with washing and soap lather. I'm telling you now that there's more to it than that. You need to be able to maintain that kind of hygiene throughout the day and use products that won't damage your skin. You will also need to consider washing habits that are congruent with your diet and exercise. For instance, you might need to wash more often when your diet comprises of spicy food (makes you sweat more profusely) or if you exercise a few times a day. With that said, we can say that while you can never neglect the importance of diet and exercise, it is equally important to think beyond soap for your daily routines.

BODY HYGIENE PRODUCTS

Look for a product that gives you a refreshing feel and contains agents that get rid of grime, grit and sweat from your body. A good body wash will moisturise, tone and make your skin softer. You can also use body scrub for cleaning off the dead cells, which will result in a smooth and soft skin. Bath salts are also excellent for a tired and sore body.

Body products made from plant ingredients are most effective for dry and tired skin. Others have skin tightening virtues which are best for softening the skin. Other creams and gels also include moisturisers, which have antioxidants to detoxify your skin. Remember to look out for UV protection when purchasing moisturisers.

YOUR HANDS

Well-groomed hands are a must for any guy looking to take it to the next level. A number of lifestyle magazines highlight the fact that hands are something women notice most often when they are on a date. Think about it in terms of the following. If you are holding her hands and indulging in some foreplay, how attractive do you think rough hands with wolverine-like nails will be? It will only offer discomfort and leave you feeling insecure and her embarrassed. Well-groomed hands that are nourished also suffer less through winter-dryness and prevent cracking nails, rough cuticles, sweaty palms, sunspots or sore skin.

Here are some hand-care tips to help you groom your hands:
- Do not bite your nails.
- Groom them by using nail clippers or nail scissors.
- Exfoliate using natural products that have granules to wash away the surface dirt.
- If you have sensitive skin and need specific products to wash with, don't use the soap dispensed in the office washroom. Instead, wash with plain water and follow this up with a moisturiser.
- Follow a basic hand-care routine, ensuring you keep your nails trimmed short, cutting straight across the top (to avoid ingrown/hang nails occurring) and cleaning underneath the tips with a nailbrush.

At the end of the day, chipped, broken and dirty nails are a major turn off to women. Regular hand grooming will make you far more appealing to members of the opposite sex.

FEET

The most important aspect of good foot hygiene lies in the cleansing methods used. You need to clean your feet at least once a day in order to prevent bacterial build up, which can result in bad odours. Here are some more recommendations on proper foot care:

- If you are prone to athlete's foot, eczema, psoriasis or general foot odour, it is advisable that highly coloured and scented products are avoided to reduce the likelihood of foot irritation.
- A basic anti-bacterial agent should suffice or the use of a product recommended by your general practitioner in the presence of skin disorders.
- If you suffer from smelly feet, it may be advisable to wash them more often. Cotton socks are advised over synthetic fibres as these allow the feet to breathe and remain cool.
- Socks should be changed daily to prevent the bacteria from building up.
- In the event of a corn or a callous developing, remember to treat it with the appropriate equipment. Never try and dig out the root of the corn or callous using sharp objects.
- If you suffer from smelly feet always remember to use foot powder.

TANNING

A tan can look healthy and attractive to the opposite sex. Tanning treatments are very useful in terms of their speed of effect as well as providing an alternative for those of you who do not like the sun. There are loads of tanning products out there, make sure you test them and eventually purchase one that works best for your skin. Do not buy the first one you see otherwise you are going to be severely embarrassed later on. Make sure you buy one that encourages the pigmentation process and not one that just dyes it.

The better quality products will give you a more natural looking tan and not an orangey effect. You will also need to make sure the product is hypoallergenic and that it moisturises your skin. This is essential, as you do not want all your pores blocked.

It is a good idea to test these types of products on a small patch of the skin before applying them all over. This will ensure that you do not have an adverse reaction to the chemicals. You can do the patch test at the store itself or ask for samples that you can take home.

Once you have found the brand you want after the patch test, what you need to do is to scrub down your body really well. You will need to get rid of the dead skin that accumulates throughout the day. This is important as if you do not get the dead skin off, the tan will become blotchy in a day or two as the dead skin peels off by itself. Pay attention to areas like the elbows and the knees, which tend to dry out easily. It may do you good to moisturise all these areas well before you apply the tan.

You are now ready to apply the lotion. Use latex gloves. Otherwise your hands will be smudged. Rub the lotion/gel into the body with circular motions. Normally it takes four to five hours for the tanning to be noticed. It would be best if you did it before you went to bed so that there is less irritation.

SMELLING FRESH

There are a number of small but useful tricks to keep you from being a stinker. If you are one of those guys who neglects dealing with body odour you are going to have to mend your habits quickly. Women are attracted to smell, it's plain and simple. Of course we all sweat, but some do so more than others and need to compensate for this.

Sweating in itself is a completely natural bodily function. It is the body's way of excreting toxins like food, smoke, alcohol or even car fumes. So a good sweat is a great way to keep the skin healthy as the pores of the skin keep on getting cleaned. The problem occurs when these toxins are not washed daily, which results in the bad odour.

Even if the odour is not offensive, it is noticeable, which remains incentive enough for people to keep their distance. Make the deodorant or perfume personal to you. Don't just go and pick out any brand. Have a reason for choosing it and make it yours. Make sure it is not too overpowering and that it lasts throughout the day. Fragrances for men are plenty. Shop around for one that suits your personality type. You can do this at most retail stores by sampling the testers. Remember, deodorant is never optional.

Make sure there is no alcohol in your deodorant as this can often cause rashes and swelling of the skin. You can also use an all-natural antiperspirant around your crotch area if you suffer from bad odours down there. But make sure it is all-natural. You can also use talc body powder on areas where you sweat profusely. This will help absorb any excess moisture and control odours.

POST GYM GROOMING

It is possible to have a great work out and still smell good. Bearing in mind that modern day gym etiquette includes meeting members of the opposite sex; it is essential to keep well groomed, as this could be an opportunity to make an impact. Don't forget, when you are doing exercise, especially toning, your skin is also having its own workout. Look out for antiperspirants that will keep you smelling fresh throughout the entire workout.

Don't forget to cool off after a heavy workout so your perspiring skin can get some relief. You will need to replenish the moisture your skin has lost by applying a light aloe Vera, eucalyptus or mint containing lotion. If you have sensitive skin, use a fragrance-free brand with seal-in moisturiser.

It is also important to dry the feet, since using communal areas like showers, exercise mats etc. can lead to fungal infections. So it is advisable to get your hands on some foot talcum powder and clean socks for your gym bag.

FINAL WORDS ON GROOMING

The bottom line is that if you want to look after your skin, attract the opposite sex and discover a well-groomed lifestyle – you are going to have to do something about it. It's all about realigning your habits. If looking after your body remains too new age for you…well, I'll close the stable door on my way out. Remember guys – it's just a few habits each week that need to be reinvented and before you know it…you will know it!

I hope you have enjoyed this section on Grooming and that it has provided you with sufficient thought to make immediate changes. From my side, it has been an absolute pleasure indulging you in a topic I am incredibly passionate about. I sincerely wish you the very best of luck.

CONCLUSION

Final Words on the "Sex, Relationships, Dating, Nutrition & Grooming" What Men Really Need to Know!

Congratulations on finishing the book. If you have endeavoured to take on board all the information and implemented the advice that has been offered, you are en route to personal and social excellence. Remember that knowledge and understanding are the first dimensions in all the sections. Only Actions will align you with fulfilment and reward that has escaped your journey so far. Make sure you re-read the contents of this book regularly to avoid falling back into old and trustless habits. Always remain steadfast in your convictions and remember:

You have all the knowledge at your disposal. Now use it!

We have embarked on a long journey and one that I hope you will have found enlightening. This exploration began five years ago when I was invited to develop an entity based on my passions alone. I was afforded the time and financial resources to develop what has now become this book. My circumstances in life led me to an adulthood that lacked genuine self awareness. But the nature of my personality has always steered me towards development. I wanted to understand why some people always looked good, had self-esteem, exuded confidence and remained assertive in the most trying of times. My conclusions led me to five core areas, which I have addressed in this book.

This exploration has led to my own personal fulfilment, more so than I could ever have imagined before embarking on this journey. My health and well-being exceeded any of my initial expectations. I lost two stone in less than a month and I embarked on a healthy regime, which culminated in me

- ✓ Cycling from London to Paris.
- ✓ Trekking the Himalayas.
- ✓ Running the Paris Marathon.
- ✓ Embarking on a Mont Blanc Summit.
- ✓ Dating the most beautiful women I could have imagined
- ✓ Pleasuring the most beautiful women in ways they could never have imagined – and that is through genuine feedback.
- ✓ And providing me with all the tools necessary to ensure love is not lost through common pitfalls.

This journey has allowed me to understand women and identify relationships, which are beneficial to both parties. I married the most exquisite woman in 2008 within three months of us meeting. She remains an absolute highlight in my short life and resulted in one of the most insightful adventures of discovery through my own personal mistakes. All the key Chapters in Dating allowed me to develop the confidence to approach her, which ultimately fashioned our union. She was ten years younger than me, degreed in international politics and exceptionally beautiful...yes, you know the story. It was an enchanting life experience and one that I remain truly grateful for.

My exploration into the dynamics of our relationship and its failures allowed me to open doors that had always previously remained shut. Understanding my own personal agendas, which for such a long time had remained a conscious mystery, geared me towards making active and attractive decisions based on fulfilment and not fear.

And when it came to sex. Let me tell you my friends, there is no greater pleasure than fulfilling someone you love. In terms of self-esteem, it rarely gets better than this.

I believe that we are all the masters of our own destiny, that personal fulfilment remains entirely dependent on ourselves. That is not to say that life is not fuelled with obstacles and trying times, because it is. But through the development of the self as well as enjoying one of the most wonderful gifts life has to offer, namely companionship and love, you are able to achieve enlightenment and discovery through choice. This book has brought me so much awareness as well as providing me with the tools to embark on a more accomplished and sophisticated adventure. I now hope you embark on your own personal journey and I wish you much personal success and love in your endeavours.

Peter Goodall

APPENDICES

APPENDICES

1. NUTRITION QUIZ

Slightly Easier Questions

1. Name the three types on macronutrients (3)
2. Other than saturated fat, name another type of fatty acid chain (1)
3. What is the average calorie intake for a male of between 19 and 50 years of age? (1 point for being within 51-299 calories here, or 2 points for being within 50 calories)
4. Milk, butter, cheese etc are all types of which products? (1)
5. Are complex carbohydrates or simple carbohydrates proven to be more beneficial to our health? (1)

Harder Questions

6. Amino acids make up what type of macronutrient? (2)
7. If a fatty acid chain contains three carbon double bonds along its length, what type of fat will it be? (2)
8. Which of the following food items would contain the most saturated fat: Steak; peanuts or bananas? (1)
9. What is the leading cause of death in the UK? (1)
10. Which of the following food items contains the best source of protein: eggs; Soya flour or jam doughnut? (1)

Answers

1. Carbohydrates, protein and fat.
2. Monounsaturated or polyunsaturated.

3. 2,550 kcals.
4. Dairy products.
5. Complex carbohydrates.
6. Protein.
7. Polyunsaturated.
8. Steak.
9. Coronary heart disease.
10. Soya flour (not eggs as is a common misapprehension).

If you achieved a score of more than 10 in this quiz, pat yourself on the back as your knowledge would be well above the national average. A score of around 6 would be the average and if you managed 12+, you've definitely studied nutrition before or were paying attention in your biology lessons.

2. GOOD CARBOHYDRATES FOR YOUR SHOPPING LIST

Make sure you include the following carbohydrates in your shopping list.

Carbohydrate Shopping (Tick Off)

- Bran
- Wheatgerm
- Barley
- Maize
- Buckwheat
- Cornmeal
- Oatmeal
- Brown Pasta
- Macaroni
- Spaghetti

- Brown rice
- Potatoes
- Root Vegetables
- Wholemeal Breads
- Granary Bread
- Brown Bread
- Pita Bread
- Bagel
- Wholegrain Cereals
- High Fibre Cereals
- Porridge Oats
- All Bran
- Weetabix
- Shredded Wheat
- Ryvita Crispbread
- Muesli
- Cassava
- Corn
- Yam
- Oatcakes
- Peas
- Beans
- Lentils

3. GOOD PROTEIN RICH FOODS FOR YOUR SHOPPING LIST

Make sure you include the following protein rich foods in your shopping list.

Protein Shopping (Tick Off)

- Tofu
- Alfalfa Seeds
- Artichokes
- Asparagus
- Avocados
- Baked Beans
- Kidney Beans
- Cowpeas
- Soybeans
- Beet Greens
- Beets
- Broccoli
- Cabbage
- Carrots
- Cauliflower
- Corn
- Lentils
- Mushrooms
- Onions
- Peas
- Spinach
- Buckwheat
- Cornmeal

- Quinoa
- Peanut Butter
- Almonds
- Brazil Nuts
- Cashew Nuts
- Peanuts
- Pine Nuts
- Hazelnuts

4. LIST OF FOODS THAT CONTAIN MONOUNSATURATED AND POLYUNSATURATED FATS FOR YOUR SHOPPING LIST

Make sure you include the following Monounsaturated and Polyunsaturated fat rich foods in your shopping list.

Good Fats Shopping (Tick Off)

- Olive Oil
- Peanut Oil
- Canola Oil
- Avocados
- Nuts
- Seeds
- Safflower Oil
- Sunflower Oil
- Soy Oil
- Flaxseeds
- Flax Oil
- Walnuts

5. VITAMIN AND MINERAL CHEAT SHEET

Nutrient	Info	Fruit Source	Vegetable Source	Nut Source
Vitamin A	Helps cell reproduction	Tomatoes, Watermelon, Peaches, Oranges, Blackberries	Sweet potato, Kale Carrots, Spinach, Avocado, Broccoli Peas, Asparagus Squash - summer Green Pepper	Pistachios Chestnuts Pumpkin Seeds Pecans, Pine Nuts/Pignolias Sunflower Seeds Almonds Filberts/Hazel nuts
Vitamin B1 (Thiamine)	Important for the production of energy	Watermelon	Peas, Avocados	
Vitamin B5	Important for metabolism of food	Oranges, bananas	Avocado, Sweet potato Potatoes, Corn, Lima Beans, Squash, Artichoke, Mushrooms Broccoli, Cauliflower Carrots	
Vitamin B6	Important for the creation of antibodies	Bananas, Watermelon	Avocado, Peas Potatoes, Carrots	
Vitamin B9	Important in producing red blood cells and components of the nervous system	Kiwi Blackberries Tomatoes Orange, Strawberry Bananas	Lima Beans, Asparagus Avocado, Peas Artichoke, Spinach Broccoli,	Peanuts Sunflower Seeds Chestnuts Walnuts Pine

		Cantaloupe	Squash Corn, Sweet potato Kale, Potatoes Carrots, Onions Green Pepper	Nuts/Pignolias Filberts/Hazel nuts Pistachios Almonds Cashews Brazil Nuts Pecans Macadamias Pumpkin Seeds
Vitamin C	Important Antioxidant	Kiwi Strawberry Orange Blackberries Cantaloupe Watermelon Tomatoes Lime, Peach Bananas, Apples Lemon, Grapes	Artichoke, Asparagus Avocado, Broccoli Carrots, Cauliflower Corn, Cucumber Green Pepper	
Vitamin D	Promotes absorption of calcium and magnesium		Mushrooms	
Vitamin E	Important antioxidant	Blackberries Bananas Apples Kiwi		Almonds Sunflower Seeds Pine Nuts/Pignolias Peanuts Brazil Nuts
Vitamin K	Critical for blood clotting	Spinach, broccoli, kale	Pine Nuts, Cashews, Chestnuts, Hazelnuts	

Calcium	Eases Insomnia and helps regulate the passage of nutrients through cell walls.	Oranges, Blackberries, Kiwi, Tomatoes, lime, strawberry, lemon, grapes, apples, bananas, peach	Artichoke, peas, squash, broccoli, lima beans, spinach, carrots, avocado, asparagus	Almonds, Brazil nuts, peanuts, walnuts, chestnuts, macadamias, peanuts, sunflower seeds, pumpkin seeds, cashews
Copper	Involved in absorption, storage and metabolism of iron and the formation of red blood cells.	Kiwi, apples, bananas, blackberries, grapes, lemon, lime, orange, peach, strawberry, tomatoes	Artichoke, avocado, broccoli, carrots, cauliflower, corn, cucumber, green peppers, kale, lima beans, mushrooms, onions, peas, potatoes, spinach, squash, sweet potato	Most nuts have traces of copper in them
Iodine	Helps regulate energy production and body weight.	Fruits grown in iodine rich soils contain iodine.	Vegetables grown in iodine rich soils contain iodine.	Nuts grown in iodine rich soils contain iodine.
Iron	Iron deficiency affects the immune system and can cause weakness and fatigue.	Blackberries, kiwi, strawberry, tomatoes, bananas, grapes	Lima beans, peas, avocado, kale, spinach, broccoli, squash, potatoes, corn, carrots, mushrooms	Most nuts have traces of iron in them.

Magnesium	Needed for cell generation, relaxing nerves and muscles, clotting blood and in energy production.	Kiwi, bananas, tomatoes, blackberries, strawberry, orange	Avocado, artichoke, peas, squash, potatoes, corn, spinach, kale, broccoli, sweet potato	Brazil nuts, cashews, almonds, pumpkin seeds, pine, peanuts, walnuts, macadamias, sunflower seeds, pecans, pistachios, chestnuts, hazelnuts
Phosphorus	Necessary for the formation of bones, teeth and nerve cells.	Kiwi, tomatoes, blackberries, bananas, strawberry, orange, peach, lime	Lima beans, peas, artichoke, avocado, corn, potatoes, asparagus, broccoli, mushrooms, sweet potato	Sunflower seeds, Brazil nuts, cashews, pine, pistachios, almonds, peanuts, walnuts, chestnuts, pecans, pumpkin seeds
Potassium	Essential for growth and maintenance of the body.	Bananas, tomatoes, blackberries, strawberry, orange, peach, grapes, apples, lemon, lime	Avocado, lima beans, potatoes, peas, squash, sweet potato, broccoli, corn, carrots, spinach, asparagus, green pepper, mushrooms, onions, cauliflower, cucumber	Chestnuts, sunflower seeds, pumpkin seeds, almonds, Brazil nuts, peanuts, cashews, pine, walnuts, pecans, macadamias, hazelnuts

Selenium	Functions as an antioxidant.	Bananas, kiwi, strawberry, blackberries tomatoes, orange, peach, apples, grapes	Lima beans, peas, mushrooms, kale, corn, sweet potato, potatoes, squash, onions, spinach	Brazil nuts, sunflower seeds, cashews, peanuts, walnuts, almonds, chestnuts, pecans
Sodium	Regulates blood pressure	In most fresh fruits.	In most fresh vegetables.	Peanuts, pumpkin seeds, cashews, chestnuts, almonds
Zinc	Important in protein and carbohydrate metabolism as well as growth and vision.	Blackberries, kiwi	Peas, lima beans, squash, potatoes, corn, sweet potato	Pumpkin seeds, pine nuts, cashews, sunflower seeds, pecans, almonds, walnuts

6. OPTIMUM MALE DIET MENU SUGGESTIONS

Carrot and Coriander Soup

Ingredients you will need:

25g margarine (Non Dairy)
500g carrots (sliced)
1 medium potato (chopped)
1 small onion (finely chopped)
1 celery stick (chopped) 1 garlic clove (finely chopped)
900ml water
1 tsp. ground coriander
Pinch of sugar alternative (*If required*)
Salt and pepper
2 tbsp. coriander (roughly one man-sized handful!)

Method:

Melt the vegetarian and non-dairy margarine in a pan, add the carrots, potato, onion, celery and garlic and cook gently for 10 minutes.

Add the ground coriander, sugar and water and season to taste. Bring to the boil. Cover and simmer for 1 hour or until the carrots are tender. Cool slightly.

Add the fresh coriander (including the stalks), reserving a few leaves for decoration. Whiz in a food processor until smooth. Add a little more water to loosen, if required, decorate the soup with coriander leaves and serve.

Delicious & Nutritious Nut Roast – The Optimum Male Diet Alternative to Meatloaf!

Ingredients you will need:

200g mixed nuts (chopped)
1 stick of celery (chopped)
1 green pepper (chopped)
1 onion (chopped)
1 medium carrot (grated)
50g mushrooms (sliced)
25g wholemeal flour
50g breadcrumbs
125ml vegetable stock
1 tbsp. vegetable oil
1 tbsp. mixed herbs
Note: These quantities will serve 2-3 people.

Method:

Preheat the oven to 190°C/375 °F/Gas mark 5.

Heat the vegetable oil in a pan and add the chopped onions, frying for several minutes. Then add the celery, mushrooms and pepper, frying for 2 minutes. Add the grated carrot and fry for a further minute. Remove the pan from the heat; add the wholemeal flour and stir. Finally, add the vegetable stock, mixed nuts, breadcrumbs, mixed herbs and season with a dash of salt and pepper. Grease the inside of a loaf tin adequately. Pour the mixture into the loaf tin and press down with a spoon. Bake in the oven for approximately 35 minutes.

Vegetable Curry in a Hurry

Ingredients you will need:

3 medium sized potatoes (chunks)
Half a cauliflower (cleaned and cut into florets)
1 carrot (peeled and sliced)
1 small tin or 300ml of processed peas
1 large onion (chopped)
2 bay leaves
1 tbsp. curry powder
2 tbsp. tomato purée
1 aubergine or green pepper, chopped (optional but tasty)
3 fl. oz of olive oil or sunflower oil

Method:

Heat the oil in a sturdy pan and fry the onion for several minutes. Add the carrot, potato chunks and cauliflower florets. Fry for a further 10 minutes. Next, add the pepper or aubergine (optional). Add the curry powder and a pinch of salt. Allow to cook for 5 to 10 minutes. Sprinkle in the processed peas, and then add the bay leaves and the tomato purée. Cover over with water, bring to the boil and then simmer for approximately 30 minutes. For a further smattering of protein, serve on a bed of rice.

Apricot and Apple Crumble

Ingredients:

3 apples, sliced thinly
2 oz dried apricots, cut into quarters
1 tbsp sugar alternative (*If required*)
4 tbsp water
For the topping you will need:
3 oz of vegetarian and non-dairy margarine
6 oz flour

Method:

Put the apples and apricots into an ovenproof dish. Sprinkle with your sugar alternative and water. Make the crumble by rubbing the margarine into the flour and then mixing in the sugar alternative. Pile the crumble on top of the apple and apricot mixture. Bake in a moderately hot oven for 45 minutes to an hour. Serve hot with vegan ice cream.

Banana Parcels

Ingredients you will need:

Bananas
Puff pastry
Soya milk
Sugar Alternative (*If Required*)

Method:

Peel one banana per person. Wrap each banana in puff pastry. Brush the pastry with Soya milk and dust with your sugar alternative. Cook in a hot oven till golden brown.

Walnut and Mushroom Pâté

Ingredients you will need:

60 ml water
100g firm tofu (mashed)
Half a medium onion (sliced)
2 crushed garlic cloves
50g walnuts (chopped)
Salt and pepper to taste

Method:

Heat some water in a pan and add the garlic, mushrooms and onion. Simmer for 5 minutes until the mixture is soft. Place the mixture and tofu into a blender and mix until smooth. Add the walnuts and season with salt and pepper. Blend for approximately 5 minutes. Transfer to serving plate.

Note: The pâté needs to be chilled in the fridge for at least 2 hours before serving.

Healthy Gravy

Ingredients you will need:

Vegetable stock
Vegan Worcestershire sauce
Balsamic vinegar
Cornflower or thickening granules

Method:

To make vegetable gravy tastier I always make it using water from boiled vegetables if I have any. Carrot water is especially nice as it has a nice sweet flavour. You need to strain off the vegetables and then boil the water down so that it reduces. Then you will have a more concentrated flavour.

If you don't have any vegetable stock made up you can make your own. Finely chop or grate 1 large onion, 1 carrot and a stick of celery. Put into a pan of boiling water cover vegetables with water then add the same amount of water again. Boil until the vegetables are really soft and the gravy has reduced down considerably. Then strain the veggies. The left over vegetables can be blended and made into soup and the stock is ready to be made into gravy.

You can of course use a stock cube to make the gravy, or to intensify the flavour of yours, but they are very salty and sometimes the flavour can be too intense for a delicate dish.

Put your stock into a saucepan and add a dash of vegetarian Worcestershire sauce, and a dash of balsamic vinegar and some salt if required. Then add slowly some thickening granules or some cornflower until the gravy is of the desired thickness. Make sure you stir it quickly so it can mix well. If you have lumps in it, strain it through a tea strainer before serving.

7. RATING YOUR DAYS

I want you to start recording a day diary, recording how you felt at the end of each day, whether you were assertive, whether you carried any hidden agendas, whether you were selfless etc

The purpose of this is to generate a measuring stick for you to accelerate to higher grades as time goes by. Don't be annoyed if you slip back into old routines; remember that life is about 70:30 and not 100. Use the following scale:

A= A truly excellent day where you have felt confident and interacted in a constructive and assertive manner.

B= All-in-all a good day. You felt reasonably confident and socialised with most people.

C= A rather average day. There may have been times where you felt confident but there were also some awkward periods where you felt a little diminished.

D= Not a good day. Decidedly lacking in confidence and compelled not to interact with others.

E= Akin to agoraphobia in that you felt inclined to isolate yourself from every one. Very low self-esteem and not a day you want to repeat in a hurry.

8. THE STEPFORD WIFE TEST

I want you to imagine the perfect partner or wife, namely 'The Stepford Wife'. Now we are going to see how lucky or unlucky your choice in partner has been.

Allocate a score of between 1-5 for your partner, based on the following questions and use a zero where they do not apply:

1. Does your partner do most of the cleaning?
2. Does your partner find you funny and laugh at your jokes when you are alone together or in a social environment?
3. Is your partner sexy?
4. How amenable is your partner to sex when you want it?
5. Is your partner agreeable?
6. Does your partner appear to be listening to you all of the time?
7. Has your partner become more attractive since the birth of your relationship?
8. Is your partner well tempered?
9. Is your partner sexually exploratory?
10. Does your partner cook for you?

If you score anywhere above 35 on the Stepford Scale, you have 70% to be grateful for. Remember, this is just for fun, so don't go banging down her door because she failed 'The Stepford Wife' test.

9. THE LOVE SCALE

As you should be aware, there varying degrees of companionship, so I thought it might be a good idea provide you with some food for thought. Remember, this is a very basic yardstick and all I want you to do is develop a little thought. If you are single, again, use one of your past relationships. Decide which of the categories your past or current partnership falls into:

1. Convenience

The relationship has no realistic chance of longevity and you are both completely aware of the fact that you are only together for convenience. There would be no denying that if something better came along, for either of you, the relationship would end and you would both separate. One night stands also feature in this category.

2. A level of fondness but no real commitment

You do or did feel something towards this person, but at the end of the day, you have no intention of remaining with her in the long run. You defend them in conversations, but that's as far as it goes.

3. Definite fondness

You hold this person in high regard. You are aware of the fact that you have feelings for her and you would be sorry if the relationship were to end. But you will not negotiate or compromise when it comes to the decision making process and having your own life is imperative when it comes to your happiness.

4. In-Love

You are on top of the world. You can't stop calling her, talking to your friends about her, you just want to have sex and spend all your time with her. She has no genuine faults; they are just endearing little habits and make you want her even more. You just want time to stop when you are together.

5. Deeper Love

The initial lustful attraction has subsided but you want this person to be involved in your life through to the very end. She has become your friend, confidant and lover and you are committed to the relationship 100%. Again, no analysis required, just a bit of personal observation.

10. THE RELATIONSHIP INVENTORY

I want you to go through the following inventory to identify areas that may require some work in your relationship. I have posed a few questions in varying categories where you will be able to assess particular domains, which will require your attention. Remember to remain genuine and connected in your responses.

Your Communication Skills

For the questions below, I want you to allocate a score of between 1 (least applicable) and 5 (most applicable).

1. Have you had an argument with your partner that resulted from a clear lack of communication on your part?

2. Has your lack of communication ever been commented on?

3. Do you feel inclined to brush issues under the carpet and avoid confrontation?

4. Does the thought of apologising make you feel vulnerable?

5. Do you mask personal agendas?

You will have a score between 0 and 25. Check your score against the following scale:

A (0-4) Your communication skills are very good - well done! Keep this up as you're definitely implementing the right level of skill here.

B (5-11) Your communication skills are average. There are a few areas you may need to keep a close eye on.

C (12-17) It is time to take action. You're communication skills are not at the level they should be to maintain a healthy relationship.

D (18-23) Very poor communication skills. Immediate and determined effort needs to be made.

E (24+) Congratulations for being so honest. However, your communication skills are non-existent. CBT or NLP are strongly recommended.

Your Self-Esteem

As above please, with the score of 1(the lowest) to 5 (the highest) for the following questions:

1. How do you feel about yourself right now?

2. Do you maintain a healthy diet?

3. Do you express concerns?

4. Do you partake in any form of exercise?

5. Do your express your successes?

Five simple questions, but they should help to ascertain your level of self-esteem. Use the following scale to determine what action is required:

A (22+) You are doing very well! You clearly feel confident and have more the sufficient levels of self-esteem

B (17-21) Very good – The occasional blunders may occur but you are still on top of things.

C (13-16) Average level of self-esteem. Take some active steps in developing this.

D (8-12) Revisit the chapter that is devoted to self-esteem. Identify areas that need to be worked on and take necessary steps.

E (0-7 Immediate action is required. You have a low opinion of yourself and should look into CBT and NLP.

How 'Loved Up' Are You?

Let's take a look at your current relationship. Maintain scores of 1(the lowest) to 5 (the highest) for the following questions:

1. Are you able to express concerns with your partner?

2. Do you feel supported by her?

3. Do you enjoy spending time together?

4. Does she encourage you?

5. Can you imagine spending the rest of your life with her?

A (21+) You are absolutely in love and good for you.

B (16-20) Your love life is definitely something to look forward to.

C (12-15) Your relationship is ok but could be better. Take some time to work out why you are more fulfilled.

E (11 and below) Your relationship is in trouble. Immediate action is required. Go through the section with your partner and discuss potential areas to work on.

Printed in Great Britain
by Amazon

35312668R10265